EU ENLARGEMENT: A LEGAL APPROACH

The enlargement of the EU to embrace Central, Eastern and Southern Europe is usually analysed from political and economic points of view, but the current process also has significant legal implications, which this edited collection aims to explore. Written by scholars and officials from both the EU and the new Member States, the contributions cover three main themes. The first chapters examine how Treaty-based accession conditions have been elaborated and controlled to meet the particular needs of the present process. The second part of the book analyses the modalities of accession and in particular the unprecedented "pre-accession strategy" established by the Union with a view to monitoring the transformation of the candidate countries' legal orders. The final group of chapters envisages the impact of enlargement on the EU institutions and policies, both internal and external.

This volume is a useful reference for anyone interested in the EU enlargement as such but also provides a valuable background to the current constitutional reform of the EU.

EU Enlargement: A Legal Approach

Edited by

Christophe Hillion
Faculty of Laws
University College, London

• HART •
PUBLISHING

OXFORD AND PORTLAND OREGON
2004

Published in North America (US and Canada) by
Hart Publishing
c/o International Specialized Book Services
5804 NE Hassalo Street
Portland, Oregon
97213-3644
USA

Hart Publishing is a specialist legal publisher based in Oxford, England. To order further copies of this book or to request a list of other publications please write to:

Hart Publishing, Salters Boatyard, Folly Bridge,
Abingdon Rd, Oxford, OX1 4LB
Telephone: +44 (0)1865 245533 Fax: +44 (0)1865 794882
email: mail@hartpub.co.uk
WEBSITE: http//:www.hartpub.co.uk

British Library Cataloguing in Publication Data
Data Available

ISBN 1-84113-376-0 (hardback)

Typeset by Olympus Infotech Pvt Ltd, India, in Palatino 10/12 pt.
Printed and bound in Great Britain by
TJ International Ltd, Padstow, Cornwall

Foreword

In welcoming this book on legal aspects of enlargement, I should like to make some brief personal reflections on the legal challenges we face. But first let this subject be seen in its context.

The great enlargement of the European Union on 1 May 2004 has in many ways a historic significance. This is not merely a matter of the numbers of new Member States, or of the size of this latest expansion. Numerically, it might be counted as the largest of the successive enlargements: from the original six Member States (in 1952), to nine (in 1973), to ten (in 1981), to 12 (in 1986), to 15 (in 1995), to 25 from 1 May 2004.

What is most significant about this, the fifth enlargement, is not the number of Member States joining the European Union, or their size — the size of their territory, or their population, or their economy.

There are perhaps two factors which, in combination, explain the exceptional significance of this enlargement. The first is that the incoming Member States include not only two Mediterranean island states, Cyprus and Malta, historically linked with Europe although geographically close to Asia and Africa respectively, but also eight Central and Eastern European states most of which were, until relatively recently, directly or indirectly within the orbit of the Soviet Union and correspondingly cut off from Western Europe.

Yet all of these states shared, with the existing Member States, a common European cultural heritage (and to some extent a legal and political heritage) long before the European Union was conceived. This enlargement of the Union can therefore be regarded as constituting, in many ways and after a long historical gap, also a reunion.

A second factor which differentiates the latest enlargement from the earlier ones is the transformation of the European Union itself. What the new Member States are joining now is very different from what it was some years ago. The Union is in many ways — some obvious and some less obvious — very different from the earlier European Communities. To mention just some of the most obvious developments, the Union has not only a common market, but a common citizenship, a common currency, and the beginnings of a common foreign and security policy. Much progress has been made towards drawing up a European Constitution.

Both factors — the reunification of Europe and the transformation of the European Union — would have seemed hardly credible until very shortly before the two processes began — at the very end of the 1980s.

Some observers of the enlargement process would criticise the delays which have occurred. Many would say however that an important part of the story of the 2004 enlargement lies in what has already been achieved. They would stress, in particular, the substantial reforms made in some of the applicant States (both those joining now, and candidates for future accession): reforms to their economies and to their political systems; improvements in the protection of minorities and human rights; the raising of environmental standards; the development of administrative and judicial infrastructures which will be essential to make the implementation of EU policies and laws a reality rather than a paper exercise.

From a legal perspective, a number of vital questions arise. Law is the foundation of the European Union, and the enlargement poses several challenges.

The most significant challenge, in my view, is to ensure that the fundamental principles of the Union's legal order — including the primacy and the direct effect of Union law — are maintained. The challenge of reconciling national constitutions and national legal systems with these principles is a constant theme, even today, in several of the 'oldest' Member States, and will certainly present itself in the 'youngest'.

More generally, there is the challenge of maintaining the uniform application of Union law in the enlarged Union. The key here lies in the effective use of the system of references from national courts to the Court of Justice. Again this must be regarded as an issue for the old as well as for the new Member States, and for the Court of Justice itself. The limited resources of the Court will certainly be over-stretched unless a more rational use can be made of the system, while preserving its essential features.

The Court of Justice will be called upon also to ensure that in its enlarged form — moving from fifteen to twenty-five judges, with eight advocates general — it works efficiently. The new structure, with the Grand Chamber to hear important cases, represents almost the first major change in the structure of the Court since its inception, and will lead to a greater rotation in the composition of the Court than it has ever experienced. It will be essential to secure consistency in the case-law, together with the capacity to adapt the law when it is necessary to do so.

And then of course there is the language issue: for many purposes, because of understandable political forces, the Court will be obliged to work in no fewer than twenty languages, even if it maintains a single working language internally. It will obviously not be possible to expect national courts to read Union legislation in all twenty authentic texts. The problems here may be less serious than they appear, since — at the risk of considerable over-simplification — any discrepancies between the different language versions of the texts are to be dealt with by looking at the aim of the provisions, considered in their context — a method which has always been the predominant approach of the Court to interpretation. Nevertheless the work of the Court of Justice, and of the national courts, will be more complex than ever.

Although the enlargement thus presents many challenges, not least in legal terms, they should be seen as precisely that: as challenges which are to be confronted, and which indeed may even lead to improvements in the working of the Union's legal system. Enlargement of the Union, handled in the right way, will bring not only problems, but benefits.

Francis G Jacobs
Luxembourg, July 2003

Contents

List of Contributors

Anneli Albi is a lecturer in EU law at the University of Kent. A graduate from the University of Tartu, she got her Ph.D from the European University Institute (Florence) in 2003, on the constitutional adaptations of Central and Eastern European countries for EU integration. She has been General Rapporteur and lecturer in the Asser Instituut's MATRA multi-country project and has published in the field of constitutional implications of CEE's EU integration. Her book *EU Enlargement: The Constitutions of Central and Eastern Europe* is forthcoming by Cambridge University Press.

Alan Dashwood, Barrister (Inner Temple), is Professor of European Law at the University of Cambridge and a fellow of Sidney Sussex College. He was previously Director in the Legal Service of the Council of the European Union.

Michael Dougan is Professor of European Law at the University of Liverpool. He previously taught at the University of Cambridge and at University College London.

Geoffrey Edwards is Reader in European Studies in the Centre of International Studies at the University of Cambridge and a Jean Monnet chair-holder in political science. A Fellow of Pembroke College, he sits on the Management Committee of the Centre for European Legal Studies in the Law Faculty in Cambridge.

Christophe Hillion is lecturer in EU Law at University College, London, and Visiting Professor at the College of Europe in Natolin (Warsaw). He was previously Deputy Director of the Centre for European Legal Studies, Cambridge.

Kirstyn Inglis qualified as a Scottish solicitor in 1990, when she moved to Brussels to practice EC law. Since 1997 she has been Senior Legal Researcher on enlargement, agri-food and environment law at the European Institute of the University of Ghent, Belgium.

Francis G Jacobs has been Advocate General at the Court of Justice of the European Communities since 1988. He was previously Professor of European Law at the University of London, and in practice at the English Bar (Queen's Counsel).

Marc Maresceau is Professor of European Law and Institutions at the Universities of Ghent and Brussels and is the Director of the European Institute at the University of Ghent, Centre of Excellence Jean Monnet.

He has been Visiting Professor at various universities, among them King's College, University of London; Hebrew University Jerusalem; College of Europe, Bruges and Natolin; Università di Bologna; Università di Pisa; Université de Bordeaux IV; Université de Rennes I; Libera Università Mediterranea, Bari. He studied at the University of Ghent, the Johns Hopkins University, Bologna and the Institut universitaire de hautes études internationales, Geneva. Many of his publications concentrate on the external relations of the European Union, in particular the relations between the European Union and Central and Eastern Europe.

Alan Mayhew is Professorial Fellow, Sussex European Institute. He is also Visiting Professor at the College of Europe Bruges/Natolin, Adviser to the Minister for European Affairs, Government of Poland, and to various governments in central and eastern Europe. He is the author of *Recreating Europe — The European Union's Policy towards Central and Eastern Europe*, published by Cambridge University Press in 1998.

Allan Rosas has been Judge at the Court of Justice of the European Communities since 2002. He was formerly Associate Professor of Public Law at the University of Turku (1978–1981) where he got his doctorate, and Armfelt Professor of Law at the Åbo Akademi University (Turku/Åbo) (1981–1996). He then became Principal Legal Adviser at the Legal Service of the European Commission (1995–2001) and Deputy Director-General of the Legal Service (2001–2002).

John R Spencer has been a Professor of Law at the University of Cambridge since 1995. From 1990 onwards he has also spent a number of periods at French universities as visiting professor. His interests include criminal evidence and comparative criminal procedure. He was part of the international team of criminal lawyers that produced the EU Corpus Juris project. In England, he was a consultant to Lord Justice Auld's Review of the Criminal Courts (published in October 2001). His publications include the 8th edition of *Jackson's Machinery of Justice* (1989), (with Rhona Flin) *The Evidence of Children, the Law and the Psychology* (2nd ed 1993), *La procédure pénale anglaise* (Que sais-je? series) (1998), and (with Mireille Delmas-Marty) *European Criminal Procedures* (2002).

Table of Cases

European Court of First Instance

European Court of Justice

United Kingdom

Table of Legislation

Treaties and Conventions

CFSP Instruments

JHA Decisions

EC Regulations

EC Directives

NATIONAL LEGISLATION

Introduction

The European Union (EU) has embarked on its most ambitious expansion to date. It is enlarging to the countries of central, eastern and southern Europe. A first wave of accession took place on 1 May 2004, adding ten new countries (the Czech Republic, Cyprus, Estonia, Hungary, Latvia, Lithuania, Malta, Poland, Slovakia and Slovenia) to the list of Member States. But several other waves should follow. Bulgaria and Romania are presently negotiating their accession, and expect to enter in 2007, perhaps together with Croatia and the Former Yugoslav Republic of Macedonia which formally applied in 2003 and 2004 respectively. Other states from the so-called Western Balkans — Albania, Bosnia & Herzegovina and Serbia & Montenegro — have been recognised as 'potential candidates' by the EU. Turkey expects to start negotiations soon after the end of 2004, and Ukraine has voiced her 'European aspirations' on several occasions. Indeed, for Iceland, Norway and Switzerland, the present enlargement might be seen as an incitement to review their current relationship with the EU. Enlargement is therefore a work in progress and it is likely to remain one of the EU's main preoccupations for a considerable time to come.

The present collection, which is intended to coincide with the first wave of this process, aims at exploring the legal foundations and some of the potential implications of this specific enlargement on the Union's functioning and policies. It is based on a conference that took place at the Cambridge Law Faculty on 12–13 July 2002, under the auspices of the Centre for European Legal Studies (CELS).

In introducing this collection, I should like to thank all the participants of the conference, and particularly the speakers: HE Tom Risdahl Jensen, Ambassador of the Kingdom of Denmark in London, who kindly opened the proceedings; Graham Avery, John Bell, Barbara Brandtner, Marise Cremona, Jenő Czuczai, Alan Dashwood, Michael Dougan, Geoffrey Edwards, Francis Jacobs, Marc Maresceau, Alan Mayhew, Allan Rosas, John Spencer, Joanna Szychowska and Myrosław Wyrzykowski. Special thanks are also due to the speakers who kindly took up the extra burden of producing a written version of their thoughts, as well as to the other contributors who accepted to be part of this venture. I am also grateful to Diane Abraham and John Bell of CELS for their help in organising the conference; to Michael Dougan and Eleanor Spaventa for their time and devotion in making a success of the conference; and to Anne Myrjord for her unlimited support in organising the event and for her help in having the written contributions finally edited. I should also gratefully acknowledge the financial support of the French Embassy — Institut Français du Royaume-Uni. Last but not least, I am indebted to Richard Hart, publisher of this book, for his wonderful patience and understanding.

Christophe Hillion
London, December 2003

1

The Copenhagen Criteria and their Progeny

CHRISTOPHE HILLION*

I. INTRODUCTION

IN JUNE 1993, the European Council meeting in Copenhagen took a firm commitment to enlarge the European Union (EU) to the central and eastern European countries (CEECs), by formally acknowledging that:

> the associated countries in central and eastern Europe that so desire *shall* become member of the European Union' (emphasis added).

It was the first time that such a promise was made to European states that had not yet formally applied for membership,[1] although at that stage, the CEECs' wish to become members was an open secret.[2] Having made this promise, the European Council also set the conditions:

> Accession will take place as soon as an associated country is able to assume the obligations of membership by satisfying the *economic and political conditions required* (emphasis added).

* University College, London. The author wishes to thank Anne Myrjord for all her valuable comments and suggestions.

[1] Hungary formally applied on 31 March 1994, Poland on 5 April 1994, Romania on 22 June 1995, Slovakia on 27 June 1995, Latvia on 27 October 1995, Estonia on 24 November 1995, Lithuania on 8 December 1995, Bulgaria on 14 December 1995, the Czech Republic on 17 January 1996 and Slovenia on 10 June 1996.

[2] The Preamble of the first Europe Agreements (EAs) concluded in December 1991 with Hungary, Poland and the Czechoslovakia (as it then was) already contained a reference to these countries' clear ambition to accede. For instance, the Preamble of the EA with Poland said in its last indent: 'Recognising the fact that the final objective of Poland is to become a member of the Community and that this association, in the view of the Parties, will help to achieve this objective'; see also the 1992 joint petition of Hungary, Poland and the Czechoslovakia asking that accession negotiations should begin with them by 1996; *Agence Europe Documents* No 1802, 8 October 1992.

Such 'political and economic conditions' were then laid down in commanding terms. In order to be able to accede, the candidate country has to show

— stability of institutions guaranteeing democracy, the rule of law, human rights and respect for and protection of minorities;
— the existence of a functioning market economy as well as the capacity to cope with competitive pressure and market forces within the Union;
— the ability to take on the obligations of membership including adherence to the aims of political, economic and monetary union.

The above standards have since then been referred to as the 'Copenhagen criteria'.[3] Expressed by the European Council as 'obligations of membership', they have to be read jointly with the relevant Treaty provisions, which in 1993 were to be found in Article O of the Treaty on European Union (TEU) signed in Maastricht:

> Any European State may apply to become a Member of the Union. It shall address its application to the Council, which shall act unanimously after consulting the Commission and after receiving the assent of the European Parliament, which shall act by an absolute majority of its component members.
>
> The conditions of admission and the adjustments to the Treaties on which the Union is founded which such admission entails shall be the subject of an agreement between the Member States and the applicant State. This agreement shall be submitted for ratification by all the Contracting States in accordance with their respective constitutional requirements.[4]

The absence of clear directions as to what the substantive conditions of entry are, has led both the Member States and the institutions[5] to supplement the Treaty provisions with various requirements. The Copenhagen

[3] The Copenhagen European Council also pointed out that enlargement depends not only on the candidates' fulfilment of accession conditions, but it is also subject to the 'Union's capacity to absorb new members, while maintaining the momentum of European integration in the general interest of both the Union and the candidate countries'; see G Edwards' chapter in this collection.

[4] These provisions had already been amended notably by the Single European Act to accommodate the European Parliament's will to take an active part in the enlargement process. Their newest version can be found in Art 49 TEU which since the Treaty of Amsterdam subordinates the admission of new states to a political conditionality by reference to the values of the EU, encapsulated in Art 6(1) TEU. See from the same author, 'Enlargement: a legal analysis' in A Arnull & D Wincott (eds), *Accountability and Legitimacy in the European Union* (Oxford, OUP, 2002), 403; F Hoffmeister, 'Earlier enlargements', in A Ott & K Inglis (eds) *Handbook on European Enlargement* (The Hague, TMC Asser, 2002) at 90–91.

[5] The European Court of Justice has however refrained from giving further indications on such conditions; Case 93/78 *Mattheus* v *Doego* [1978] ECR 2203.

European Council conclusions offer a good illustration of this trend, but it is certainly not the only one. In practice, each enlargement has been an occasion for the Member States and the institutions to reflect and elaborate on the conditions of entry, not least because of the constant evolution of the Community/Union and of its legal order, but also as a reaction to the steady increase of membership applications.

Comparing the Copenhagen criteria and previous membership requirements will suggest that the former undoubtedly consolidate previous practice (Section II). At the same time, they have enlarged the corpus of accession conditions as well as subtly modified their nature, notably by converting them progressively into more objective 'benchmarks' (to use a trendy concept) which are controlled more systematically by an increasingly institutionalised framework (Section III). The novelty of the Copenhagen criteria also lies in the way the obligations they embody have been enforced: their gradual 'constitutionalisation' has resulted in them being applied more strictly (Section IV). However, the criteria have paradoxically entailed flexible and evolving requirements as a result of the regular adjustment and refinement by the EU of their meaning, scope and function (Section V).

II. THE COPENHAGEN CRITERIA: 'PLUS ÇÀ CHANGE ...'

A brief analysis of existing accession conditions shows that most of the Copenhagen criteria set out by the European Council in 1993 have deep roots in previous institutional practice.

A. The Political Criteria: The Consolidation of a Customary Prerequisite to Accession

The Copenhagen political criteria predate the provisions of Article 49 TEU as revised by the Amsterdam Treaty. Since then, membership has been open to European states that respect the principles set out in Article 6(1) TEU, namely the principles of liberty, democracy, respect for human rights and fundamental freedoms and the rule of law. Article 49 TEU thus epitomises, and partly 'constitutionalises', the previously established Copenhagen political conditionality.[6] But the latter is not new either. The

[6] See in this sense the Commission Regular Report of 2002; COM(2002)700, (http://europa.eu.int/comm/enlargement/report2002/#report2002) which reads as follows: 'Since the entry into force of the Treaty of Amsterdam in May 1999, these [political] requirements have been enshrined as *constitutional principles* in the Treaty on European Union...' (emphasis added).

political profile of a candidate state has always been decisive in determining the admissibility of its application for membership. Furthermore, one may suggest that the political conditionality has been implicit in the Community legal order from the very outset, and made progressively more explicit.

It should be recalled that the Treaty establishing the European Economic Community (EEC) was signed only a few years after the failure of the Treaty setting up a European Political Community (EPC) whose draft already subjected membership to the fulfilment of a political condition. Article 116(1) EPC provided that:

> Accession to the Community shall be open to the Member States of the Council of Europe and to any other European State which guarantees the protection of human rights and fundamental freedoms...[7]

While the EPC Treaty never entered into force, the political requirement connected with membership to the Communities nonetheless remained, albeit much less explicitly.[8] On the occasion of the signature of the Treaty establishing the European Coal and Steel Community (ECSC) in Paris, the then French Foreign Minister Robert Schuman emphasised that the Community would be open to all 'free' European states. The Preamble of the EEC Treaties made this point somewhat clearer by referring to a Community aimed at preserving and strengthening 'liberty', and open to other peoples of Europe who share the Member States' 'ideal'. It thereby suggested that membership implied more than a mere trade and economic endeavour.

Although these statements were essentially meant to preclude accession of European 'popular democracies', the political conditionality first materialised in the context of the EEC relations with Greece, Portugal and Spain. Discussions on their potential membership were made conditional to their acceptance and establishment of democracy. Indeed, the development of Greece's relations with the EEC was frozen following the coup of the 'Colonels',[9] while Spain and Portugal had to

[7] 'Draft Treaty embodying the Statute of the European Community', Information and Official Documents of the Constitutional Committee published by the Secretariat of the Constitutional Committee (Paris, 1952–53). The Preamble of the Treaty also envisaged enlargement in its last indent: Member States were 'determined to invite other European Peoples, *inspired with the same ideal*, to join with [them] in [their] endeavour' (emphasis added).

[8] It has been suggested that one of the ambitions was to 'de-politicise' the new Treaty to ensure its approval by the six Member States after the failure of both the EDC and the EPC; P Craig and G de Búrca, *EU Law* (Oxford, OUP, 2003) at 318.

[9] The Community suspended the application of the Association agreement it had previously concluded with Greece with a view to preparing its membership; (OJ 1963 No 26/93); J Raux, 'Relations Extérieures' (Editions Techniques — *Juris-Classeurs*, 1990), Fascicule 2201 at 4.

free themselves from their dictatorships before they could eventually be regarded as admissible states.[10]

Then, the European Council, meeting in Copenhagen in April 1978, expressed in forceful terms the political condition to which accession would be subject:

> respect for and maintenance of representative democracy and human rights in each member State *are essential elements of membership* in the European Communities (emphasis added).[11]

This statement echoed a *Common Declaration on Fundamental Rights* which had already been signed on 5 April 1977 by the presidents of the European Parliament, the Commission and the Council.[12] At that point, Greece and Portugal had made clear their ambition to accede, and Spain was about to make a formal application.[13] Pointing out that all Member States were Contracting Parties to the European Convention on Human Rights, and noting the European Court of Justice's case law on fundamental rights,[14] the three presidents committed the institutions to ensure respect for fundamental rights in the exercise of their powers and in pursuance of the aims of the European Communities.

While the political requirement expressed by the European Council did not appear in the Accession Treaties, the Preamble of the Commission's opinions on the applications of the three southern candidates nonetheless underlined that:

> the principles of pluralist democracy and respect for human rights form part of the common heritage of the peoples of the States brought together in the European Communities and *are therefore essential elements of membership of the said Communities*' (emphasis added).[15]

[10] Spain had first approached the EEC in 1962. The Socialist group in the Assembly [as it was then called] opposed the possibility of opening the Community to Spain under Franco's rule. A report of Assembly member Willy Birkelbach was instrumental in blocking Spain and Portugal's admissibility; *Rapport devant le Parlement européen*, document de séance No 122, 15 January 1962.

[11] Declaration on Democracy, Copenhagen European Council, 7–8 April 1978, Bull EC 3/78, 6.

[12] Bull EC 3/77, 5 and OJ 1977 C103/1.

[13] Greece applied in June 1975, Portugal in March 1977 and Spain in July 1977.

[14] At that stage, the European Court of Justice was developing its own 'fundamental rights case law': eg Case 11/70 *Internationale Handelsgesellschaft* [1970] ECR 1125, Case 4/73 *Nold* [1974] ECR 3727.

[15] OJ 1979 L291/3 and OJ 1985 L302/3, respectively. The Commission had already indicated in its first Opinion on the Greek application that the principles of pluralistic government and the respect for human rights were prerequisite of EC membership; Bull EC Suppl 2/76. It is also noteworthy that it is during that period that the Commission suggested that the Community should become party to the European Convention on Human Rights and Fundamental Freedoms; Bull EC Suppl 2/79.

It may be assumed that the presidents' Common Declaration also inspired the Stuttgart *Declaration on Respect of Democracy and Human Rights* of 19 June 1983,[16] as well as the provisions of the European Parliament's *European Union Treaty*, whose Article 2 referred to an accession open to '[a]ny *democratic* European State' (emphasis added). This condition of democracy was indeed regarded as a reflection of the existing Com-munity practice.[17]

In the context of fundamental transformation in central and eastern Europe, the 1991 Maastricht European Council emphasised the political condition of accession to the newly born European Union. Somewhat anticipating the Amsterdam drafting of Article 49 TEU, it noted in its conclusions that:

> The Treaty on European Union, which the Heads of State or Government have now agreed provides that any European State *whose system of government is founded on the principle of democracy* may apply to become a member of the Union' (emphasis added).[18]

The progressive institutional acknowledgement of a political conditionality was also supported by the academic community. For instance, back in 1968, Soldatos and Vandersanden suggested that an important condition for the admissibility of an application was that the applicant state belongs to the 'free' Europe. Relying on the Preamble of the EEC and its reference to the Contracting Parties' pledge 'to preserve and strengthen peace and liberty', they deduced that the potential member country must be a democracy, functioning according to the 'classical' constitutional model, the latter being understood as the antonym of the Eastern bloc constitutional system.[19]

While the fulfilment of the political condition became necessary, practice shows that it was nevertheless insufficient for a state to be able to join the Community.

[16] D Simon, 'Article 237' in V Constantinesco, J–P Jacqué, R Kovar et D Simon, *Traité instituant la CEE — Commentaire article par article* (Economica, 1988) at 1551.
[17] F Capotorti, M Hilf, F G Jacobs and J–P Jacqué, *The European Union Treaty — Commentary on the draft adopted by the European Parliament on 14 February 1984* (Oxford, Clarendon Press, 1986). The European Parliament had already adopted a Declaration on Fundamental Rights and Freedoms (OJ 1989 C120/51). Interestingly, Art 25 of the Declaration provided that it should apply 'in the field of application of Community law'. It could thus apply to Art 237 EEC (now Art 49 TEU) which already provided that enlargement required the EP's assent. Having adopted this Declaration, the EP was, in principle, committed to take it into account before granting its assent to the accession of a state to the Community.
[18] See also the Commission Report 'Europe and the Challenge of Enlargement', Bull EC Suppl 3/92, 11, pt 8.
[19] P Soldatos and G Vandersanden, 'L'admission dans la Communauté Economique Européenne' (1968) *CDE* 674.

B. The Economic Criteria: Ensuring the Candidate's Aptitude to Participate in the Common Market

The Copenhagen criteria that relate to the candidate's economic situation, also find their origins in previous practice. Already in the context of the UK's accession to the Community, the six Member States of the time, France in particular, through the voice of President de Gaulle, declared that the UK was not ready to accede, inter alia because of its economic situation which was found to be an obstacle to its participation in the Common Market.[20] This ad hoc economic condition was invoked again in 1967 in the context of the 'second' UK application. A declaration by the Council of Ministers pointed out that 'one Member State considered that the re-establishment of the British economy must be completed before Great Britain's request can be considered'.[21] The *admissibility* of the application was therefore subject to the candidate's economic recovery.

Similarly, the candidates' economic situation was discussed in the context of Greece, Portugal and Spain's accessions to the Community.[22] Although wealth and economic fitness were not explicit prerequisites to their participation in the Common Market, their economic difficulties were nonetheless a cause of concern, as underlined in the Commission opinions.[23] Indeed, the Community provided substantial assistance to help the process of adaptation of their economies.[24] In the case of Greece, the Commission even envisaged a pre-accession assistance programme that the Council however rejected on the ground that it would delay accession.

Somewhat surprisingly considering the economic profile of the candidates concerned, the formalisation of the economic condition came about on the occasion of the later EU enlargement to the EFTA states (Austria, Finland, [Norway] and Sweden); the Commission pointed out that membership presupposes 'a functioning and competitive market economy'.[25]

[20] C Preston, 'Obstacles to EU Enlargement: the Classical Method and the Prospects for a Wider Europe' (1995) 33 *JCMS* 451 at 452.

[21] The Commission also considered in its opinion that accession was subject to adjustment of the Sterling to fit into the EC's evolving monetary system and the restoration of the British balance of payment equilibrium. F Nicholson & R East, *From Six to Twelve: The Enlargement of the European Communities* (Harlow, Essex, Longman, 1987) at 56; C Preston, *Enlargement and Integration in the European Union* (Routledge, 1997) at 31; J–P Puissochet, *L'Elargissement des Communautés Européennes* (Editions Techniques et Economiques, 1974) at 16.

[22] M Sohier, 'Observations comparatives sur les conditions d'adhésion de l'Espagne et du Portugal' (1985) *CDE* 584 ; Hoffmeister, above n 4 at 96.

[23] Commission Opinion on the Greek application in Bull EC Suppl No 2/76; Commission Opinion on the Spanish application in Bull EC Suppl No 9/78, Commission Opinion on the Portuguese application in Bull EC Suppl No 5/78.

[24] Editorial Comments, 'The Greek Accession Treaty' (1979) 16 *CMLRev* 342; Editorial, 'the Second Enlargement' (1982) 19 *CMLRev* 213; P Dagtoglou, 'The Southern Enlargement of the European Community' (1984) 21 *CMLRev* 149.

[25] 'Europe and the Challenge of Enlargement', EC Bull Suppl 3/92, 11: the Commission underlined that 'an applicant country without these characteristics could not be effectively

Having progressively been established as an accession condition, the candidates' economic fitness is also connected to their capacity fully to participate in the Common Market. Observing the economic provisions of the EC Treaty implies that a Member State is a market economy.[26] Indeed, the appropriateness of the candidate's economic situation has become all the more significant given the provisions on the Economic and Monetary Union introduced by the Maastricht Treaty.[27] For the new Member States, fulfilling the 'convergence criteria' requires a prior and tighter adaptation of their economic structures.[28] Meeting the economic condition thus links up with the applicants' obligation to observe the acquis communautaire.

C. Adopting the Acquis: A Condition Inherent to Membership

The last Copenhagen criteria equally relate to a long-standing accession condition.[29] The applicant country has to show its ability to take on the 'obligations of membership', which entail the acceptance and observance of the so-called *acquis communautaire*; viz. the broadly defined Community/Union's rules and objectives.

The origin of this obligation can be traced back to the 1969 Hague Conference of the Heads of State or Government[30] which dealt with the second application of Britain, Denmark, Ireland and Norway. On this

integrated; in fact, membership would be more likely to harm than benefit the economy of such a country'.

[26] H Smit & P Herzog point out that an applicant must have an economy that is largely based on private enterprise and a free market and be able to abide by the Treaty rules on the free movement of goods, persons, services and capital and on the right of establishment; see *The law of the European Community: a commentary on the EEC Treaty* (Matthew Bender & Co, Vol 6, 1989) at 370; also Müller-Graff who suggests that the example of former East Germany is an indication of what happens to an economy that lacks a market order and the economic strength to withstand Community wide-competition, 'The legal framework for the enlargement of the internal market' (1999) 6 *Maastricht Journal of European and Comparative Law* 192.

[27] The Commission progress Report of 2002 pointed out that the economic criteria 'are consistent with the principles for economic policies as enshrined in the EC Treaty by the Maastricht Treaty…' M Cremona, 'Accession to the European Union: membership conditionality and accession criteria' (2001) 25 *Polish Yearbook of International Law* 219.

[28] See the remarks of Pedro Solbes, European Commissioner for Monetary Affairs, reported in *Agence Europe*, No 8411, 11 March 2003.

[29] On the British application, M. Couve de Murville, French Minister of Foreign Affairs, under President de Gaulle, considered that: '[l]orsque la Grande Bretagne *aura la possibilité d'accepter les dispositions du traité de Rome*, rien ne pourra l'empêcher d'entrer dans le Marché Commun' (emphasis added) in 'Dix ans de guerre froide franco-britannique', *Le Monde*, 1 January 1973.

[30] See further Puissochet above n 21; J L Brinkhorst and M J Kuiper, 'The integration of the new Member States in the Community legal order' (1972) 9 *CMLRev* 364 at 367.

occasion, the six Member States agreed to enlarge the Community on the following terms:

> *In so far as the applicant states accept the Treaties and their political aims, the decisions taken since the entry into force of the Treaties and the options adopted in the sphere of development*, the Heads of State or Government have indicated their agreement to the opening of negotiations between the Community on the one hand and the applicant States on the other (emphasis added).

This initial approach was later confirmed in the context of subsequent enlargements. As a matter of principle, it is the candidate's duty to adapt its legal order to make it compatible with that of the EC/EU. This obligation of 'legal approximation' is supplemented by another principle established by the Council of Ministers in March 1970. According to the latter, candidates' difficulties to approximate their legal order should be solved through the establishment of transitional measures rather than by reforming existing Community rules.[31] In other words, the expression 'adjustments of the treaties which admission entails' contained in Article 49 (2) TEU (and previously in Article O TEU, and Article 237 EC) has been interpreted narrowly.[32] The Member States and the candidate do not renegotiate the acquis, they only discuss technical changes such as the number of the new Member's seats in the European Parliament and other committees, as well as its voting rights in the Council.[33] Apart from these arithmetical changes, and the setting up of transitional periods, it is very much a take-it-or-leave-it negotiation.[34]

Whether that interpretation has been entirely adhered to in the context of the current enlargement has been subject to debate, at least for a moment following the negative Irish referendum on the Nice Treaty. On various occasions, it was suggested that the accession treaty could be used

[31] As recalled by Sir Con O'Neill, this approach has since then become the paradigm for the opening of all accession negotiations. The EC statements made at the opening of negotiations with Greece, with Spain and Portugal, the EFTA states, the CEECs and Cyprus 'have all been cast in the same mould'; D Hannay (ed), *Britain's Entry into the European Community* (Frank Cass Publishers, 2000), 24 at footnote 1.

[32] On the rationale of this interpretation, Puissochet (above n 21 at 19–20) explains that politically, none of the founding Member States wanted to run the risk of jeopardizing the acquis; legally, Arts 98 ECSC, 237 EEC and 205 EAEC only provide for 'adjustments' and not for genuine amendments to the Treaties; and in practical terms, accession negotiations would have never ended if, for the sake of perfection, the parties had wanted to take that opportunity to renegotiate part of the Treaties or secondary legislation. This approach has been confirmed in practice.

[33] Sohier (above n 22 at 593) underlines that as an exception to the rule of limited adjustments Art 11 of the Act of Accession of Spain and Portugal modified the rule on the rotating presidency, introducing a new differentiated system including two cycles of six years each.

[34] M Maresceau, 'The EU Pre-Accession Strategies: a Political and Legal Analysis' in M Maresceau and E Lannon (eds), *The EU's Enlargement and Mediterranean strategies* (Basingstoke, Palgrave-Macmillan Press, 2001), 3.

to introduce the reforms necessitated by new accessions.[35] Had this scenario materialised, it would have been one of the first times that the term 'adjustments' would have implied more fundamental institutional change to the Treaties.[36] Whether this reform would have been genuinely negotiated with the candidates — as Article 49 TEU seems to require, is a moot point.[37] Indeed, the legality of that option would have had to be double-checked in order to avoid any evasion of the constitutional requirements of Article 48 TEU procedure for amending the Treaties.

Be that as it may, the foregoing remarks suggest that the Copenhagen criteria broadly echo the conditions of admission to the EC/EU, which had previously been established by the institutions and the Member States. As the next section should demonstrate, these criteria nevertheless imply more than a mere confirmation of a long practice. They add further elements to the corpus of accession rules, both in substantive and institutional terms.

III. THE COPENHAGEN CRITERIA: A GRADUAL 'CONSTITUTIONALISATION' OF ACCESSION CONDITIONS

While confirming previous accession conditions, on several accounts the Copenhagen criteria nonetheless elaborate on their substance. Such an elaboration has been accompanied by the setting up of an ad hoc monitoring process, with the Commission playing a key role, and which has become increasingly institutionalised as accession negotiations and preparation have gained pace.

A. Elaborating Accession Conditions

As the EU legal order is constantly reviewed and enriched through the legislative activities of the institutions, the 'acquis' criterion has naturally

[35] See Geoffrey Edwards' chapter in this collection.

[36] The Accession Treaty with the UK brought about a significant substantive change in the fisheries policy (eg Chapter 3 of Act of accession, OJ 1972 L73) as recalled by the Court of Justice in Case 3, 4 and 6/76 *Kramer* [1976] ECR 1279.

[37] In principle, candidates as such are not involved in the reform of EU law, at least so long as the Accession Treaty has not entered into force. A first noticeable — although partial — exception is their participation in the 'Convention on the future of Europe' that drafted the 'Treaty establishing a Constitution for Europe'; see the Laeken Declaration, SN 300/1/01 REV 1, 24. More remarkable perhaps is their full participation to the Inter-Governmental Conference that started under the Italian Presidency, and thus before they officially became Members on 1 May 2004. Further: the respective chapters of Geoffrey Edwards and Alan Dashwood, in this collection.

become more demanding for the latest candidates. More remarkable perhaps is the elaboration of the other accession conditions formalised in Copenhagen, viz. the 'political and economic criteria'.

One noticeable novelty is the inclusion of the 'respect for and protection of minorities' in the political conditionality.[38] Agenda 2000 justifies this addition by arguing that the candidate countries have allegedly more minority populations than the current Member States.[39] It is also pointed out that satisfactory integration of minorities into society is a condition for democratic and international stability.[40] It is therefore part of the democratisation process rather than a criterion of its own. It is not the aim of this chapter to analyse this innovation in any more detail,[41] suffice it to say that it seemingly fleshes out the political conditionality as previously envisaged. It is however noteworthy that it does not correspond to a Union's particular policy or even competence. Indeed, the Amsterdam Treaty, which 'constitutionalised' the political accession criteria, remained silent on that point: Article 6(1) TEU does not contain any explicit reference to the protection of minorities.[42]

The elaboration of accession conditions is even more apparent in Agenda 2000, in which the Commission gave its opinion on the CEECs' applications for membership to the Union. The other Copenhagen political as well as economic criteria were spelled out in more specific terms, were each of them being divided into a number of indicators which in

[38] It has been suggested that the Commission's note on the positive and non-discriminatory treatment of the Sami minority by the Norwegian authorities had already introduced the treatment of minorities in accession conditions; E Tucny, *L'élargissement de l'Union Européenne aux Pays d'Europe centrale et orientale — La conditionnalité politique* (Paris, L'Harmattan, 2000), 21–22.
[39] Agenda 2000, 'The Challenge of Enlargement', Part II, COM(1997)2000; cp. the report of the Minority Rights Group, 'EU Accession Exposes Double Standards on Minority Rights', 15/04/2003 available on http://www.minorityrights.org/news_detail.asp?ID=107; also Open Society Institute, *Monitoring the EU accession process: Minority Protection* (2002) http://www.eumap.org
[40] Agenda 2000, above n 39.
[41] Further: B de Witte, 'Politics versus law in the EU's approach to the issue of ethnic minorities', European University Institute, Robert Schuman Centre Policy Paper No 2000/4; also: 'the impact of enlargement on the Constitution of the European Union', in M Cremona *The Enlargement of the European Union* (Oxford, OUP, 2003), 209 at 239; K Henrard, 'The impact of the enlargement process on the development of a minority protection policy within the EU: another aspect of responsibility/burden sharing?' (2002) 9 *Maastricht Journal of European and Comparative Law* 357; G Toggenburg, 'A rough orientation through a delicate relationship: The European Union's endeavours for (its) minorities' (2000) 16 *European Integration online Papers*.
[42] For more on this point: C Hillion, 'Enlargement of the European Union — the discrepancy between membership obligations and accession conditions as regards the protection of minorities', (2004) 27 *Fordham International Law Journal* forthcoming; M Nowak, 'Human Rights 'conditionality' in relation to, and full participation in, the EU' in P Alston, *The EU and Human Rights* (Oxford, OUP, 1999), 687 at 692; also G Amato and J Batt, 'Minority rights and enlargement to the East', European University Institute, Robert Schuman Centre Policy Paper No 98/5.

practice became no less than sub-conditions. As regards the economic criteria, the 'existence of a market economy' has been assessed notably by reference to whether the equilibrium between demand and supply is established by the free interplay of market forces; whether prices as well as trade are liberalised; whether significant barriers to market entry (establishment of new firms) and exit (bankruptcies) are absent; whether the legal system, including the regulation of property rights, is in place; whether laws and contracts can be enforced. Similarly, the 'capacity to withstand competitive pressure and market forces within the Union' was divided into several sub-conditions. Particularly, the Commission has checked whether there is a sufficient amount, at an appropriate cost, of human and physical capital, including infrastructure (energy supply, telecommunication, transport, etc.), education and research, and 'future development in this field'.[43]

The elaboration [or 'bullet-pointing'] of the Copenhagen criteria described above could suggest that accession conditions has been made progressively more articulate and systematic. This should have the advantage of giving further direction to the candidates, at least in principle.[44] It also helps the Commission in its role as assessor of the candidates' progressive compliance with Copenhagen criteria, as it will be further seen later.

What it denotes more generally is an attempt by the EU to carve the 'model' Member States. One could even speak of 'super Member States', given that various conditions do not have to be fulfilled, as a matter of Community law, by the current Members themselves, at least not to the extent foreseen in relation to the candidates. The protection of minorities is again a case in point. In practical terms, the Copenhagen criteria have thus become the basis for determining the policy agenda in the applicant countries; economic and political measures being defined in view of fulfilling the criteria, under the supervision of the Commission. However debatable it can be,[45] the elaboration of the accession conditions has been blessed and further stimulated by the authoritative role of the European Council. It has also led to a progressive *institutionalisation* of compliance checks.

[43] Agenda 2000 mentions a number of other indicators which are taken into account by the Commission when assessing candidates' economic progress. As regards the Commission's political benchmarks, Agenda 2000 refers to eg the holding of free and fair elections, the level of independence of the judiciary, the constitutional protection of democratic freedoms. The Commission's regular progress reports on each of the candidates are also informative as to what constitute the Copenhagen economic and political criteria: the reports contain a number of suggested measures which should be adopted by the candidate in order to fulfil the criteria.

[44] See below, Section IV.

[45] Further: P Nicolaides, 'Preparing for accession to the EU' in Cremona, above n 41.

B. Institutionalised Control of Compliance

While Article 49(2) TEU provides for the main aspects of the enlargement procedure,[46] it does not contain any particular provisions on the preparation of accession. By contrast, the *adoption* of the Copenhagen criteria by the European Council, on the suggestion of the Commission,[47] represents the launching of a genuine *policy* to prepare the candidates' accession. This policy is not only based on an expanding set of substantive rules, but it also involves an ad hoc, although progressively more settled inter-institutional cooperation.

In proclaiming that 'accession will take place as soon as an associated country is able to assume the *obligations of membership by satisfying the economic and political conditions required*' (emphasis added), and mostly by setting out what these conditions are, the European Council supplemented the general provisions of Article 49 TEU and re-defined the constitutional framework for enlarging the Union. This new framework has led to the development of additional instruments which epitomise the normative nature of the Copenhagen criteria. A case in point is the Council Regulation establishing the Accession Partnership (AP), which was adopted on the subsidiary basis of Article 308 EC, following a Commission proposal. The AP includes a set of priorities together with a system of conditionality for the candidates to meet the Copenhagen criteria.[48]

On the basis of the AP and more generally in the pre-accession framework, the Commission has been granted a pivotal function as a 'screening actor'.[49] Its traditional role of 'guardian of the [EC] Treaty' operates not only vis-à-vis the current Member States but seemingly also in relation to potential future members, as it defends and promotes the wider *Union's* acquis.[50] Its enhanced role materialises particularly through the abundant production of opinions on the candidate's suitability for membership. In contrast to previous accession procedures in which *two* Commission opinions were given,[51] the current enlargement has led to many more assessments. On the

[46] As recalled by the European Court of Justice in Case 93/75 *Mattheus* v *Doego* [1978] ECR 2203.
[47] A Mayhew, *Recreating Europe* (Cambridge, CUP, 1998), 25.
[48] M Maresceau 'Pre-accession' in Cremona above n 41, 9 at 37; Hillion, above n 4 at 419; from the same author, 'EU shapes for Eastern Enlargement' (1998) 10 *EU Focus*.
[49] M Everson and H G Krenzler, *Preparing for the Acquis Communautaire*, European University Institute, Robert Schuman Centre, Policy Paper No 98/6, esp. section III. 1. As regards more particularly the scrutiny of the political conditionality: A Williams, 'Enlargement of the Union and human rights conditionality: a policy' (2000) 25 *ELRev* 601 at 609.
[50] The Commission also supervises the progress made by the candidate in adopting the acquis in Justice and Home Affairs, and CFSP; see chapters 24 and 27 of the regular reports for each candidate country.
[51] The Commission usually gives an informal opinion to the Council before the latter decides to start the negotiations, and a formal Opinion — as required by Art 49 TEU — once the

invitation of the European Council,[52] Commission reports have been delivered on an annual basis, thereby allowing a regular evaluation and close monitoring of the candidates' progress in fulfilling the accession criteria.[53] On the basis of those reports, the Council has been in a position to decide, subject to the final approval of the European Council, to alter the pace of the pre-accession process and the conduct of negotiations. Such an institutionalised monitoring of the candidates progress by the Commission suggests a more systematic and allegedly 'depoliticised' process relying on more *objective* criteria.[54] It also supplements the meagre procedural aspects of accession provided for in Article 49(2) TEU.

Moreover, it is noteworthy that the conditions have become well-established standards for assessing the applications of other associated countries, notably the countries from south-east Europe and Turkey.[55] Indeed, the criteria are being increasingly referred to by the institutions, particularly the Commission, in relation to the current and future EU *neighbouring* countries.[56] It is also suggested that the *methodology* elaborated in this enlargement process, could be used outside the context of EU enlargement *stricto sensu*, in other external relations frameworks. It has seemingly become embedded in the Commission functioning in more general terms.[57]

accession negotiations are concluded; K Lenaerts and P van Nuffel, *The Constitutional law of the European Union* (London, Sweet and Maxwell, 1999), 276.

[52] The Luxembourg European Council of 1997 invited the Commission to draw up regular reports on the progress towards accession by each of the candidate countries.
[53] The progress reports contain a concluding section where the Commission makes 'recommendations to the European Council'; see for instance Composite Paper 1999, Part VI 'Formal Conclusions'.
[54] The expression 'depoliticisation' comes from Everson and Krenzler, above n 49.
[55] In particular, the Conclusions of the 2002 Copenhagen European Council reaffirm in pt 18 that 'Turkey is a candidate state destined to join the Union *on the basis of the same criteria as applied to the other candidate states*. As regards the so-called 'Western Balkans', pt 23 reads as follows: 'the European Council recalls *the criteria defined at the Copenhagen European Council in June 1993* and reaffirms the European perspective of the countries for the Western Balkans in the Stabilisation and Association Process' (emphasis added). This does not mean that other criteria may not be added to the list, as already suggested by the Commission's composite paper of 1999, 37. See also the 'Thessaloniki Agenda for the Western Balkans' (Doc 10369/03), approved by the European Council in Thessaloniki, June 2003.
[56] President Prodi aired the idea to use Copenhagen-like criteria also vis-à-vis EU neighbours, in a speech he gave on the occasion of the ECSA World Conference, in Brussels, December 2002. Further: M Maresceau, in this collection.
[57] The Director General for Enlargement, M Landaburu, has already suggested that if the EU is to succeed with its 'good neighbour policy', it will need 'additional instruments', which proved their worth in the current process of enlargement, eg increased financial aid, regular reports as to whether the targets set have been achieved (the transfer of EU aid would be linked to these targets, under the principle of conditionality — as in the case with the candidate countries), the possibility of taking part in Community programmes; *Agence Europe*, No 8461, 10. During a visit to Israel, Enlargement Commissioner Günter Verheugen referred to the idea that Israel could become a member of the EEA considering that it fulfils the 'economic and political requirements' of EEA membership; see *Financial Times*, 18 June 2003.

Hence, the Copenhagen criteria, initially established in the specific context of the EU eastern enlargement, have become entrenched conditions for enlarging the Union. What is more, a subtle shift has taken place as regards their nature. Thus far, accession conditions were essentially political and subjective in nature. Since the 1993 Copenhagen European Council, they have seemingly become more 'objective' standards which are used as a basis for a more articulate policy based on benchmarking, conditionality and compilation of regular reports, and monitored in an institutionalised framework. This entrenchment of membership conditionality could partly explain why the conditions can be applied more strictly.

C. A Stricter Application

As accession preparation has become more systematised, membership criteria have been applied more strictly than in previous enlargements. That is particularly the case with the condition regarding the adoption by the candidates of the EU acquis. In the present enlargement, both Member States and Commission have insisted on the requirement that, in principle, the candidates should take up the Union's acquis as a whole *before* accession.[58] This position contrasts with the approach adopted in the context of the southern enlargement when the Commission recommended some flexibility in the use of transitional periods to help the candidates' legal adaptation *after* accession.[59] In the present enlargement context, approximation is envisaged essentially as a pre-accession obligation. Such a shift is all the more significant that none of the opt-outs hitherto granted to Member States are allowed to the candidates. Accession thus implies absorption by the new Member State of the Schengen and Economic and Monetary Union (EMU) acquis. As already suggested earlier, the level of required adaptation seems therefore higher for candidate states than for current Member States.

In addition, the definition of the acquis to be adopted by the candidates is unsettled. It includes not only 'hard-law' legislation but also additional principles established by the Court's case law and practices developed by

[58] Agenda 2000, above n 39; also the 'General EU position' presented at the Ministerial meeting opening the intergovernmental conference on accession of Hungary to the EU, CONF-H 2/98, 26 March 1998; para 10.

[59] Report 'The transitional period and the institutional implications of enlargement', Bull EC Suppl 2/78, 6. In another Communication on 'the Problems of Enlargement' presented at the Copenhagen European Council of December 1982, the Commission noted that 'differentiated application of community measures and instruments in the applicant countries' could be increasingly used throughout the transition period. It added that 'in general ... possibilities for differentiation compatible with the treaties already exist[ed]'; Bull EC Suppl 8/83, 7.

the institutions, as they are on the day of accession.[60] The EU opening statement for accession negotiations with Hungary also pointed out that the acquis includes a fuzzy category of 'statements and resolutions adopted within the Union framework'.[61] In this regard, the introduction of the EU Charter of Fundamental Rights in the Commission's regular reports is particularly remarkable.[62] It tends to illustrate the wide and evolving understanding of the candidates' duty to 'approximate'. Both in the Commission 2001 and 2002 Strategy Papers, the Charter is mentioned as an instrument which 'emphasises' the political requirements to be complied with by the candidate countries, viz. the Copenhagen political criteria and the principles of Article 6(1) TEU. The Commission considers the Charter as a useful reference for assessing the candidate's political progress.[63] Seen in this light, it could be wondered whether the political requirements have not been widened as a result of the reference to the Charter, given that it is now well established that it goes beyond the mere EU acquis.[64]

IV. 'CATCH ME IF YOU CAN': THE CONTINUOUS ADJUSTMENT OF THE OBLIGATIONS DERIVED FROM THE COPENHAGEN CRITERIA

Although more strictly applied, the Copenhagen criteria are not devoid of flexibility and evolution. As a result of a regular adjustment

[60] The concept of *acquis communautaire* was first mentioned in the Commission Opinion on Denmark, Ireland, Norway and UK accession to the Communities, Bull EC Suppl 9/10 — 1969. More recently, there is been a shift to the 'EU acquis' notably in the context of enlargement. On this concept, C Delcourt, 'The *acquis communautaire*: Has the concept had its day?' (2001) 38 *CMLRev* 829; R Goebel, 'The European Union Grows' (1992) 18 *Fordham International Law Journal* 1092.
[61] See the 'General Position', above n 58.
[62] The author has here benefited from the remarks made by Dr Jenö Czuczai during the Cambridge conference on enlargement, July 2002. See also E Tanchev, 'The impact of the EU Charter of Fundamental Rights on the Candidate Countries', in A Kellermann, J de Zwaan & J Czuczai, *EU Enlargement: The Constitutional Impact at EU and National Level* (The Hague, TMC Asser Press, 2001), 35.
[63] Being proclaimed by the three political institutions in Nice, the Charter has also been recognised as an inter-institutional instrument that the three institutions have to take into account in exercising their powers. There is no apparent reason why this instrument should not also concern the powers exercised in the context of the pre-accession process, particularly since such 'political' declarations played a significant role in the past, as suggested earlier; see above, section II. A.
[64] Cp for instance the provisions of the Charter on non-discrimination and those of Art 13 EC. For more on the Charter, see eg P Eeckhout, 'The EU Charter of Fundamental Rights and the federal question' (2002) 39 *CMLRev* 945; J Dutheil de la Rochère, 'The Charter of Fundamental Rights and Beyond' (2001) 4 *Cambridge Yearbook European Legal Studies* 133; F Jacobs, 'The EU Charter of Fundamental Rights, in Arnull & Wincott, above n 4 at 275; G de Búrca, 'The Drafting of the European Union Charter of Fundamental Rights' (2001) 26 *ELRev* 126.

of their meaning, scope and function they have entailed changing obligations.

A. Adding New Dimensions to the Copenhagen Criteria

As pointed out earlier, the substantive growth of the Union's legal order partly explains the continuous adjustment of accession conditions. But the latter's moving character also results from the adaptation, by the European Council and the European Commission, of the Copenhagen criteria themselves.

For instance, supplementing the 'acpuis' criterion, the 1995 Madrid European Council considered that in order to ensure the effective implementation of the acquis before entry, applicant countries should also create the conditions for their integration through the *adjustment of their administrative and judicial structures*. This additional institutional and administrative criterion was confirmed and built on by the subsequent European Councils.[65] The 2002 Seville European Council reiterated in forceful terms that 'the candidate countries must take all necessary measures to bring their administrative and judicial capacity up to the required level'.[66]

Moreover, the 1999 Helsinki European Council added a 'good-neighbour' criterion to the list of accession conditions,[67] the underlying idea being not to import conflicts into the Union. Regional cooperation and 'good-neighbourliness' thereby became an important prerequisite to membership,[68] although enforced with varying strictness.

The EU approach vis-à-vis Cyprus is quite illustrative of a case-by-case definition of that obligation. Despite the Union's support for the reunification of the island in view of its accession[69] it eventually had to

[65] See eg the Conclusions of the Feira, Nice and Göteborg European Councils. Also, the Laeken European Council of December 2001 upheld the Commission proposal to set up a framework to monitor the administrative and judicial adjustment in the candidate countries.

[66] See pt 20, Seville European Council Conclusions, 21–22 June 2002.

[67] Agenda 2000 already contained a section on 'Border disputes' where it was suggested that 'applicants should make every effort to resolve any outstanding border dispute among themselves or involving third countries. Failing this they should agree that the dispute be referred to the International Court of Justice'.

[68] Cremona, above n 27, 231. Karen Smith has pointed out that 'good neighbourliness' already appeared in the context of the Greek accession. Greece had to acknowledge that it would not impede the strengthening of ties with Turkey; see 'the evolution and application of EU membership conditionality' in Cremona, above n 41, 105 at 110. On the other hand, it was not conceived as a full fledge condition, further: J–F Drevet, *L'elargissement de l'UE, jusqu'où?* (Paris, L'Harmattan, 2001), 132.

[69] See pt 12, Copenhagen European Council Conclusions, 12–13 December 2002.

acknowledge the possibility of enlarging only to the Greek Cypriot part of the island,

> … in the absence of a settlement, the application of the acquis to the Northern part of the Island shall be suspended, until the Council decides unanimously otherwise, on the basis of a proposal by the Commission. Meanwhile, the Council invites the Commission, in consultation with the government of Cyprus, to consider ways of promoting economic development of the northern part of Cyprus and bringing it closer to the Union.[70]

Considering that the whole enlargement process would have probably been put on hold by Greece had Cyprus not acceded, although only in part, the 'good-neighbourliness' obligation had to be slightly bended.[71] The relations between Estonia and Latvia on the one hand, and the Russian Federation, on the other hand, have also raised difficulties. The absence of an agreement on the recognition of borders, while problematic from the point of view of the good-neighbourliness condition, did not create any particular obstacle to their final admission to the Union. By contrast, the obligation has been reaffirmed in forceful terms in relation to the Western Balkans.[72]

The foregoing illustrates not only the suggestion that candidates' obligations as initially set out in Copenhagen have been adapted and supplemented.[73] It also shows a pragmatic attitude of the EU as regards the application of the conditions, which contrasts with the systematic

[70] *Ibid.*

[71] The settlement of the 'Cyprus problem' has become part of the accession conditionality applied to Turkey. In its 2003 Progress Report, the Commission recalled that 'efforts to resolve the Cyprus problem form part of the enhanced political dialogue between the European Union and Turkey. As repeatedly stressed by the European Council, Turkey, together with all parties concerned, has a decisive interest in providing determined support for efforts towards a comprehensive settlement of the Cyprus problem. The Commission considers that there are favourable conditions for the two communities to reach a comprehensive settlement of the Cyprus problem before Cyprus' accession to the EU on 1 May 2004. *The absence of a settlement could become a serious obstacle to Turkey's EU aspirations*' (emphasis added); see: http://europa.eu.int/comm/enlargement/report_2003/pdf/strategy_paper2003_full_en.pdf

[72] See in particular the Thessaloniki Agenda, above n 55, and the Zagreb Summit Final Declaration of November 2000, http://europa.eu.int/comm/external_relations/see/sum_11_00/statement.htm

[73] One could also mention that nuclear safety has become an important pre-accession requirement. The 1999 Cologne European Council emphasised in pt 60 of its conclusions: 'the importance of high standards of nuclear safety in Central and Eastern Europe. It stresses the importance of this issue in the context of the Union's enlargement and calls on the Commission to examine this issue thoroughly in its next regular progress reports on the applicant countries, due in autumn 1999'. In its 1999 Composite Paper, the Commission indeed recommended that the opening of negotiations with Bulgaria should be 'conditional upon decision by the Bulgarian authorities… on acceptable closure dates for Units 1–4 in Kozloduy nuclear power plant'.

approach that was portrayed earlier. This flexibility is also reflected in the evolution in the *function* of the criteria.

B. Changing Function of the Criteria: The Progressive Differentiation of Status Among the Candidates

The approach adopted by the EU as regards the function of the accession criteria has changed overtime. At the outset, the candidate had to fulfil the Copenhagen political conditions and prove 'to be ready to take the necessary measures to comply with the economic criteria', before negotiations could be opened. In other words, these requirements were the constitutive elements of an *admissibility* test proposed and applied by the Commission in Agenda 2000.[74] On the basis of this test, the Commission considered that although progress had still to be made in a number of applicant states, only Slovakia did not satisfy the Copenhagen political criteria, which constituted a 'necessary but insufficient condition for opening negotiations'.[75] This first understanding of the political criteria, in terms of their function in the accession conditionality, was later upheld by the Luxembourg European Council in 1997.[76]

As to the fulfilment of the economic criteria, which was assessed in a more 'dynamic' fashion, the Commission found that Hungary and Poland came 'closest to meeting them, while the Czech Republic and Slovenia [were] not far behind.' It was also felt that Estonia, while meeting the first criterion, would need to make progress to fulfil the second.

Considering that the Czech Republic, Estonia, Hungary, Poland, Slovenia could be in a position to satisfy all the conditions of membership in the medium term, the Commission recommended that negotiations should start only with these five candidates as well as with Cyprus ('5+1'). Both analysis and recommendation were endorsed by the 1997 Luxembourg European Council, and accession negotiations started in March 1998 with the 5+1.

This first approach to accession conditionality suggests that a country *aspiring* to accede can be *eligible* without being *admissible* (Bulgaria, Latvia, Lithuania, Romania inadmissible on economic grounds; Slovakia on political grounds). *Eligibility* is based on the fulfilment of the constitutional requirement, viz. 'Europeaness' (under the pre-Amsterdam version of the TEU provisions on accession).[77] *Admissibility* depends on the fulfilment of

[74] Composite Paper 1999, Part VI.
[75] Agenda 2000, above n 39 at 49.
[76] Following the Commission Composite paper 1999, the approach was later confirmed by the 1999 Cologne European Council, pt 59 of the Conclusions.
[77] A Commission report presented in June 1992, at the Lisbon European Council, shed some light on the concept of Europeaness: the term European '...combines geographical, historical

the Copenhagen political condition and the tangible proof of the ability to fulfil the economic criteria in the medium term. An admissible candidate can then start accession negotiations. *Admission* takes place after the successful conclusion of the negotiation process, when the Accession Treaty is finally signed and ratified by the Member States and the acceding state.

The first approach has changed overtime. Particularly in 1999, in the context of the Kosovo crisis, the Helsinki European Council moved on to a more inclusive approach based on a more flexible application of the admissibility test. In view of the increasing heterogeneity within the group of negotiating countries, and the non-negotiating applicants' progress to meet the criteria, the Member States decided to open negotiations to all the initially non-admissible-eligible candidates from central and eastern Europe.[78] Accession negotiations also started with Malta, after the change of government.[79] Turkey, however, was still found to have failed the admissibility test, on the grounds that it did not meet the political criteria, although some of the latter's constitutive elements were applied more softly in the case of CEECs. It has notably been argued that the protection of minorities, which belongs to the political conditionality, had not been satisfactory in some candidate states.[80] Either it suggests that the protection of minorities plays a less significant role in the political accession conditionality, or it tends to mean that the criteria are not applied consistently.

Be it as it may, Turkey was recognised as an 'official' candidate and thus made formally *eligible*,[81] despite the fact that most of the components of the Copenhagen political criteria were 'constitutionalised', by being inserted in Article 49 TEU. One could have assumed that such

and cultural elements which all contribute to the European identity. The shared experience of proximity, ideas, values and historical interaction cannot be condensed into a simple formula, and is subject to review by each succeeding generation'; Europe and the Challenge of Enlargement, Suppl 3/92 Bull CE 1992, particularly the section on the 'Conditions for new Members', 11. This initial 'open' definition seems to be put into question in the post-enlargement context. On various occasions, Romano Prodi has asked for the borders to be defined once and for all; see eg the speech he gave on the occasion of the ECSA World Conference in Brussels, December 2002.

[78] F de la Serre, 'L'Elargissement de l'Union Européenne: à qui, quand, avec quelles réformes préalables?' (2000) 3 *Cahiers Européens de Science-Po*, 1.
[79] Maresceau, above n 34.
[80] See *Monitoring the EU Accession*, above n 38; P van Elsuwege, 'The Baltic States on the Road to EU Accession: Opportunities and Challenges' (2002) 7 *European Foreign Affairs Review* 171. It is symptomatic that the issue of Russian minorities has re-appeared on the EU-Russia agenda after Copenhagen 2002, despite the fact that Russia had previously tried to on several occasions. See 'Russia warns of "vacuum" after enlargement' *EU observer*, 4 February 2004.
[81] This recognition suggests that a country's *aspirations* to become a member (which does not mean official candidature) have to be officially acknowledged by the EU: an 'aspiring' country have to be regarded as an official 'candidate' in order to be 'eligible.' This has not been the case for Ukraine and Moldova.

constitutionalisation should have implied that eligibility would be determined not only by reference to the European identity of the applicant, but also in consideration of its fulfilment of the political criteria now set out in Article 6(1) TEU. The new approach was nonetheless confirmed by the Copenhagen European Council of December 2002:

> If the European Council in December 2004, on the basis of a report and a recommendation from the Commission, decides that Turkey *fulfils the Copenhagen political criteria*, the European Union will open accession negotiations without delay' (emphasis added).[82]

The European Council has thus confirmed that the political criteria, although partly inserted in the Treaty, still determines the *admissibility* of a candidate rather than its *eligibility*,[83] suggesting a hierarchy between the two conditions of Article 49(1) TEU.

Another noteworthy point, in view of the constitutionalisation of the political criteria, is that the European Council, when addressing the question of enlargement, still refers to the 'Copenhagen political criteria' rather than simply invoking the political condition of Article 49(1) TEU. This choice probably indicates that the former still imply stricter conditions than Article 6(1) TEU, as it would hardly be conceivable that the European Council would refer to a lower political standard than that set out in Article 49(1) TEU. This suggestion is further supported by the absence of the 'protection of minorities' criterion in Article 6(1) TEU. The European Council thus suggests that the Copenhagen criteria remain better tailored to monitor accession. Pt 23 of the 2002 Copenhagen Conclusions which concern the Balkans, seems to confirm this point:

> The European Council *recalls the criteria defined at the Copenhagen European Council in June 1993* and reaffirms the European perspective of the countries of the Western Balkans in the Stabilisation and Association Process as stipulated by the European Council in Feira. The Council underlines its determination to support their efforts to move closer to the EU (emphasis added).

On the other hand, the European Council's choice could also support a widespread view that, in spite of the provisions of Article 49(1) TEU, two sets of standards apply: one for the candidates, based on the stricter Copenhagen political criteria and one for the Member States, based on Article 6(1) TEU.

[82] Copenhagen European Council, Presidency Conclusions, 12–13 December 2002, pt 19.
[83] When Croatia submitted its formal request for membership in February 2003, the Commission recalled that 'all European countries have the right to ask to join'; *Agence Europe* No 8406, 22 February 2003, 7.

V. CONCLUSIONS

The chapter has suggested that the Copenhagen criteria have crystallised and developed further the existing corpus of accession conditions. Initially established in relation to the CEECs, they have since then become standard accession criteria. They supplement the provisions Article 49(1) TEU to the extent that one can speak of the progressive 'constitutionalisation' of the Copenhagen criteria.[84]

Indeed they constitute the basis of a dynamic *policy* which elaborates the accession procedure set out in Article 49(2) TEU. Such a policy aims at preparing the candidates to meet the accession conditions. It endows the Commission and the European Council with far reaching guiding and supervisory roles to ensure compliance with these conditions by the candidate states.

The use of strict accession conditionality together with evolving obligations has allowed the Union and its Member States to shape the 'model' Member State before its accession. It has even involved obligations with no clear basis in the Treaties — EU or EC — themselves. In that, accession conditionality and membership conditionality are not interchangeable concepts.

[84] It is noteworthy that the House of Lords Select Committee on the European Union suggested that Art 57 of the Draft Constitution of the Convention on the Future of Europe which concerns Union Membership should include a statement of the Copenhagen criteria; House of Lords, session 2002–03, 18th Report.

2

Reforming the Union's Institutional Framework: A New EU Obligation?

GEOFFREY EDWARDS*

I. INTRODUCTION

THE COPENHAGEN EUROPEAN Council of June 1993 agreed not only on the criteria to be met by any new prospective candidates for EU membership of the EU, but it also gave the Union itself a new responsibility of ensuring its own capacity to absorb any new members while maintaining the momentum of integration.[1] It was, to quote the Copenhagen Presidency Conclusions, regarded as an 'important consideration in the general interest of both the Union and the candidate countries'. It was not, perhaps, a particularly dramatic statement compared to the criteria to be met by the candidates. In part, this was because of the context: the Maastricht Treaty itself had not yet been ratified by all Member States. But nor was the undertaking seen as particularly challenging in that further reform — or at least a review of Treaty changes — was already on the political agenda under the TEU. Institutional reform, in other words, has been a constant in the EC/EU's history. It became increasingly pressing with the limited outcome of the review process that resulted in the Amsterdam Treaty of 1997, together with the slow but determined pace of enlargement negotiations to admit the countries of Central and Eastern Europe and Malta and Cyprus. The inability of Member governments to agree on institutional reform at Amsterdam meant that a further intergovernmental conference (IGC) was necessary to deal with these so-called Amsterdam 'left-overs' (the size of the Commission, voting weights in the Council and on further moves

* Pembroke College, University of Cambridge.
[1] Copenhagen European Council, Presidency Conclusions, pt 7A(iii).

towards qualified majority voting (QMV)). Under a Protocol attached to the Treaty, these were to be tackled within the framework of a further 'comprehensive review' of the institutions before the membership of the Union reached twenty States.[2] Whether the IGC that convened in Nice met the requirements of a comprehensive review may be debatable since the Heads of State or Government meeting called for a yet another review. However, they also deemed the Nice Treaty as a sufficiently sound basis from which to face the potential consequences of enlargement.[3]

The Irish rejection of the Nice Treaty in its first referendum on the issue in June 2001, threw the whole process into doubt. On the one hand, the more optimistic could look to the precedent of the Danish referendums on the Maastricht Treaty which suggested that carefully crafted declarations of the European Council might be enough to assuage Irish concerns and persuade enough to vote 'yes' without further Treaty amendment in a second referendum. On the other hand, the more pessimistic, aware that Irish polls seemed to suggest that opinion was reluctant to change, were increasingly concerned that the Union would not be seen as having met its obligation to ensure its capacity to absorb new members. Whether the obligation was regarded merely as a practical, political undertaking, or whether, through constant repetition in Presidency Conclusions and the Protocol attached to the Amsterdam Treaty — along with a Declaration attached by several Member States to the Treaty that institutional reform was 'an indispensable condition' for the conclusion of accession negotiations — it had become a moral and even legal obligation, it became of vital importance to the enlargement process. For Pierre Moscovici, for example, then French Minister for European Affairs, the protocol had the force of law, which was why, 'in Nice, we stayed around the table until we reached agreement'.[4] The seeming obligatory nature of the commitment, therefore, had all the potential for creating a political crisis. The possibility was reinforced by repeated declarations that there was no 'Plan B'.[5] The implication was that without Nice, enlargement could not take place according to the agreed 'roadmap' or timetable.

It is, of course, possible that such declarations were, in large measure, designed to bring pressure on Irish voters to accept the Nice Treaty or be held responsible for holding up the accession of a group of mostly small, relatively poor, newly democratised European states. Rumours were rife,

[2] Art 2 of the Protocol on the institutions with the prospect of enlargement of the European Union attached to the TEU.
[3] Pt 4 of the Nice European Council Presidency Conclusions.
[4] Pierre Moscovici in Dublin, 13 December 2001; French Embassy Statements SAC/01.303.
[5] See, for example, EUObserver with reports inter alia of the Danish Prime Minister (27 May 2002 and especially 16 October 2002) and various Commission spokespersons (ibid, 10 June, 2nd September and 21 September 2002); http://www.euobserver.com.

though, that several Plan Bs had, in fact, been drawn up in the event of a second 'no' vote, most focusing on incorporating as much as possible of Nice in the accession treaties. And there was, too, the prospect of yet another IGC in 2004, called for by the Nice European Council to deal with what Heads of State or Government had had neither the time nor the inclination to tackle. By December 2001, this 'post-Nice agenda' had been overtaken by a list of some 60 questions agreed at the Laeken European Council, which were to be discussed in a Convention on Europe's Future. The Convention's chairman, the former French President, Valery Giscard d'Estaing, drew somewhat ambitious parallels between the Convention and that held in Philadelphia which had drawn up the constitution for the United States of America. One implication of this was that the Irish result was no longer relevant; by one means or another, the Union was clearly determined to provide itself with the capacity to continue the integration process and enlarge at the same time.

In the event, confronted by near-marginalisation, the Irish people voted in favour of the Nice Treaty in the second referendum in October 2002, thereby making the question of the nature of the EU's obligation to reform before enlargement somewhat redundant. Academic though it may have become, the issue is nonetheless of interest as an example of the way in which the EU attempts to bind itself to political goals by creating expectations and obligations.

This habit has been characterised in a number of ways in and within different academic disciplines. From one political science perspective, for example, one might talk in terms of the institutionalisation of the reform or integration process, with, from the Maastricht Treaty on, repeated Treaty provision for reviews within specified periods.[6] European Council Conclusions that reiterate the commitment could be seen to reinforce this. Similarly, if from a different theoretical basis, one might talk of a process of spillover taking place, with the central institutions, including the European Council, pressing for further reforms to promote or, perhaps, to protect the institutional structures and decision-making processes as well as extending the competences of the EU. Moreover, even if the reform process has been one of 'Brusselisation',[7] of moving decision making to Brussels-based institutions rather than 'communitarisation' (ie of retaining the more classical supranational dimension of the Community and the more traditional role of the Commission), there has been a certain

[6] G Edwards and A Pijpers, *The Politics of European Treaty Reform* (London, Cassell, 1997); J P Olsen, 'Reforming European Institutions of Governance', ARENA Working Papers WP 01/7, U Sverdrup 'An Institutional Perspective on Treaty Reform: Contextualising the Amsterdam and Nice Treaties', ARENA Working Papers WP 01/27.

[7] A process suggested initially by J O Kiso 'CFSP heads into unchartered waters' in *The European Voice*, 4 September, 1997.

degree of path-dependency in that the agenda of succeeding IGCs has been set largely by the limits of the preceding Treaty. Progress, as the (first) Irish referendum suggested, was neither inevitable nor necessarily smooth, though it could be argued that the costs — real or potential — of stepping outside the paths of consensus can be and have sometimes been considerable, as perhaps the second Irish referendum showed. But from a more rationalist or utilitarian perspective, institutional reform was much more an issue of efficiency: the prospect of such a huge enlargement inevitably challenged an already sub-optimal policy-making machinery. Or, from a more social constructivist perspective, the growing sense of crisis that the EU had not met its obligation to reform and thereby might not allow enlargement, was created by a challenge to the legitimacy of the Union itself — how could the moral basis and political legitimacy of the EU be maintained if it denied membership to other eligible European states?[8]

Significantly, several of these concepts overlap with those in legal studies, especially, perhaps, the sense of moral obligation and the concept of soft law. The latter has been used by a number of commentators over the last decade or so, leading one of them to suggest that we may have entered into 'an era of soft law',[9] an era characterised by the proliferation of 'regulation by publication'.[10] For most lawyers, the concept appears to be one that describes 'a category of acts which, though not identified as binding, are capable, at least in some circumstances, of having legal effect'.[11] In other words, measures that 'have been or may be used in a court of law to determine the obligations of parties to a dispute'.[12] The list of what *might be* considered soft law could be long; a recommendation, opinion, code of conduct etc may turn out to be 'soft law' if later taken up by a court and 'hardened up'. Indeed, others seem to take an even broader approach; Snyder, for example, has suggested that soft law comprises 'rules of conduct which, in principle, have no legally binding force but which nevertheless may have practical effects'.[13] There is perhaps a

[8] L Friis and A Murphy 'Enlargement: A Complex Juggling Act' in M Green Cowles and M Smith (eds) *The State of the European Union vol. 5: Risks, Reform, Resistance, and Revival* (Oxford, OUP, 2000).
[9] B Flynn 'Subsidiarity and the rise of 'soft law' in EU environmental policy', University College Dublin Occasional Paper No. 40, 1997, quoted by M Cini 'The soft law approach: Commission rule-making in the EU's state aid regime' (2001) 8 *Journal of European Public Policy* 193.
[10] F Snyder, 'Soft Law and Institutional Practice in the European Community', European University Institute, LAW Working Paper No 93/5, 3.
[11] F Beveridge and S Nott, 'A hard look at soft law' in Paul Craig and Carol Harlow (eds), *Law Making in the European Union* (The Hague, Kluwer Law International, 1998), 291.
[12] *Ibid.*
[13] Snyder, above n 2, quoting Snyder, 'The effectiveness of European Community Law: Institutions, Processes, Tools and Techniques' (1993) *Modern Law Review* 56.

tendency, as Klabbers[14] has pointed out, that soft law is often used to describe things that are simply difficult to describe as hard law:

> 'guidelines, codes of conduct, resolutions, recommendations and action programmes, indeterminate provisions of treaties, unratified conventions, perhaps even the opinions of advocates general ...they may all perhaps be qualified as 'soft law'. Clearly they are not hard law; clearly they are not totally irrelevant either, so *viola:* soft law it must be.'

Rather more constructively, Dehousse and Weiler have suggested that an historical perspective is needed: 'the 'soft law' concept may be useful in understanding how pragmatic arrangements have slowly crystallised into binding rules of law'.[15]

The Presidency Conclusions agreed at the Copenhagen European Council of 1993 cannot be seen as 'soft law' in the sense that they were later tested in a court of law, though the provisions included in the Protocol attached to the Amsterdam Treaty could be seen as a 'hardening up'. It was clear, as we shall see, that a growing number of Member States did see institutional reform as an essential prerequisite to further enlargement. And it could be argued that, after the Luxembourg European Council of 1997,[16] the initial 'wave' of admissions increasingly looked as if it would take the number of Member States beyond the twenty indicated in the Protocol, there was a legal requirement to introduce reform. But it is equally plausible to argue that the way in which successive Presidency Conclusions reinforced this obligatory dimension suggests that the soft law concept in providing a strong normative bias may still be useful — not least in pointing up the overlap between political and legal approaches. As Beveridge and Nott put it, the 'much cited study' of Wellens and Borchadt,[17] suggests a number of possibilities, the following being of particular relevance for our purposes:

- soft law may provide a legal basis for State action;
- the soft law may in future serve as a basis for negotiation, thus acting as a precursor for hard law;
- soft law may create expectations about conduct, raising the question of 'legitimate expectations';

[14] J Klabbers 'The Undesirability of Soft Law' (1998) 67 *Nordic Journal of International Law* 384/5.
[15] R Dehousse & J H H Weiler, 'EPC and the Single Act: From Soft Law to Hard Law?' European University Institute, EPU Working Paper 90/1, 6.
[16] The Luxembourg Council agreed to the opening of negotiations with Cyprus, the Czech Republic, Estonia, Hungary, Poland and Slovenia.
[17] K C Wellens and G M Borchardt 'Soft Law in European Community Law' (1989) 14 *ELRev* 267.

— during the process of creation of hard law, soft law can have a legitimising effect on conduct;
— soft law may bind the institutions themselves, carrying a 'hard law character in the internal organisational and institutional system' …

What follows therefore examines the ways in which Member governments dealt with the original Copenhagen commitment to institutional reform in the light of these possibilities.

II. PRESIDENCY CONCLUSIONS AND BEYOND

The Presidency Conclusions of the Copenhagen European Council of 21–22 June 1993 added, under 7A(iii), not only three requirements of the candidate countries but also:

> 'The Union's capacity to absorb new members, while maintaining the momentum of European integration, is also an important consideration in the general interest of both the Union and the candidate countries.'

It was a timely reminder to the Member governments themselves as well as a marker for the future in that the Maastricht Treaty had not at that point been ratified. Delays and uncertainties had been created by the results of the Danish and French referendums (the Danes voting 'no', the French, a 'petit oui'), the growth of Eurosceptic nationalism within the British Conservative Party and the consequent delays in putting the necessary bill before Parliament, and the reference of the Maastricht Treaty to the German Constitutional Court. And while public attention after Copenhagen was immediately very much more focused on the willingness of the Union to open itself up to enlargement to the East, a number of governments and parties were particularly concerned about the consequences of that enlargement for the institutional structure of the Union.

In part this was due to the unavoidability of further debate on Treaty reform. Not only was it called for under Art N(2) of the Treaty on European Union, but there was clearly dissatisfaction with the Maastricht outcome. As Ian Davidson put it in the *Financial Times*:

> 'The treaty is a ramshackle structure with disparate pieces tacked together, some of which were improvised in haste in response to German unification. And the consequences of improvisation and ambiguity, and of the impact of outside events, is that it does not look viable as framed …'[18]

[18] *Financial Times*, 27 September 1993.

Davidson was responding to a report produced by Karl Lamers of the German CDU, which inter alia, declared:

> 'The expansion of the Community ... must not be allowed to weaken the degree of integration already achieved by the present core; on the contrary this must be strengthened. Otherwise the European Union will not be able to help solve the increasingly life-threatening crises of the nations that make it up ...'[19]

Lamers, who went on to produce an even more influential report for the CDU/CSU with the CDU Deputy Leaders, Wolfgang Schäuble, the following year (see below), was not alone. Jacques Delors, in his last year as Commission President, also expressed his concern over the fissiparous pressures that appeared to be gathering strength, not least in the UK:

> 'What I see is a European construction drifting towards a free trade zone, that is to say, an English-style Europe which I reject and which is against the spirit of the founding fathers of the Treaty of Rome.'[20]

It was not simply a question of the viability of the TEU, but the institutional and decision-making changes consequent to the EFTAn enlargement that reinforced such concerns as those of Delors. What particularly concerned the British — with the Spanish and the Italians somewhere in support until the dénouement — was the loss of voting strength in the Council with the advent of four, ultimately three after Norway's rejection of accession, small EFTAn states. Enlargement to include Austria, Finland, Norway and Sweden had generally been regarded as unlikely to cause difficulties. Britain's seeming willingness to delay the enlargement process, even when in a minority of one, aroused considerable hostility, the Greek European Minister, Theodore Pangalos (rarely noted for his quiet tact or diplomacy), describing British moves as 'blackmail tactics'.[21] The Danish Foreign Minister expressed it thus:

> 'Denmark cannot and will not accept that enlargement to the north is put in danger by Britain's incomprehensible insistence on an obsolete set of rules. We cannot accept it also because a successful enlargement to the north is an absolute condition for the EU to fulfil the next, decisive task: the integration of the new democracies in Central and Eastern Europe. Europe's future is at stake, no more, no less.'[22]

[19] *Ibid.*
[20] *The Guardian*, 19 October 1993.
[21] *The Guardian*, 28 March 1994.
[22] *The Independent*, 17 March 1994.

It was not, of course, the first — or last — time that momentous chapters in the EC/EU's history have been subordinated to domestic concerns by Member governments. And there was, indeed, a certain irony in the Greek and French declarations of irritation: both had threatened to block Iberian accession in the early 1980s — the Greek Prime Minister, Andreas Papandreou, for the sake of a better aid package, and President Chirac, when Prime Minister, in the interests of maintaining the protection of French agriculture. What it did, though, was to reaffirm the need to focus on adequate institutional reform. If the Iaonnina Compromise that resulted from British intransigence was to last only until further Treaty reform could be agreed,[23] that simply emphasised the pressing nature of the necessary reforms — hence the priority given to reform by the Reflection Group set up by the subsequent Corfu European Council in June 1994. The Group was to look at the weighting of votes, the threshold for qualified decisions, the number of members of the Commission and any other reform 'deemed necessary to facilitate the work of the institutions and guarantee their effective operation in the perspective of enlargement'.[24] In addition, the Conclusions declared:

> 'The institutional conditions for ensuring the proper functioning of the Union must be created at the 1996 Intergovernmental Conference, which for that reason must take place before accession negotiations begin'.[25]

Chancellor Kohl and the German Government were particularly keen to push the pace of enlargement beyond the EFTAns towards Eastern Europe with Kohl 'convinced that he can persuade his EU partners that anxiety over stability in eastern and central Europe is not a selfish German preoccupation'.[26] In fact, the French had already shown themselves receptive at least to meeting security concerns, but not necessarily by means of enlargement; Edouard Balladur, the French Prime Minister had put forward his proposals for a Stability Pact in June 1993.[27] For their

[23] The Compromise held that 'If Members of the Council representing a total of 23 to 26 votes indicate their intention to oppose the adoption by the Council of a decision by qualified majority, the Council will do all in its power to reach, within a reasonable time and without prejudicing obligatory time limits laid down by the Treaties and by secondary law, such as in Articles 189 B and 189 C of the Treaty establishing the European Community, a satisfactory solution that could be adopted by at least 68 votes …'

[24] *Financial Times*, 27 June 1994.

[25] Insofar as the Conclusions call for reform before negotiations opened and it was precisely those institutional 'left-overs' that remained after Amsterdam, the opening of negotiations in 1998 might suggest the unreliability of Presidency Conclusions as a guide to future behaviour.

[26] *The European*, 4–10 March 1994.

[27] For details see T Ueta 'The Stability Pact: from the Balladur Initiative to the EU Joint Action' in M Holland (ed) *Common Foreign and Security Policy: The Record and Reforms* (London, Pinter, 1997).

part, the British, still wedded to the idea that a wider Europe meant a looser Europe, tended to reinforce both French and particularly German interest in more radical reform and the concept of flexibility, variable geometry etc, as a way of overcoming the vagaries of national vetoes.[28] But the CDU, at least in the form of the Schäuble-Lamers paper, went considerably further. It was particularly concerned that differences in socio-economic development, structural economic change and unemployment, 'regressive' nationalism, and overstretched national and European institutions pointed to the conclusion that 'the process of European unification has reached a critical juncture'.[29] In looking to a Franco-German hard core of the inner circle, the paper's impact was considerable, not only on the German Government but also in terms of the adverse reaction it created, especially in the UK. While distancing itself from the paper, the German Presidency (July-December 1994) nonetheless had to press particularly hard on both the enlargement and reform fronts, though the Essen European Council of December 1994 simply repeated the language agreed at Corfu, that 'the institutional conditions for ensuring the proper functioning of the Union must be created at the 1996 Intergovernmental Conference, which for that reason must take place before accession negotiations begin.'

III. THE TREATY OF AMSTERDAM

The mandate for that IGC had already been set out in Art N of the TEU which was to analyse the extent that:

> 'The policies and forms of cooperation introduced by this Treaty may need to be revised with the aim of ensuring the effectiveness of the mechanisms and the institutions of the Community.'

The target was especially the pillar structure, with a further opportunity provided for tying up some of the loose ends that remained from the final

[28] The Schäuble-Lamers paper for the CDU-CSU fraction (*Überlegungen zur europäischen Politik*) which outlined the possibilities of a hard core group of states was published in Bonn in September 1994 immediately after that of Balladur, whose contribution included that of variable geometry. See inter alia Edwards & Pijpers, above n 6. The French position was reiterated by Alain Juppé, Balladur's successor in March 1996, when he declared: Let's have the courage to say it. Tomorrow's Union will no doubt be made up of two distinct levels: a Union of common law, comprising the fifteen present members and those with a vocation to join it; at the heart of this Union ... a second circle of states at the centre of which will be France and Germany, nations prepared and willing to go further or faster than the others on subjects such as the currency or defence', *Agence Europe*, 15 March 1996.

[29] Edwards and Pijpers, above n 6.

Treaty negotiations, particularly in relation to the Common Foreign and Security Policy (CFSP), the extent of co-decision and the extension of Community competences. These possibilities had been overtaken by the interrelated issues of enlargement and institutional reform. However, these, too, seemed to jostle for priority with another concern, the legitimacy of the EU itself. President Chirac put it this way after an informal meeting of Heads of State or Government in Majorca in September 1995, that, 'in the first place', the IGC should:

> 'be limited to the institutional aspects, in other words, be preparing for the opening-up, enlargement of the EU, which, as everyone realizes, requires the institutions to be modified. But at the same time ... the enlargement mustn't overshadow aspects closer to home, those which more directly affect the Europeans, ie specifically, on the one hand, everything to do with the fight against organised crime, drugs and terrorism, particularly where security is involved, and, on the other, of course, everything relating to the fight against unemployment and for jobs.'[30]

The final mandate taken up by the Reflection Group from the Madrid European Council later in 1995 as expressed in their Report was that the main objectives of the IGC should be:

- — making Europe more relevant to its citizens;
- — making the Union work better and preparing it for enlargement;
- — giving the Union greater capacity for external action.

The order of the objectives indicate clearly the alertness of the Group to the issue of the political legitimacy of the EU and the need, if Member governments were to avoid the problems of ratifying the Maastricht Treaty, 'to ensure that European construction becomes a venture to which citizens can relate'. The Group's Report added: '... the Union's principle internal challenge is to reconcile itself with its citizens. Therefore, enhancing its legitimacy in their eyes will have to be the prime objective of the coming reform'.[31] However, while there may have been a consensus on the necessity of improving the democratic legitimacy of the institutions and strengthening their effectiveness with a view to enlargement, quite how this was to be achieved divided the Group and the Member States at the subsequent IGC.

[30] Press Conference 23 September 1995; SAC/95/220 Ambassade de France à Londres.
[31] General Secretariat of the Council of the EU *1996 Intergovernmental Conference: Reflection Group Report* Brussels 1995, 36. Some of the language of the Report was to resonate throughout the debates on Amsterdam, Nice and through to the Convention on Europe's Future, the Report declared: The Union is not and does not want to be a super-state ... The right way for the Union to regain the commitment of its citizens is to focus on what needs to be done at European level to address the issues that matter most to them ...'.

In the event, and typical of so much of EU decision-making, the IGC was to a considerable extent hijacked by another more immediate if no less momentous issue, Economic and Monetary Union. As one German journalist put it:

> 'If Maastricht had been about making sure that a united Germany stays firmly committed to the European project, Amsterdam has been about making sure that France remains committed to EMU and to the Stability Pact to which Germany attached high symbolic importance.'[32]

The result was a distinct down-grading of many of Germany's other more ambitious goals for Amsterdam.

For many, therefore, the Treaty was regarded as disappointing. If the objective had been to apply the 'principles of efficiency, democracy, transparency and solidarity in the EU', as recommended by the Reflection Group, the resulting Treaty, to quote one MEP, deserved 'a first prize for complexity, lack of clarity and transparency'.[33] It reflected, according to Moravscik and Nicolaïdes,

> 'the lack of compelling and compatible substantive national interests in deeper, more uniform cooperation ...' and 'the absence of clear substantive interests in [moving forward in] ... new areas sufficient to justify substantial sacrifices of sovereignty'.[34]

Despite having so often declared that institutional reform was an absolute priority before enlargement, they managed only to agree to postpone the effort to agree on it.[35]

Although there were some changes in extending co-decision with the European Parliament and on qualified majority voting, Heads of State or Government could agree only on a two-stage approach to more comprehensive institutional reform. According to the Protocol:

> 'At the date of entry into force of the first enlargement of the Union... the Commission shall comprise one national of each of the Member States,

[32] C Bertram (*Die Zeit*) in European Policy Centre (ed), *Challenge Europe: Making Sense of the Amsterdam Treaty* (Brussels, European Policy Centre, 1997), 64.
[33] L Brinkhorst, ibid at 49.
[34] A Moravscik and K Nicolaïdes, 'Federal Ideals and Constitutional Realities in the Amsterdam Treaty' in G Edwards and G Wiessala, *The European Union 1997* (1998) *JCMS* 17.
[35] As Ian Davidson put it: The Amsterdam meeting was the most unsuccessful European summit for many years ... The omens at Amsterdam were all negative. The most striking was that governments failed to agree on any of the institutional reforms necessary if the European Union is to take in 10 or more new members from eastern Europe. They had long said that institutional reform was an absolute priority before enlargement, as a mega-Europe could not function without overhauling the decision-making rules; but last week they simply gave up the attempt to agree, and put off the problem to another day ...' *Financial Times*, 25 June 97.

provided that, by that date, the weighting of votes in the Council has been modified ... At least one year before the membership of the European Union exceeds twenty ... [a new IGC shall be convened to] carry out a comprehensive review of the provisions of the Treaties on the composition and functioning of the institutions.'

Not content with such a commitment, the Belgian, French and Italian governments registered their disappointment in the Treaty by attaching a Declaration to it which held that since it did not meet the need for substantial progress towards reinforcing the institutions, they:

'...consider that such reinforcement is an indispensable condition for the conclusion of the first accession negotiations. They are determined to give the fullest effect appropriate to the protocol as regards the composition of the Commission and the weighting of votes and consider that a significant extension of recourse to qualified majority voting forms part of the relevant factors which should be taken into account.'

But even while the 'Amsterdam left-overs' remained to be dealt with, the European Council at Luxembourg agreed to launch an accession process for the 10 Central and Eastern European countries and Cyprus, with negotiations beginning with Cyprus, the Czech Republic, Estonia, Hungary, Poland, and Slovenia. The prospect of agreement, together with the growing embarrassment of being unable to begin to meet the demands of the applicants, thus seemed enough to modify the existing position reaffirmed at Essen that institutional reform 'must' precede accession negotiations. The Luxembourg Presidency Conclusions merely added:

'As a prerequisite for the enlargement of the Union, the operation of the institutions must be strengthened and improved in keeping with the institutional provisions of the Amsterdam Treaty.'

The predicament in which Member governments now found themselves was particularly well put by the three 'Wise Men' (Richard von Weizsäcker, Jean-Luc Dehaene and Lord (David) Simon), who had been called on by the Commission to report on the institutional implications of enlargement. In their Report, delivered in October 1999, they wrote:

'There is also agreement among Member States that enlargement is an objective of such political and historical importance, both for the Union and candidate countries, that it cannot be delayed or postponed because institutional reform is incomplete. The challenge for the present generation of European leaders is to attain the fundamental objective of enlargement while also resolving, in the same time frame, one of its consequences, namely the need for such reform as will enable an enlarged Union to perform effectively.'[36]

IV. TOWARDS NICE AND BEYOND

Much of the debate between Amsterdam and Nice turned on the scope of the agenda for the IGC. Agreement came only after decisions on membership of the single currency and preparation of Agenda 2000 (on agriculture, structural funds etc) within the context of enlargement. The issue on the IGC agenda, as Gray and Stubb have pointed out, was largely whether a narrow agenda based on the Amsterdam leftovers would bring about a rapidly concluded IGC and early enlargement — with the probability of the need for a further IGC later — or whether it was wiser to have a broader agenda, the prospect of a lengthier IGC and the postponement of enlargement.[37] The Cologne European Council in June 1999 decided on the former, a decision confirmed at Helsinki in December 1999 but then modified at Feira in June 2000 to include further consideration of provisions for enhanced cooperation.[38] The task of the French Presidency to bring about agreement in Nice was made more difficult not only by the parallel discussions on a European Security and Defence Policy and on the nature of the Charter of Fundamental Rights, but by the opening up of perhaps the most important debate ever on Europe's future by the German Foreign Minister, Joschka Fischer in his speech at Humboldt University in May 2000.[39]

But the Nice IGC at least settled the Amsterdam left-overs. The Commission was to include one Commissioner from each Member State until it reached 27 members when a rotation system would be introduced. On the reweighting of votes — perhaps the most difficult for a French Presidency insofar as it did not want to breach parity with Germany — the final decision was a highly complicated and not wholly coherent (or consistent) triple majority. Reweighting was tied to a the

[36] Richard von Weizsäcker, Jean-Luc Dehaene and Lord (David) Simon, *The Institutional Implications of Enlargement — Report to the European Commission.* Report called for President designate of the Commission, Romano Prodi. Brussels, October 1999.
[37] M Gray and A Stubb 'The Treaty of Nice: Negotiating a Poisoned Chalice' in G Edwards and G Wiessala (eds), *The European Union 2000–2001* (2001) *JCMS* 8.
[38] Significantly, the Helsinki Council, which, in addition launched negotiations with Bulgaria, Latvia, Lithuania, Malta, Romania and Slovakia, agreed, to quote the Presidency Conclusions:
The Union has made a firm political commitment to make every effort to complete the Intergovernmental Conference on institutional reform by December 2000, to be followed by ratification. After ratification of the results of that Conference the Union should be in a position to welcome new Member States from the end of 2002 as soon as they have demonstrated their ability to assume the obligations of membership and once the negotiating process has been successfully completed.'
[39] For the text of Fischer's speech and a good range of governmental responses to it, see M Leonard (ed), *The Future Shape of Europe* (London, Foreign Policy Centre, 2000).

numbers of MEPs, which had been capped at Amsterdam at 700 but now increased to 732 — with the Presidency handing out 'extra seats like loose change'.[40] QMV was extended to a substantial number of areas — estimated by Peter Ludlow at 40 out of a possible 75 that had been raised.[41] And the provisions on enhanced cooperation were modified by removing the veto, reducing the number of states required to initiate the process and relaxing other conditions. Reform of the Court of Justice and the Court of First Instance was also added — agreed by jurists rather than negotiated by Heads of State or Government.

Most importantly from the perspective of this chapter, the Nice Presidency Conclusions declared:

> 'This new treaty strengthens the legitimacy, effectiveness and public acceptability of the institutions and enables the Union's firm commitment to the enlargement process to be reaffirmed. The European Council considers that, as from the date of entry into force of the Treaty of Nice, the Union will be in a position to welcome new Member States once they have demonstrated their ability to assume the obligations of accession and the negotiations have been brought to a successful conclusion.'

There was, perhaps a certain lack of conviction in the statement, the exhausted Heads of State or Government (the Nice European Council was the longest on record) recognising the need for further constitutional debate — with the association of the candidates for membership. As Declaration 23 attached to the Treaty put it, while the Treaty may have completed 'the institutional changes necessary for the accession of new Member States', and opened the way for enlargement, it was hardly enough to ensure ' the democratic legitimacy and transparency of the Union and its institutions, in order to bring them closer to the citizens of the Member States'. In other words, it did not guarantee any continued momentum towards integration. It therefore called for yet another IGC in 2004, initially at least to deal with the issues of the powers of the EU and the Member States, the status of the Charter of Fundamental Rights, a simplification of the Treaties and the role of national parliaments.[42]

The rejection of the Nice Treaty in the Irish referendum of 7 June 2001 was seen by many as creating the risk of serious delays to the whole process of enlargement.[43] Indeed, it seemed initially that only the

[40] Gray and Stubb, above n 37 at 16.
[41] P Ludlow 'The Treaty of Nice: Neither Triumph nor Disaster' (2001) 14 *European Community Studies Association Review.*
[42] Declaration on the Future of the Union.
[43] See, for example, reports of the Swedish Prime Minister on the 'risk' *Financial Times,* 12 June 2001. The result of the referendum was 53.87 per cent against with only 41.13 per cent in favour in a turn out of only 34.8 per cent of the vote (figures taken from B Laffan 'The Nice Treaty: the Irish Vote' *Notre Europe,* 6 July 2001).

Commission President believed that enlargement could go ahead without Nice being ratified though even he was obliged to admit that it was required 'as a political condition for enlargement.[44] The referendum result was a shock, most politicians in Europe — even in Dublin — had assumed that the Irish, as long-term beneficiaries of EU membership, would have voted with their purses. The reasons for the rejection included wariness of the institutional arrangements under Nice — not least after the clear divergences between big and small states at the IGC — as well as usual Irish concerns over its military neutrality. The 'No' camp's position had been given a further boost with the intervention of a former Irish Attorney General, John Rogers, who declared that '... it is clear that the capacity of an Irish citizen to influence decisions which will intimately affect his/her life will be significantly reduced by the impact of the Nice Treaty'.[45] In what was a hurried, lack-lustre campaign, a somewhat overly-complacent government had been relatively easily portrayed as being out of touch with the people. It was not particularly surprising in such circumstances, that the Taoiseach, Bertie Ahern, should echo the concerns of so many in the past that 'there is unfortunately a widespread sense of disconnection between the institutions and its citizens'. He went on to say:

> 'There is a frustration at what is sometimes seen as an absence of clarity, openness and responsiveness in how the Union goes about its business. There is a real and urgent need to focus on how we can make the Union more meaningful to our citizens and how its democratic accountability can be strengthened.'[46]

While such concerns duly found there way into the Laeken Declaration on the future of Europe in December 2001 which, inter alia, called for institutions to be brought closer to Europe's citizens, there was a certain irony in the reactions of the European Council meeting in Göteborg to the Irish results.

The Heads of State or Government were agreed that the Nice ratification process would continue 'so that the Union is in a position to welcome new Member States from the end of 2002'.[47] While supporting their conclusions, they did not repeat the text of their Foreign Ministers that they 'excluded any reopening of the text signed in Nice',[48] but merely echoed

[44] *Financial Times*, 23/24 June 2001. Prodi had given an interview to the *Irish* Times on 21 June suggesting enlargement could go ahead. The reaction of many governments and others was immediate — the German government, for example, being reported in the *Financial Times* as saying that his remarks sent 'completely the wrong signal'.
[45] *Financial Times*, 4 June 2001. See also Laffan, above n 43.
[46] *Financial Times*, 18 June 2001.
[47] Göteborg European Council Presidency Conclusions, pt I.4.
[48] General Affairs Committee 11 June 2001 Press Release.

their willingness to help the Irish Government 'find a way forward'. As Laffan has suggested, the result was that the domestic management of the issue by the Irish Government became more difficult:

> 'Although the Government repeatedly said it would respect the outcome of the referendum, the determination of the other states to ratify the treaty was interpreted as pressure on Ireland to hold another referendum to secure the 'right' outcome!'[49]

Moreover, the Heads of State or Government declared that the 'enlargement process is irreversible.'[50] In addition, they applauded the Swedish Presidency (and themselves) in achieving significant breakthroughs in the accession negotiations, so that 'Provided that progress towards meeting the accession criteria continues at an unabated pace, the roadmap should make it possible to complete negotiations by the end of 2002 for those candidate countries that are ready'.

The possibility that the irreversible process of enlargement might be at least seriously delayed by an Irish vote, whether or not the result of an electorate's unhappiness with its Government or because of opposition to Nice or towards enlargement,[51] imposed growing pressures on the Irish Government. This was particularly the case as 2002 progressed when there seemed so little change in the opinion polls, and even though the Government had established a 'National Forum on Europe' in October 2001 designed to facilitate a broad discussion of issues relevant to Ireland's membership of an enlarged EU.[52] Indeed, polls seemed unchanged despite the assurances won by the newly re-elected Taoiseach at the Seville European Council in June 2002 that recognised Ireland's traditional policy of military neutrality. This had been a primary issue in the Forum, kept alive for many in the 'No' lobby by the Irish and EU support for the United States in the fight against terrorism.[53] But, significantly, the

[49] Laffan, above n 43 at 8.
[50] Presidency Conclusions, pt I. 8
[51] The Minister for Foreign Affairs, for example, declared that such an 'historic issue like the enlargement of the Union' was too important to become 'a scapegoat for the protest vote in respect of disappointments people may have about a whole range of issues, most of them domestic policy issues unrelated to EU matters'. Press release, 12 June 2001, Department of Foreign Affairs. Quoted in D Sweeney 'The two referenda on Nice, the security debate in Ireland and the limits of Europeanization'; Paper given to the Biennial meeting of the European Union Studies Association, Nashville, 27–9 March 2003.
[52] For opinion polls see various reports in EU observer taken from Economist Intelligence Unit polls.
[53] The *Financial Times*, 19 October 2001 had reported one leading member of the 'No' lobby as saying: It was always our objective to keep neutrality at the centre of the forum discussions. It will certainly be easier now that there is a war going on.'

Presidency Conclusions, after taking cognisance of the Irish declaration went on:

> 'The European Council welcomed the Irish Government's determination to have the Treaty of Nice approved, this being a condition for enlargement to take place within the scheduled timescale.'[54]

The question that became increasingly pressing therefore was how seriously delayed accession would have to be if the Irish electorate rejected Nice a second time. The initial optimism — expressed, for example, by the Swedish Presidency[55] — that the Danish precedent post-Maastricht of appropriate 'opt-outs' seemed misplaced when the polls remained unfavourable. Indeed, polls in later September and early October still suggested the results were too close to call.[56] Inevitably, considerable attention was focused on possible alternative options if the vote did go against ratification. One report suggested that the Irish Government would make a formal declaration that the vote was not one against enlargement as such and that therefore it should go ahead.[57] A similar report had apparently circulated in the immediate aftermath of the first vote and had been rejected then. And as one junior minister in the Irish Government declared in October 2002:

> 'A No vote is a vote against enlargement. We have an option on Saturday week we can decide to proceed with the other member states, on the agreed basis for enlargement or we can decide to reject that and start fresh negotiations. That will delay enlargement, no doubt about that.'[58]

A number of other options were rumoured to be under consideration, all of which were denied with varying degrees of vehemence. *Der Spiegel* had a report that the German Government was working on a new treaty that would exclude Ireland — a report flatly denied as 'nonsense' by the Government.[59] The Commission was alleged to be working on what

[54] Seville Presidency Conclusions pt 8, 21–2 June 2002.

[55] A Presidency statement had suggested: 'Solutions can be found and there are already precedents ... To put these solutions in place, we must understand the reasons behind the Irish No vote and then find an adequate response.' *Financial Times*, 12 June 2001.

[56] *The Independent* 20 September reported one poll with 29% in favour, 19% against but with 44% don't knows. The position seemed to have changed little in the Economist Intelligence Unit poll of 7 October 2002.

[57] One report suggested that EU Foreign Ministers had discussed the possibility at their informal meeting in Denmark on 31 August 2002; EurActiv.com Portal — Document 18 October 2002.

[58] *Financial Times*, 11 October 2002.

[59] *The Irish Times*, 27 May 2002. A spokeman in the German Foreign Ministry added that 'It wasn't the Foreign Ministry but the legal wing of the European Commission which tested the legality of this idea'.

came to be known as Plan B, though in June 2002 Romano Prodi was declaring that 'If the Irish decide to block enlargement, there is no alternative', and 'There is no Plan B. There is no back door or side door without the Nice Treaty'.[60] Whether Plan B, C or D, one proposal seriously considered was that the more technical aspects of the Nice Treaty should be incorporated in the accession treaties with the new Member States. There were, however, a number of drawbacks to such a scheme. Given the acrimony in which Nice had been negotiated, for example, there was no guarantee that attempting to agree on the technical issues to be included would not reopen the various deals finally done. Secondly, the final accession treaties would need to be ratified by all the Member States, including Ireland, unless the so-called 'German plan' was adopted of excluding Ireland. However much the Irish Government had argued that the vote was not against enlargement, such a clear expedient to by-pass a democratic vote would have been likely to arouse controversy well beyond Ireland itself.

The establishment of the Convention on the Future of Europe in February 2002, with the prospect of yet another IGC in 2004, called for by the Nice European Council were not regarded as serious alternatives to the ratification of Nice. The Convention may have been called on to deal with what Heads of State or Government had been unable or unwilling to tackle at Nice (the IGC had, after all, already been the longest on record), to which had been added the agenda of 60-odd questions agreed by the Laeken European Council, but the prospect was one of added complexity and confusion rather than clarity. The Convention's chairman, the former French President, Valery Giscard d'Estaing, had drawn somewhat ambitious parallels between the Convention and that held in Philadelphia which had drawn up the constitution for the United States of America but any inference that the end result of a European Union constitution would make the Irish result irrelevant was easily discarded.

The EU and its Member governments and institutions, and indeed, the candidate countries had perforce to rely on maintaining pressure on the Irish Government to be rather more proactive than during the first referendum and to lobby as effectively as they could without it becoming counter-productive. The incoming Danish Presidency placed the successful conclusion of the enlargement negotiations at the top of its list of priorities, with the aim of completing the cycle of Copenhagen to Copenhagen, 1993–2002. It was therefore very clearly anxious that the Irish should not impede the process. As the Danish Prime Minister put it:

> 'If they [the Irish] can block enlargement from a formal point of view, politically can you imagine the disappointment that such a thing would

[60] *EU Observer*, 8 July 2002.

produce in the candidate countries. It would be a political disaster and the judgement of posterity will be severe, if this happens.'[61]

Some four days before the second referendum, the Prime Minister also visited Dublin pointing out that, while he had no wish to interfere in the campaign, a second rejection of Nice would mean an unprecedented crisis for enlargement, there was no Plan B.[62] A similar point was made by Ministers representing the 10 candidate countries, who, while expressing respect for the Irish people to make their own decision on Nice, added:

> 'We are strongly convinced that Irish people are fully aware of the opportunities that the participation in the European integration process brings. We also believe that they clearly see the chances created by EU enlargement. In this context we want to underline that the ratification of the Treaty of Nice by all the Member States is one of the elements of EU internal preparations for the admission of new members which will enable all of us to meet in the Union in 2004.'[63]

In the event, the result on 19 October was a vote in favour of Nice of 62.89 per cent against a 'no' vote of 37.11 per cent with a turnout of some 49 per cent. The crisis was over.

V. CONCLUSION

The October referendum result brought an end to the speculation about whether the criteria laid down at Copenhagen that the EU's ability to absorb new members 'while maintaining the momentum of European integration' had been met insofar as Nice had been accepted by the 15 Member States as opening the way towards enlargement. The fourth Copenhagen criterion appeared to have been achieved. And yet the path to the final Irish ratification of Nice raises interesting questions about the ways in which the EU and its member states commit themselves politically and legally to future actions. There have been numerous occasions in the past where the Member governments have committed themselves to particular deadlines — 1992 and the completion of the single market was perhaps the most notable. On occasions, clocks have been stopped in order to allow governments to bring about a final compromise. But, arguably, few issues have been on quite the scale of the commitments

[61] *Ibid.*
[62] *EU Observer,* 16 October 2002 and *RTĒ Interactive News,* 15 October 2002.
[63] Joint press release adopted by the meeting of the Ministers and State secretaries for European Affairs and Heads of delegations of Cyprus, the Czech Republic, Estonia, Hungary, Latvia, Lithuania, Malta, Poland, Slovakia and Slovenia in Warsaw, 25 September 2002. EurActiv.com Portal — Document 26 September 2002.

undertaken at Copenhagen in 1993 to bring about the enlargement of the EU to the countries of Central and Eastern Europe and the Mediterranean.

It was clear from Member government reactions to the failure of the Amsterdam Treaty to resolve the final institutional, decision-making issues, that they saw such reform as a prerequisite for enlargement. The Protocol attached to the Treaty was clear enough, that enlargement had to take place with the reform of the Commission and a reweighting of the votes on the Council and that before the EU reached 20 members an IGC would carry out a comprehensive review of the composition and functioning of the institutions. Such a review and reform was regarded — at least by the Belgians, French and Italian governments in their Declaration attached to Amsterdam — as 'an indispensable condition' for enlargement. There was a consensus that without such reform, enlargement would carry the danger of immobilism and a complete incapacity of the EU to act. The Nice Treaty may have been regarded as somewhat minimal and not wholly satisfactory for all, but it was deemed to be enough — along with, ie agreement to hold yet another IGC to review the issues that Heads of State or Government had been unable or unwilling to agree to.

What had begun therefore as a political commitment under the Danish Presidency had gradually become regarded as a legal obligation. There may in the immediate aftermath of the first Irish vote have been some wobbling on the part of the Commission — or at least its President — unready perhaps to see enlargement delayed by a few thousand votes, but there were no clear or easy alternative plans to the Nice Treaty. Hypothetical possibilities were, inevitably, under review but were, equally inevitably, denied.

Member governments had reiterated their commitment to institutional reform through constant repetition through successive Presidency Conclusions. In some instances, they had used the same formulation. It could perhaps be seen as the creation of soft law — at least in the sense that Dehousse and Weiler have used the term.[64] In one respect, the Conclusions may have created a binding commitment — even if, in detail, they were not wholly reliable. Having declared from Corfu onwards that the IGC bringing about such reforms should take place before accession negotiations began, the Luxembourg European Council Conclusions of 1997 allowed negotiations to begin and reform to be accomplished before accession, despite the inability of the Amsterdam IGC to resolve the problems of institutional reform. Nonetheless, the commitment had become a legal requirement within the Protocol attached to the Amsterdam Treaty.

Why Member governments made it a legal commitment is perhaps obvious from the preceding discussion — the EU had to be able to act, to

[64] Above n 15.

reach decisions with a degree of efficiency and effectiveness. Equity, in the sense that they had placed even more onerous and often politically more difficult obligations on the applicant states, played little part.[65] The EU's capacity to absorb new states was itself the critically important issue — alongside, of course, the fact that the majority of Member governments actually wished to see the momentum of integration maintained.[66] The combination of political necessity and legal flexibility creates a powerful force — even if, in this case, it took two IGCs and two national referendums to achieve it. And the momentum continues with institutional reform again a part of the agenda in the Convention of the Future of Europe and the IGC of 2003–04.

[65] The shift to placing the burden on the applicants to meet the changes demanded of EC/EU membership before accession is noted by Christophe Hillion in this collection.

[66] Hence the preparedness of the majority to envisage 'enhanced cooperation' of flexibility in order to circumvent the few who didn't wish to maintain that momentum, particularly, of course, the British Government throughout much of the 1990s.

3

The Impact of Enlargement on the Union's Institutions

ALAN DASHWOOD*

I. INTRODUCTION

AT THE TIME when I gave the talk which was the origin of this chapter, in July 2002, the Convention on the Future of Europe had been working only for a few months, and the nature and extent of any changes to the institutional structure of the European Union that it might propose, remained purely speculative. In my talk, I explored a number of ideas — some of them radical, and some pretty mundane and obvious — for better adapting the institutions of the Union to the likely stresses of enlargement, with a view to completing the job that had been done at Nice in December 2000 only partially, and to almost nobody's satisfaction.

This final version of the chapter has been written in the light of the outcome of the Convention's deliberations, which were presented by the Chairman, Mr Valery Giscard d'Estaing — in the form of a Draft Treaty Establishing a Constitution for Europe — to the European Council of Thessaloniki in June 2003.[1] The institutional provisions of the Convention text, as it will be referred to here, are among its more controversial elements and they are unlikely to emerge unscathed from the Intergovernmental Conference (IGC) which began, under the Italian Presidency, in October 2003, and which is expected to conclude, at the latest, some time early in 2004, under the Irish Presidency. In the new political conjuncture — bringing together the most ambitious enlargement of the Union to date, and the most thorough overhaul of the complex set of primary legal arrangements under which Union activities are carried on — the ideas that were canvassed back in July 2002 are here

* Sidney Sussex College, University of Cambridge.

[1] The proposals discussed in this chapter are the ones found in Document No CONV 850/03, dated 18 July 2003.

reconsidered and compared with those proposals contained in the Convention text which may be thought to have a bearing on the issues they were intended to address. The focus of the chapter, therefore, remains on the impact of enlargement. No pretence is made of providing a systematic analysis of the whole range of institutional changes that a new Constitutional Treaty based on the Convention text would bring about.

The single institutional framework of the Union is said by Article I–18 (2) of the Convention text to comprise: the European Parliament; the European Council; the Council of Ministers (presently named 'Council of the European Union'); the European Commission (presently, the 'Commission of the European Communities'); and the Court of Justice.[2] The discussion that follows will be confined, as my original talk was, to the four main political institutions.

II. THE EUROPEAN PARLIAMENT

Article 2 (1) of the Nice Protocol on the enlargement of the European Union[3] provided for the replacement, on 1 January 2004, of the first sub-paragraph of Article 190 (2) EC,[4] by a new table redistributing seats in the European Parliament among the present Member States of the Union, with effect from the start of the 2004/2009 parliamentary term. According to paragraph 2 of the same Article of the Enlargement Protocol, during the 2004/2009 term the total number of MEPs was to be that laid down by the amended Article 190 (2) EC 'plus the number of representatives of the new Member States resulting from the accession treaties signed by January 2004 at the latest'. Table 1 of the Nice Declaration on the enlargement of the European Union[5] established the distribution of MEPs in a Union composed of 27 Member States, including Bulgaria and Romania, giving a total of 732.[6] Should there be a smaller number of accessions, the Council was empowered by Article 2 (3) of the Enlargement Protocol to

[2] See the list of Community institutions in Art 7 EC. This does not include the European Council, which has its present Treaty basis in Art 4 TEU; it does, however, include the Court of Auditors. There are certain to be Member States unwilling to countenance the apparent downgrading of the Court of Auditors, and its addition by the IGC to the list comprising the institutional framework of the Union seems probable.

[3] The Protocol was annexed by the Treaty of Nice to the TEU and to the Community Treaties; hereinafter, the 'Enlargement Protocol'.

[4] Also of Art 108(2) EURATOM.

[5] Declaration No 20 to the Final Act of the Conference; hereinafter, the 'Enlargement Declaration'.

[6] This was an increase over the maximum of 700 fixed by the Treaty of Amsterdam. Anecdotal evidence suggests that the explanation for this increase lies in a political 'deal' that was struck in order to assuage the dissatisfaction of the smaller Member States with the re-weighting of the qualified majority for voting within the Council.

adopt a decision making a pro rata correction of the distribution of seats in the Parliament, in order to bring the total as close as possible to 732, but without giving any of the present Member States more MEPs than they have under Article 190 (2) before its amendment. If further accessions should take place after the adoption of such a decision, Article 2(4) would allow the total of MEPs temporarily to exceed 732, and the new Member States would benefit from the same pro rata correction.

In the event the operation of the rules of Article 2 of the Enlargement Protocol has been pre-empted by the Treaty of Accession of 2003 in respect of the 10 candidate countries with which negotiations have been successfully completed.[7] The distribution of MEPs which is there provided for takes account of the pro rata correction referred to in Article 2 (3) of the Enlargement Protocol, through re-allocation of the 33 Romanian seats and the 17 Bulgarian seats that were foreseen in the Enlargement Declaration.[8] The only Member States not to receive additional parliamentary representatives are Germany and Luxembourg, caught by the rule requiring there to be no increase above the numbers applicable under the pre-Nice arrangements, and the smallest of the acceding States — Cyprus, Estonia, Malta and Slovenia — owing, presumably, to arithmetical logic.[9]

The Convention text would maintain the distribution of MEPs as determined by the Accession Treaty throughout the 2004/2009 parliamentary term.[10] However, Article I–19 (2) of the text provides for a possible increase in the total membership of the European Parliament to 736, and also that '[r]epresentation of European citizens shall be degressively proportional, with a minimum threshold of four members per Member State'. A law establishing the composition of the Parliament in accordance with those principles must be adopted by the European Council, acting unanimously on the basis of a proposal from, and with the consent of, the Parliament, '[s]ufficiently in advance of the European Parliamentary elections in 2009, and, as necessary thereafter for further elections ...'.[11]

A minimum threshold of four MEPs per Member State is acceptable, since it would allow different political tendencies in even the smallest countries to be given a voice at the level of the Union; its justification lies, therefore, in the values of representative democracy. However, the same

[7] See OJ 2003 L236/17. Hereinafter, 'the Accession Treaty'.
[8] Act of Accession, Art 11.
[9] The allocation of MEPs is as follows: Germany, 99; France, Italy and the United Kingdom, 78 each (ex 72); Spain and Poland, 54 each (ex 50); The Netherlands, 27 (ex 25); Belgium, Greece, Hungary, Portugal and the Czech Republic, 24 each; Sweden, 19 (ex 18); Austria, 18 (ex 17); Denmark, Finland and Slovakia, 14 each (ex 13); Ireland and Lithuania, 13 each (ex 12); Latvia, 9 (ex 8); Slovenia, 7; Cyprus, Estonia and Luxembourg, 6; and Malta, 5.
[10] Protocol on the representation of citizens in the European Parliament and the weighting of votes in the European Council and the Council of Ministers, Art 1.
[11] Convention text, Art 19 (2), second subpara.

values require that the body of MEPs be much more representative of the Union's population as a whole, than they will be even after the redistribution of seats initiated by the Treaty of Nice, which still grossly favours the smaller Member States. The principle which, the Convention text proposes, should govern the distribution of parliamentary seats — that representation be 'degressively proportional' — will not much encourage those hopeful of seeing the democratic legitimacy of the Parliament enhanced. When the European Council of an enlarged Union with even more small Members, comes to adopt the new law on the composition of the Parliament some time in 2007 or 2008 — assuming Article I–19 (2) survives the IGC — considerations of national *amour propre* seem sadly likely to outweigh any will to create a Parliament that genuinely represents the people of the Union as a whole, rather than the separate peoples of its Member States.

The functions of the European Parliament, identified in paragraph 1 of Article I–19, comprise the enactment of legislation and the adoption of the budget, both of which it does jointly with the Council, as well as 'functions of political control and consultation'; in addition, '[i]t shall elect the President of the Commission'.

The co-decision procedure of Article 251 EC has been brought, by successive Treaty amendments, to a point at which the European Parliament is now recognised as an equal co-partner with the Council in legislating on the matters to which the procedure applies. The Convention text would take the further step of generalising co-decision, designating it 'the ordinary legislative procedure', to be used for the adoption of all legislative acts, except in those specific cases where the Constitution provides otherwise.[12] Similarly, in the budgetary procedure provided for by Article III–306 of the Convention text, the outmoded distinction between 'compulsory expenditure' (now, in practice, confined to agricultural expenditure), on which the Council has the last word, and 'non-compulsory expenditure' (covering everything else), on which the Parliament has the last word, would no longer apply; and the budget as a whole would be adopted, in the form of a European law, under a variant of co-decision, designed to put the Parliament and the Council under strong pressure to iron out any differences between them in a Conciliation Committee.[13]

[12] Convention text, Art I–33.

[13] Para 8 of Art III–306 provides that if, within 21 days, the Conciliation Committee does not approve a joint text, or if the Council rejects the joint text, the Parliament, acting by a majority of its component members and three fifths of the votes cast, may confirm its amendments to the Council position; however, where an amendment is not so confirmed, the Council position on the item in question shall be deemed to have been adopted. Obduracy would, therefore, carry risks for both branches of the budgetary authority. If the Parliament were to reject the joint text by a majority of its component members and three fifths of the votes cast, it may ask for as new draft to be submitted, thus restarting the procedure.

Those are certainly welcome changes, which go a long way towards meeting the criticism — always, in my view, exaggerated — that the legislative and budgetary processes of the Union suffer from a 'democratic deficit'. Unfortunately, experience teaches that institutional and procedural reforms, necessary though they may be, will never, in themselves, be sufficient to supply the *legitimacy* deficit, which is the Union's real problem. MEPs have yet to establish themselves in the eyes of their electorates as politicians with a specific job to do, rather than as supernumeraries of national political parties. Through the European political parties, they need to get on with creating a genuine democratic process at Union level, with which individual citizens can engage. That is something, I believe, can be achieved only through organised political activity — and for that very reason, of course, it is a lot easier said than done.[14]

The reference in Article I–19 (1) of the Convention text to 'election' of the Commission President is deceptive, since it implies that the selection process is to be under the control of the Parliament: in reality, the procedure provided for by Article I–26 (1) effectively remains one in which a candidate chosen by the Heads of State or Government is put forward to the Parliament for its approval.[15] My quarrel is with the false impression created by the drafting of Article I–19 (1), not with the procedure itself, since it is indispensable that the Commission President be a person commanding the confidence of the Governments of the Member States. A difference, as compared with the procedure laid down by the present Article 214 (2) EC, is that it is spelled out in the third sentence of Article I–26 (1) that, if the candidate first proposed does not receive the support of a majority of MEPs, the European Council must put forward a new candidate within one month. This makes clear that it would not be an option for the European Council to try to have its way, by re-nominating the same person, or by refusing to put forward another name.

III. THE EUROPEAN COUNCIL AND THE COUNCIL

I share the widely held view that the present system, under which the Presidency of the European Council and of all Council bodies, down to

[14] I have made the same point on other occasions, also noting the need for Ministers to be held more effectively to account by their national parliaments for what they get up to in the Council: see 'The Constitution of the European Union after Nice: Law-making Procedures', (2001) 26 *ELRev* 215; 'Issues of Decision-making in the European Union after Nice' in A Arnull & D Wincott (eds), *Accountability and Legitimacy in the European Union* (Oxford, OUP, 2002), 13.

[15] Under the present Art 214(2) EC, as amended by the Treaty of Nice, the Commission President is nominated by the Council meeting in the formation of Heads of State or Government. The proposed Art I–26 would give the power of nomination to the European Council. The explanation of this change is that, in the system of the Convention text, the European Council, as such, is able to act by a qualified majority: see below.

the humblest working party, is held for six months by Member States in rotation,[16] will not be viable in a Union of 25 Member States. If the opportunity to exercise the functions of the Presidency were to occur only once every 12 to 13 years, the educative value of the experience would have been dissipated before a country's next turn came round, facing Ministers and their civil servants with an excessively steep learning curve.

As regards the European Council, in particular, the more Member States there are, the harder the President's task of facilitating cohesion and consensus. To take a concrete example: the preparation for a European Council customarily entails a visit by the President to the capitals of all the Member States in the fortnight or so before a meeting. Under the existing arrangements, that round of visits — which are not courtesy calls, but often involve substantive discussions — has to be combined with all the other responsibilities that fall on the shoulders of a person holding the office of Prime Minister. The job has become one, to which a person, who also has to act as his/her country's Head of Government, cannot be expected to give all the attention it requires.

The enlargement of the Union has thus brought to a head a constitutional issue that has been flirted with for too long. As I suggested in my original talk, the European Council is needed to fill a gap in the institutional system of the Union as it has evolved, namely that of setting the policy agenda. I had in mind something closer to the decision-making process than the broad task of providing the Union 'with the necessary impetus for its development' and defining 'the general political guidelines thereof', as laid down by the present Article 4 (1) TEU. The democratic leaders of the Member States acting collectively, together with the President of the Commission, are the right body, in my view, to establish the programme of policy objectives and priorities to be achieved by the Union over a given period, while leaving it to the Union's other political institutions to implement the programme in accordance with their respective powers.

However, I argued and still believe, the European Council can only perform that role adequately, if its business is strongly directed, and not by a Presidency which, under the existing system of six-monthly rotation, is inevitably driven by particular national concerns. That was why, I explained, I had come to favour the proposal then being hotly debated, that there should be a European Council President chosen by the Heads of State or Government for a term of two and a half years; and I am pleased that the Presidium, and ultimately the Convention, adopted this idea.

Article I–21 of the Convention text is the basic provision on the new office, which is designated in the English-language version — with

[16] Art 203 (2) EC.

political correctness, if inelegantly — 'the European Council Chair'.[17] According to paragraph 1 of Article I–21, the Chair would be elected by the European Council, acting by a qualified majority, for a term of two and a half years, which would be renewable once; and, in the event of an impediment or serious misconduct, the mandate of the person concerned could be ended under the same procedure. Paragraph 2 of the Article defines the Chair's role as being: to preside over the European Council and 'drive forward its work'; to 'ensure proper preparation and continuity' (this in cooperation with the Commission President, and on the basis of the work of the General Affairs Council); and to 'endeavour to facilitate cohesion and consensus within the European Council'. In my opinion, the European Council Chair ought also to have been given the task of presiding over the Council (of Ministers) in its General Affairs formation, which is charged with preparing, and ensuring follow-up to, meetings of the European Council, since he/she would be best placed to ensure that Council performs more effectively than it has been doing hitherto.[18] I hope the IGC will remedy this omission.

The smaller Member States are said to be concerned that the establishment of the post of European Council Chair will diminish the standing of the President of the Commission, tipping the institutional balance against the Commission, which they see as their protector. It has also been suggested that rivalry between the two Presidents might impair the functioning of the institutions. I believe those concerns to be misplaced. All that is needed to maintain the standing of the Commission President is that the right person be chosen for the job — a Jacques Delors would surely be a match for any European Council Chair.

Nor should it be forgotten that the President of the Commission is a Member of the European Council, and participates fully in its deliberations; though, most unfortunately, there is ambiguity in the Convention text as to his/her voting rights. On the one hand, Article I–20 (4) says: 'Except where the Constitution provides otherwise, decisions of the European Council shall be taken by consensus'. Paragraph 2 of the same Article defines the European Council as consisting of 'the Heads of State or Government of the Member States, together with its President and the President of the Commission', while the 'Foreign Minister' (of whom more below) is said to 'take part in its work'. Read together, those paragraphs suggest to me that the two Presidents, but not the 'Foreign Minister', are intended to be full members of the European Council, and any consensus would therefore have to include them. On the other hand,

[17] The designation 'European Council Chair' is found in the heading of the Article, but 'President of the European Council' is the phrase used in the body of the text. More detailed provisions on the organisation of the European Council are laid down by Art III–244.
[18] Convention text, Art I–23 (1), second subpara.

Article I–24, which is about qualified majority voting, provides in paragraph 5: 'Within the European Council, its President and the President of the Commission do not vote'. The issue is whether the word 'vote' must be understood to include all cases where decisions are reached formally by the European Council, even when it acts by consensus. Or does the exclusion of the two Presidents apply only in the rare instances where the European Council is empowered to act by a qualified majority — since how could they possibly be included in the system of weighting? I hope that the IGC will clarify the issue in the latter sense. The interaction between Member State representatives and the Commission lies at the heart of the constitutional order. It is right that, when the European Council is setting the political agenda of the Union, the Commission President should be part of the consensus.

A proposal in the Convention text of which I am strongly critical is that for the creation of the post of 'Union Minister for Foreign Affairs'.[19] The idea is that the Foreign Minister should conduct the common foreign and security policy as mandated by the Council, and chair the Council in its Foreign Affairs formation,[20] while also being a Commission Vice-President, and subject to the discipline of collegiality in respect of the responsibilities that fall on the Commission in the sphere of external relations. The proposed 'double-hatting' of the Foreign Minister has nothing to do with the impact of enlargement on the institutions, and it would be inappropriate for me to repeat at length the serious objections that I have to it.[21] Suffice it to say that I do not believe that an individual can be, at one and the same time, a loyal servant of the Council and a faithful member of the College of Commissioners, owing to the creative tension that exists between the two institutions — a tension that should not be seen as aberrant but as a sign of good health in the Union order.

As for Council formations other than Foreign Affairs (and, I have suggested, General Affairs), Article 23 (6) provides for the Presidency to be held by representatives of the Member States 'on the basis of equal rotation, for periods of at least a year'. The European Council is to adopt a decision establishing the rules of such rotation, 'taking into account European political and geographic balance and the diversity of Member States'. The proposal is a good one, which should guarantee greater continuity than at present, while making it possible for all of the Member States to benefit from the educative experience of managing Council business in a given area, with a reasonable degree of frequency. Though the

[19] Convention text, Art 27.
[20] Convention, text, Art 23 (2), *in fine*.
[21] See my article, 'The Draft EU Constitution — First Impressions' (2002/2003) 5 *Cambridge Yearbook of European Legal Studies* 395.

task of formulating a balanced decision on the rotation of Presidencies will be a challenging one.

Like the ending of the six-monthly rotation of the Council Presidency, the extension of qualified majority voting (QMV) is generally accepted as a necessary consequence of the enlargement of the Union. This will mainly be achieved through the generalisation of the co-decision procedure. The wishes of different Member States to preserve the unanimity rule, in certain areas of particular sensitivity for them, appear to have been largely satisfied by the Convention. Thus, for instance, the United Kingdom's concern that legislation on the harmonisation of indirect taxation should continue to require unanimity, has been respected in the drafting of Article III–62 (1). It is true that paragraph 2 of the Article would allow the adoption by QMV of measures relating to administrative cooperation or for combating tax fraud or tax evasion, but only where there has been a unanimous finding by the Council that such are genuinely the objectives of a given measure. That qualification would, in my view, fully have justified refusal to have recourse to QMV in the famously controversial case of the proposal for a withholding tax on savings, which had as much to do with protecting the financial services markets of the Member States levying such taxes, as with fighting fraud.

Another example of the preservation of unanimity at the strong insistence of a Member State is found in the second subparagraph of Article III–217, on the common commercial policy. The French Government was able to secure the insertion of a paragraph that requires the Council to act unanimously

> 'for the negotiation and conclusion of agreements in the field of trade in cultural and audiovisual services, where these risk prejudicing the Union's cultural and linguistic diversity'.

The insertion was made well past the eleventh hour, seemingly by the Praesidium, since it does not figure in the text dated 12 June 2003, which was the last one seen by the full Convention.[22]

A provision attracting controversy is the so-called *passarelle* in Article I–24 (4), second subparagraph. This gives power to the European Council, acting on its own initiative and by unanimity, to decide on the substitution of QMV for the unanimity rule in any of the provisions of Part III of the Constitution. It seems wrong at first sight that a decision on a matter of constitutional significance should be adopted by Heads of State or Government on their own, without any requirement of national

[22] See Art III–212 of the text contained in Document No CONV 802/03. Cf the Article now numbered III–217 in Document No CONV 850/03, dated 23 July 2003.

ratification. However, it is provided that any such initiative by the European Council must be sent to National Parliaments no less than four months before any decision is taken on it. This means that a change of voting rule could not be slipped quietly past national parliamentarians, who, once alerted to the intentions of the European Council, would be able to bring pressure to bear on their government, if they disapproved.

A final comment relating to the Council concerns the composition of the qualified majority. Enlargement provided the pretext for an adjustment of the weighting of votes, to reduce the bias in favour of the smaller Member States. The acrimonious struggle at the Nice IGC in December 2000 resulted in a deeply unattractive compromise. So that nobody would be seen to be giving up votes, the number of votes allocated to each Council member was increased, proportionately a little more in the case of the larger Member States. Spain (and Poland, as a candidate country) came off best, receiving 27 votes, as compared with the 29 allocated to each of the Big Four. Also part of the compromise were two new rules: that the votes attaining the qualified majority threshold must represent a majority of the Member States; and that, at the request of any Council member, a check must be made to ensure that the Member States comprising the qualified majority represent at least 62 per cent of the Union's population, and if they do not, the decision will not be adopted. The arrangements, which were agreed at the Nice IGC, and have been incorporated into the Treaty of Accession,[23] would be preserved by the Convention text until 1 November 2009.[24] Thereafter, Article I–24 would substitute a simpler rule, under which the qualified majority (for the European Council, as well as for the Council of Ministers) would consist of a majority of the Member States representing at least three fifths (60 per cent) of the Union's population.[25] That would be a distinct improvement on the horrendous arithmetic of Nice, but is said to be opposed in the IGC by Spain and Poland, defending the deal they secured in Nice, which was such an undeservedly good one. A probable outcome at the IGC is thought to be that the population threshold will simply be raised from 60 to 66 per cent, and honour will then be satisfied.

[23] Act of Accession, Art 12. The allocation of Council votes is as follows: Germany, France, Italy and the United Kingdom, 29 each; Spain and Poland, 27 each; The Netherlands, 13; Belgium, the Czech Republic, Greece, Hungary and Portugal, 12 each; Austria and Sweden, 10 each; Denmark, Ireland, Lithuania, Slovakia and Finland, 7 each; Estonia, Cyprus, Latvia, Luxembourg and Slovenia, 4 each; and Malta, 3.

[24] Protocol on the representation of citizens in the European Parliament and the weighting of votes in the European Council and the Council of Ministers, Art 2.

[25] The threshold goes up to two thirds of the Member States, in cases where no proposal by the Commission or the Foreign Minister is required: Art I–24 (2).

IV. THE COMMISSION

The Convention resisted the blandishments of those who would address the legitimacy deficit by having the President of the Commission, or even the entire College, either directly elected, or designated by the political majority in the European Parliament. Such an attempt to politicise the Commission would almost certainly be a flop, bringing the Union into even greater disrepute, since the individuals up for election would scarcely be household names outside their Member States of origin. Even if European voters were sold the idea that they could help determine the political colour of the Commission, for the latter to be tied politically to a majority within the Parliament, and to the programme on which that majority was elected, would upset the institutional balance, and render the Commission less capable, if not wholly incapable, of performing its traditional role, which is that of promoting an honestly formed conception of the general interest of the Union as a whole. Those who believe the Commission should be 'democratised' seem to think of it as a kind of caterpillar, munching away glumly at a bunch of old leaves labelled 'right of initiative', 'guardian of the Treaties', and so on, while it waits to be transformed into the gorgeous butterfly of a European Government. That transformation is not going to happen, nor should it. The Commission is already an exotic creature of great beauty and utility, with a particular niche in the ecology of the European Union, which only it can fill — the indispensable function of counteracting the centrifugal tendency of a constitutional order composed of sovereign States. For that, the Commission does not need to be democratically accountable: it needs to be independent.

I do, however, take issue with the proposal in the Convention text that, as from 1 November 2009, the size of the Commission should be reduced to 15 voting members, selected on the basis of a system of equal rotation among the Member States.[26] I have the same problems with that idea as with the arrangement, which was agreed at Nice, that, once membership of the Union reached 27, there should be a smaller number of (rotating) Commission posts, the actual number of Commissioners remaining unspecified.[27] A first objection is that, rightly or wrongly, the Member States, and especially the smaller ones, find it reassuring that one of their nationals should be a member of the College. The reduction of the number of Commissioners would almost certainly damage the legitimacy of the institution, and hence of the Union. A second objection is that, in political reality, it would be harder for the Commission to take firm action, eg in a state aid matter, against a large and powerful

[26] Convention text, Art 25 (3).
[27] Enlargement Protocol, Art 4.

Member State, which happened at the time not to have a voting Commissioner. I am less convinced than I once was that enlargement will make an already over-sized Commission hopelessly unwieldy. There may well not be enough interesting jobs for each Member of the Commission to be given his/her private empire, but the answer is to group Commissioners in teams, which would also help counter any tendency for a given policy area to become a national preserve. At all events, any possible advantage of a slimmed-down Commission has been sacrificed by the proposal that the Commission President be empowered to appoint non-voting Commissioners from the Member States, which do not have a national among the 15.[28] So there would 25 Commissioners after all (and subsequently more), with the added disadvantage that differences of status, between individuals enjoying equivalent prestige in their respective countries of origin, would be liable to lead to internal tensions. My prediction is that the IGC will endorse the common sense solution of one Commissioner per Member State.

V. CONCLUSION

The foregoing survey covers what appear to me to be the most interesting changes to the rules governing the main political institutions of the European Union, which are proposed in the Convention text, and which it is plausible to regard as having been influenced, whether directly or indirectly, by the prospect of the Union's enlargement. A somewhat unhappy proposal, clearly reflecting the expected impact of enlargement on the efficacy of the Commission, is the one just discussed, regarding the reduction in the number of Commissioners. On the other hand, the perception that continuation of the present system of Presidency rotation would not be practicable in a Union of 25, has made it possible to grasp the nettle of establishing a fixed-term Presidency of the European Council. Similarly, the generalisation of the co-decision procedure, for which I have long been arguing, may well have been facilitated by the necessity of extending QMV, in order to avoid gridlock in a Council with 25 Members. There was, it seems, great wisdom in the decision that was taken in Laeken to establish a Convention on the Future of Europe, at a moment when the imminence of enlargement was concentrating minds wonderfully.

[28] Convention text, Art 25 (3), second subpara.

4

Referendums in the CEE Candidate Countries: Implications for the EU Treaty Amendment Procedure

ANNELI ALBI*

I. INTRODUCTION

AS PART OF the discussions on reorganising the Treaties, the Convention on the Future of Europe considered the possibility of facilitating the EU treaty amendment procedure, which currently requires unanimous ratification 'under the national constitutional procedures' (Article 48 TEU). The fragility of this procedure was well demonstrated by the first Irish referendum on the Nice Treaty, where 33 per cent of the voters of a small country could paralyse its entrance into force. Considering the dramatic increase in the number of Member States after the forthcoming enlargement, many political and academic actors have pointed out that an easier amendment procedure is needed. However, touching a core area of Member States' sovereignty, the revision of the amendment procedure has been amongst the most sensitive and controversial issues in the Convention's agenda.

This chapter adds an argument to the camp of those advocating the facilitation of the amendment procedure. It argues that the risk of paralysis in the amendment process does not just increase by virtue of higher number of Member States, but, more importantly, the 'national constitutional procedures' in the acceding CEE countries involve distinct procedural and practical complications. The chapter first points out that the ratification of future treaty amendments is likely to involve the passing of

* University of Kent. This manuscript was completed in February 2003, before the accession referendums took place (March–September 2003). Although these demonstrated high support for EU membership (90–92% in Slovakia, Slovenia and Lithuania; 84% in Hungary; 77% in Poland and Czech Republic; 67–68% in Estonia and Latvia), the concerns raised in this paper are likely to remain relevant in future. The Draft Constitution for Europe, produced by the Convention on July 2003, largely retains the current treaty amendment procedure.

a constitutional amendment and accompanying referendum in several future CEE Member States, because the new CEE constitutions are up-to-date, clear and directly applicable legal documents and have a distinctly 'souverainist' character, in comparison with the constitutions of current Member States. It then points out that in those countries which would not need to amend their constitutions, there is nevertheless a likelihood of ordinary referendums being held on the ratification of future treaty amendments, because CEE countries have a tradition of holding referendums frequently. These referendums involve a risk of paralysis in the treaty amendment process, because several future CEE Member States have high minimum turnout requirements, relatively euro-sceptic public opinion, high percentage of unsuccessful referendums, and a prohibition to reinitiate a referendum within 1–4 years.

Finally, this contribution points out that these complications also had an impact on the Central and Eastern European positions in the Convention on EU Future, because 'selling' a federal Union would have made it more difficult to secure a successful accession referendum, as the issue of sovereignty remains sensitive in the countries which have (re) established their sovereignty merely a little more than a decade ago. Indeed, a brief study of the speeches of CEE politicians on the EU future shows that they predominantly advocate an incremental integration, preferring a 'union of nation-states' to a federation, a constitutional *treaty* rather than an EU constitution, and a gradual strengthening of the Community method instead of major institutional changes.

II. CEE CONSTITUTIONS: 'SOUVERAINIST' CHARACTER AND COMPLEX AMENDMENT PROCEDURES

Previous amendments of EU treaties have consistently narrowed the Member States' sovereignty and, after the eventual adoption of the European constitutional treaty, this trend is unlikely to stop, considering the organisational difficulties of accommodating an increasing number of Member States. In words of Peter-Christian Müller-Graff, an effective decrease in the need for amendments would presume that the Basic Treaty would be reduced to 'a minimum of undisputed and highly abstract principles', while it is difficult to find a final solution for the institutional structure with a view to the continuous contest between 'different forces of supranationality, national sovereignty and democracy'.[1] In order to legitimise successive transfers of sovereign competences, the treaty amendments require unanimous consent of the

[1] PC Müller-Graff, 'The Future of the European Treaties — A Systematic Approach to a Basic Treaty', Heidelberg, 2001, www.ecsanet.org/post_nice/contributions/MÜLLER-GRAFF-2.doc, at 16.

member countries and ratification under their 'national constitutional procedures', as established in Article 48 TEU. However, on several occasions, this system has experienced challenges to the entrance into force of a treaty by a single state, most notoriously Ireland or Denmark where the ratification process involves a referendum. The concern that a dramatically increasing number of Member States may eventually lead to a paralysis has brought the issue of revising this system on the Convention's agenda. Several alternative modes of amendment have been put forward (see Section VI), but the revision of the current procedure is one of the politically most sensitive issues, encountering a strong resistance, as the national authorisation of treaty amendments is regarded as a core area of preserving a Member State's sovereignty.

However, besides the increase in the number of countries, the Future Debate has largely overlooked the fact that the current amendment procedure would be set even more under pressure by the 'national constitutional procedures' of the acceding CEE countries. Several CEE countries have cumbersome constitutional amendment and referendum procedures, which resemble those of Denmark and Ireland or are even more challenging to the current treaty amendment procedure. This chapter will subsequently explain the procedural and practical difficulties in the CEE 'national constitutional procedures' which may increase the likelihood of a paralysis in the future efforts to amend EU treaties, in case of continuing with the current Article 48 procedure. This Section deals with the procedures of constitutional amendment and Section III addresses the procedures and experience of referendums in the CEE accession countries.

As concerns the constitutional amendment procedures, it is important to point out that the ratification of future treaty amendments is likely to lead to prior constitutional amendments and corresponding referendums in several future CEE Member States, because in comparison with the current Member States' constitutions, CEE constitutions protect sovereignty very highly. I have characterised these constitutions as 'souverainist' because they share the following features.[2]

First, the CEE Candidate Countries' constitutions[3] set forth numerous and complex sovereignty provisions (available in detail in Table 1) and all except the Slovak constitution distinguish between *sovereignty* and *independence*. The former implies internal sovereignty, referring to the state's power competences vested in the people; the latter signifies external sovereignty, implying independent statehood in international relations. The Baltic and Romanian constitutions are the most protectionist, while the Polish new

[2] This argument draws on A Albi, 'Post-modern versus Retrospective Sovereignty: Two Different Sovereignty Discourses in the EU and Candidate Countries?' in N Walker (ed), *Sovereignty in Transition* (Oxford, Hart Publishing, 2003).
[3] Available in English at the website 'Consolidating European Public Law', European University Institute, www.iue.it/LAW/conseulaw/english/constitutions.htm#.

1997 constitution is relatively liberal towards international cooperation. In comparison, six constitutions amongst the fourteen written constitutions of the EU Member States do not mention sovereignty at all, declaring simply that the people form the source of power.[4] Another four use a one-sentence formula that sovereignty belongs to the people,[5] regarding external and internal sovereignty as a unified phenomenon. Only three constitutions draw a distinction between sovereignty and independence: Luxembourg (Articles 1 and 32), Portugal (Preamble, Articles 1, 2, 3.1 and 7.1) and Ireland (Preamble and Article 5).

Table 1: Provisions on Sovereignty and Independence and their Safeguards.[6]

Estonia	Preamble: established on the inextinguishable right of the people of Estonia to ***national self-determination …*** 1. Estonia is an ***independent*** and ***sovereign*** democratic republic, wherein the ***supreme power of state is vested in the people***. 1.2. The ***independence*** and ***sovereignty*** of Estonia are ***timeless and inalienable***. 54. An Estonian citizen has a duty … to defend the ***independence*** of Estonia. 123.1. The Republic of Estonia shall not conclude international treaties which are in conflict with the Constitution.
Lithuania	Preamble: having for centuries defended its … ***independence***; embodying the inborn right of each person and the People to live and create freely in … the ***independent State*** of Lithuania. 1. The State of Lithuania shall be an ***independent*** and democratic republic. 2. ***Sovereignty*** shall be ***vested in the People***. 3.1. No one may limit or restrict the ***sovereignty of the People*** or make claims to the ***sovereign powers of the People***. 3.2. The People and each citizen shall have the right to oppose anyone who encroaches on the ***independence*** … of Lithuania by force. 135.1. In conducting foreign policy, the Republic of Lithuania … shall strive to ***safeguard … independence …*** 136. The Republic of Lithuania shall participate in international organisations provided that they do not contradict the … ***independence*** of the State.
Latvia	1. Latvia shall be an ***independent*** democratic Republic. 2. The ***sovereign power*** of the Latvian State shall belong to the ***People of Latvia***.
Romania	1.1. Romania is a ***sovereign, independent, unitary, and indivisible Nation State***. 2.1. ***National sovereignty*** resides with the Romanian people …. 2.2. No group or person may exercise ***sovereignty*** in one's own name.

Continued…

[4] Germany, Belgium, Sweden, Austria, the Netherlands and Denmark.
[5] Italy, France, Spain and Greece. The Finnish Constitution has two separate sentences in this regard.
[6] This table is from Albi, above n 2.

Table 1 Continued...

	8.2. Political parties ... contribute to the definition and expression of the political will of the citizens, while observing ***national sovereignty*** ... 37.2. Any political parties or organisations which ... militate against ... the ***sovereignty, integrity***, or ***independence*** of Romania shall be unconstitutional. 80.1(1) The President ... is the safeguard of the ***national independence*** ... 82.2. President's oath: 'I solemnly swear ... to defend ... Romania's ***sovereignty, independence*** ...'. 117.1. The Armed Forces shall ... guarantee the ***sovereignty, independence*** ... .of the State. 148.1. prohibits amendment of the provisions on the ***national, independent character of the state***.
Hungary	2.1 The Republic of Hungary shall be an ***independent***, democratic constitutional state. 2.2 In the Republic of Hungary all ***power is vested in the people***, who exercise their ***sovereignty*** through elected **representatives** and directly. 5. The State of the Republic of Hungary shall defend...***sovereignty of the people***, the ***independence*** ... of the country. 6.1 The Republic of Hungary ... shall refrain from the use of force and the threat thereof against the ***independence*** ... of other states. 19.2. Exercising its rights based on the ***sovereignty of the people***, the Parliament shall ensure the constitutional order of society .... 51.1. The General Prosecutor and the Office of the Public Prosecutor ... shall prosecute to the full extent of the law any act which violates or endangers the ... ***independence*** of the country. 68.1. The national and ethnic minorities living in the Republic of Hungary participate in the ***sovereign power of the people***.
Czech R.	Preamble: at the time of the renewal of an ***independent*** Czech state.... 1. The Czech Republic is a ***sovereign***, unified, and democratic law-observing state ... 2.1. All ***state power*** derives from the people .... 9.2. Any change of fundamental attributes of the democratic law-observing state is inadmissible.
Slovakia	Preamble: proceeding from the natural right of nations to ***self-determination*** .... 1. The Slovak Republic is a ***sovereign***, democratic, and law-governed state. 2.1. ***State power*** is derived from citizens .... 34.3. The enactment of the rights of citizens belonging to national minorities and ethnic groups ... must not be conducive to jeopardizing the ***sovereignty*** ... of the Slovak Republic .... 106. The National Council of the Slovak Republic can recall the president from his post if the president is engaged in activity directed against the ***sovereignty*** ... of the Slovak Republic.
Bulgaria	Preamble: in awareness of our irrevocable duty to guard the ***national and state integrity*** of Bulgaria ... 1.2. The entire ***power of the state*** shall derive from the people.

Continued...

Table 1 Continued...

	1.3. No part of the people, no political party nor any other organisation, state institution, or individual shall usurp the expression of the ***popular sovereignty***. 9. The armed forces shall guarantee the ***sovereignty***... and ***independence*** of the country .... 44.2. No organisation shall act to the detriment of the country's ***sovereignty*** and ***national integrity***, or the ***unity of the nation***. ... 18.2 and 3. The state shall exercise ***sovereign rights***.... 24.2 The foreign policy of ... Bulgaria shall have as its uppermost objective the ... ***independence*** of the country ....
Bulgaria	
Slovenia	Preamble: Whereas it is in keeping with the Basic Constitutional Charter on ***Independence*** and ***Sovereignty*** of the Republic of Slovenia .... Acknowledging that we Slovenians created our own national identity and attained our nationhood based on ... the fundamental and permanent right of the Slovenian people to ***self-determination***.... 3.1. Slovenia is a state of all its citizens and is based on the ***permanent*** and ***inalienable*** right of the Slovenian people to ***self-determination.*** 3.2 [Title '***sovereignty***'] ...the supreme power is vested in the people.
Poland	Preamble: ... Homeland, which recovered ... the possibility of a ***sovereign*** and democratic determination of its fate .... 4.1. ***Supreme power*** in the Republic of Poland shall be vested in the Nation. 5. The Republic of Poland shall safeguard the ***independence*** and integrity of its territory .... 104.2 Deputies' oath: 'I do solemnly swear ... to safeguard the ***sovereignty***.... of the State ...'. 126.2. The President of the Republic shall ... safeguard the ***sovereignty*** ... of the State ....

Second, the CEE constitutions add numerous safeguards to the provisions on sovereignty and independence. For instance, in Hungary, the state has to defend sovereignty and independence and the Prosecutor's Office has to prosecute acts against Hungary's independence. In Romania, the political organisations have to respect, and the president and the army have to safeguard the sovereignty and independence of the state; sovereignty may not be exercised in the name of any group or person. In Slovakia, the president is to be recalled for activities against sovereignty. Poland has to safeguard its independence, while the Deputies and the President have to safeguard the sovereignty of the state. Bulgaria's foreign policy and the army have to protect and all organisations have to respect the country's sovereignty, independence and national integrity; the constitution prohibits the usurpation of popular sovereignty and recalls the irrevocable duty to guard Bulgaria's national and state integrity. The Lithuanian constitution prohibits limitation, restriction or claims to the sovereign powers of the people; the foreign policy has to safeguard Lithuania's independence.

Third, nine constitutions out of the ten CEE candidate countries did not contain until recently provisions on transferring competences to international organisations. Only the Lithuanian constitution had a provision with this regard (Article 136), subject to the condition of preserving Lithuania's independence and prohibition on joining organisations based on the former USSR (Article 150). The Slovak constitution authorised the entrance into a 'state alliance' (Article 7), which was aimed at a closer relationship with the Czech Republic.[7] However, Poland has provisions on international organisations since adopting the new constitution in 1997; the Czech and Slovak constitutions were amended in 2001 and Hungary's in 2002, in order to join the EU. According to the new provisions in the Czech Republic and Poland, the ratification of a treaty on joining international organisations may be preceded by a referendum. In comparison, all the constitutions of the EU Member States have a clause on delegating powers to international organisations and six of them also to the EU. However, in contrast to their stance concerning international organisations, several commentators have correctly pointed out that the CEE constitutions have an 'international law-friendly' character,[8] as a number of them clearly establish supremacy and direct applicability of international law.

Fourthly, the amendment of sovereignty provisions is rather difficult. Some constitutions prohibit the amendment of the fundamental provisions. The Romanian constitution prohibits the amendment of the national and independent character of the state. The Czech constitution prohibits the amendment of 'the fundamental attributes of the democratic law-observing state'. The Estonian constitution declares that sovereignty and independence are timeless and inalienable and also mentions the inextinguishable right of the Estonian people to self-determination. The Slovenian constitution underlines the permanence and inalienability of the right to self-determination.

Fifthly, and of direct importance to this chapter, many CEE constitutions subject the amendment of sovereignty provisions to a mandatory or optional referendum, requiring a high political and popular consensus. The Romanian constitution requires a referendum for all constitutional amendments; the constitutions of Estonia, Latvia and Lithuania for amending the fundamental provisions, including sovereignty. In Latvia and Estonia, the amendment of ordinary provisions may also optionally

[7] M Hoskova, 'Legal Aspects of the Integration of the Czech Republic and Slovakia into European Security and Economic Structures' (1994) 37 *German Yearbook of International Law* 68 at 91.

[8] Eg V Korkelia, 'New Trends Regarding the Relationship between International and National Law (with a special view towards the states of Eastern Europe)' (1997) *Review of Central and Eastern European Law* 227 at 227.

be subject to a referendum and in Estonia, it is prohibited to conclude treaties which are in conflict with the constitution. Poland provides a special optional referendum for amending the state-fundamental provisions of Chapter I. The Slovenian constitution provides a referendum for any constitutional amendments, if it is so required by thirty Deputies. In Bulgaria, constitutional amendment may not be submitted to a referendum, but the Grand National Assembly has to be specially elected to amend issues concerning, inter alia, the changes related to the form of state or the form of government, direct applicability of the constitution, supremacy of international law and ratification of any international instruments envisaging such problems. The constitutions of Romania and the Baltic States share the most restrictive constitutional amendment procedures, while the Slovak, Czech and Hungarian amendment procedures are relatively liberal. In comparison, referendums generally have an unimportant role in the constitutional amendment procedures of the EU Member States and six of them do not hold referendums at all.[9]

Further, referendums require high minimum turnout rates — most extremely in Lithuania, where 3/4 of all citizens who have voting rights must consent to amend Article 1 (independence). The majority of recent referendums have failed to achieve the required quorums, and unsuccessful referendums may not be reinitiated for several years — a more detailed account of these issues will be provided in the next section.

The pattern of constitutional amendments so far shows that the post-Communist constitutions have been amended relatively frequently: up to 2002, the constitutions have been amended five times in Latvia, four times in Hungary, three times in the Czech Republic, Slovakia, Lithuania and twice in Slovenia. These amendments have concerned issues such as the changes in the distribution of powers between the branches of government, creation of new institutions and fulfilment of obligations under treaties. On the other hand, three constitutions — Estonian, Romanian and Bulgarian — have not been amended, regardless of a number of initiatives, and it is noteworthy that the two former have the most rigid amendment procedure. In addition, in the countries where the amendment of sovereignty provisions requires a referendum, none of the amendments have yet concerned the fundamental provisions of sovereignty.

These facts let us predict that ratifications of future treaty amendments which cause changes to the distribution of powers are likely to lead to constitutional amendments and may cause procedural tensions in the countries where the amendment of sovereignty provisions involves a referendum. Besides the 'souverainist' character of the constitutions, the Central and Eastern European countries are more likely to amend their

[9] Germany, Luxembourg, Belgium, Spain, Greece and the Netherlands.

constitutions instead of interpreting them broadly also for the reason that these constitutions are legal rather than political documents. Compared to some Western European constitutions, the CEE constitutions are new or comprehensively revised and they establish with detail and precision the mechanisms and procedures of exercising power and the interrelationship of governing institutions. They are clear, up-to-date and directly applicable documents, as a reaction to the countries' fifty-year experience with the declaratory Soviet constitutions, in which the mechanisms for exercising power and guarantees against state intervention remained illusory.

III. REFERENDUMS: PROCEDURAL AND PRACTICAL COMPLICATIONS

Besides the constitutional amendment referendums provided for in some CEE Candidate Countries, most of them also establish in their constitutions or referendum laws a possibility of holding referendums for deciding issues of national importance, which may be used for obtaining a public approval for ratifying potential future EU treaty amendments.[10] The following paragraphs discuss the procedure and practice of CEE referendums, pointing out four factors which should be kept in mind when discussing the future of the EU treaty amendment system.

First, Central and Eastern countries have a tradition of holding referendums frequently: there have been at least 25 referendums since 1989 in the ten Candidate Countries, before the current waive of accession referendums which are held in all eight acceding CEE countries (Bulgaria and Romania are expected to join at a later stage). These referendums have concerned issues of varying importance, from privatisation to NATO membership (see for recent referendums Table 3).[11] Referendums have been most numerous in Lithuania — altogether seven, and Slovakia — altogether four, since the countries' independence in 1991 and 1993 respectively. In addition, there have been abundant referendum initiatives which have not materialised; recent examples from 2001 include the restitution of the Royal Castle in Romania and the indexing of pensions and the amendments to the Labour Code in Hungary. In this light, the ratification of potential future EU treaty amendments are likely to undergo a referendum in a number of CEE countries.

[10] With the exception of Latvia, where the Referendum Act allows initiating referendums only in four procedural cases, and the Czech Republic, where the Referendum Act provides referendum exclusively for EU accession. Note also that in Estonia and Latvia, the constitutions prohibit referendums on treaties; in Hungary, referendums are prohibited on treaties in force.

[11] See for details of referendums in individual countries the Direct Democracy website http://c2d.unige.ch/ and in country reports in the *East European Constitutional Review*.

Second, it is important to point out that in the CEE countries, referendums are subject to high quorum requirements. In most countries, the minimum turnout rate is at least 50 per cent of the eligible voters — the details are provided in Table 2.

Thirdly, more than half of referendums within recent years have failed to meet these high quorums. Apart from enthusiastic participation in the

Table 2: Minimum Turnout Requirements.

Country	Minimum turnout	Type of referendum	No repetition
Lithuania	3/4 of all citizens who have voting rights	Referendum on amending Article 1 on independence	1 year for constit. amend. refer.
	50% turnout	Ordinary referendums and referendums on amending ordinary constitutional provisions	
Latvia	50% turnout	Constitutional amendment referendums	–
	Half of the turnout of previous elections	Ordinary referendums	
Slovakia	50% turnout	All referendums	3 years
Bulgaria	50% turnout	All referendums	
Slovenia	50% turnout	Constitutional amendment referendums	1 year
	Simple majority	Ordinary referendums	
Poland	50% turnout	Ordinary referendums, in order to be binding (otherwise consultative referendum)	4 years
	Simple majority	Constitutional amendment referendums	
Hungary	25% approval of all citizens who have voting right	Since 1997 for all referendums as a result of amendment adopted before NATO-referendum	–
	50% turnout	Before 1997 for all referendums	
Estonia	Simple majority	All referendums	1 year for constit. amend. refer.
Romania	50%	All referendums	
Czech Rep.	Simple majority	Currently referendum may be held only for EU accession	2 years

referendums of the early 1990s on independence and adoption of the constitutions, Table 3 shows that 9 out of 16 referendums from 1994 onwards have been invalid due to low turnout rates. In fact, the turnout remained far below 50 per cent in 14 cases, but Hungary reduced the minimum turnout requirement of 50 per cent shortly in anticipation of the NATO referendum and other referendums were declared valid on various procedural grounds explained in Table 3.

Table 3: Referendum Results during Recent Years.

Country	Year	Issue	Turnout
Lithuania	1994	Illegal privatisation; savings compensation for inflation victims; early parliament elections	36.8%, **invalid**
	Oct 1996	Expenditure of state budget; compensation of the loss of assets prior to 1990; decrease in number of parliament members	52%
	Nov 1996	Purchase of agricultural land by EU nationals	40%, **invalid**
Slovakia	1994	Transparency of privatisation	19.98%, **invalid**
	1997	NATO membership; nuclear weaponry and military basis	9.5%, **invalid**
	1998	Privatisation of main state companies	44%, **invalid**
	2000	Early elections	20%, **invalid**
Poland	1997	New constitution	43% (no minimum for constitutional amendment referendums)
	1996	Privatisation	32.5% (consultative)
Hungary	1997	NATO membership	49% (threshold majority 25% of the electorate)
Latvia	1998	Amendments to the Citizenship law	67%
	1999	Amendments to the Pensions law	25%, **invalid**
Slovenia	1996	Amendments to the electoral law	38% (declared successful by the Constitutional Court)
	1998	Consultative referendum on reform of local government system	Less than half, but only electors of affected border

Continued...

Table 3 Continued...

Country	Year	Issue	Turnout
			areas were asked to participate
	1999	Referendum on funding the construction of power plant TET3	27%, **invalid**
	2001	Amendments to Law on Infertility Treatment	33%, **invalid**

Estonia and Romania have had no referendums after the early 1990s, Bulgaria and the Czech Republic have had no referendums in last couple of decades.

Fourthly, besides the danger of an invalid result, the future referendums on potential treaty amendments also involve the risk of a negative result, as the public opinion of the candidate countries has been rather eurosceptic, although ahead of accession the support for EU has been increasing. In 2000–2001, national polls reported that support for accession was under 50 per cent in six Candidate Countries: 44 per cent in Poland, 42 per cent in Czech Republic and Slovenia, 48 per cent in Estonia,[12] 37.6 per cent in Latvia[13] and 47 per cent in Lithuania.[14] In Estonia, 59 per cent would have voted against joining EU in May 2001,[15] but after Estonia's victorious performance in the Eurovision song contest later that month, the support rates have been consistently increasing. The populations of Estonia, Latvia, Lithuania and the Czech Republic have also earlier been famous for their consistently low support rates for the EU membership, fluctuating over the years between 22–45 per cent.[16] The reasons for euroscepticism vary in different countries, but amongst main concerns are the fear of losing sovereignty and national identity with a view to the recent experience with another 'Union', and the cost of speedy adoption of the EU technical, environmental and social standards. As the comparative experience with the Member States who have joined previously shows, support for the EU has a tendency to decrease rather than increase after accession.

Finally, an unsuccessful referendum may block a treaty for several years. In the case of an invalid or a negative result, a new referendum on the issue may not be re-initiated within 4 years in Poland, 3 years in

[12] All reported by Reuters, cited in 'Majority of Hungarians Would Vote for Joining EU', *RFE/RL Newsline*, 5 (140), Part II, 26 July 2001.

[13] BNS News, Reported in *Postimees*, 13.06.2001.

[14] In October 2000, poll conducted by Vilmorus, http://rope.euro.lt/indexeng/html, cited in V Vadapalas 'Lithuania: The Constitutional Impact of the Enlargement at National Level' in A Kellermann, J De Zwaan & J Czuczai (eds), *EU Enlargement — The Constitutional Impact at EU and National Level* (The Hague, TMC Asser Press, 2001), 351.

[15] Reported respectively in *Postimees*, 19 May 2001.

[16] See Central and Eastern Eurobarometers, http://europa.eu.int/comm/dg10/epo/ceeb.html.

Slovakia, 2 years in the Czech Republic and 1 year in Slovenia and, in case of constitutional amendment referendums, in Estonia and Lithuania. In Estonia, the parliament is also to be dissolved.

VI. REVISION OF THE TREATIES' AMENDMENT PROCEDURE

A number of political and academic actors have pointed out that the dramatic increase in the number of member states after the imminent enlargement will necessitate an easier amendment procedure of the Treaties in order to avoid a paralysis. The previous sections of this chapter have highlighted the procedural and practical complications of the 'national constitutional procedures' in the acceding Central and Eastern countries, which may increase the likelihood of a paralysis and support thus the calls for facilitating the EU treaty amendment procedure.

The proposals for facilitating the treaty amendment procedure mainly proceeded from the division of the treaties into two parts. The fundamental part, which would set forth the political guidelines, citizens' rights, institutional framework and the basis for the division of competences, would be amended infrequently and in accordance with the 'national constitutional procedures'. The second part, which would comprise the provisions of technical, functional and implementing nature and would not directly affect the Member States' sovereignty, would be subject to an easier amendment procedure by the EU institutions. The idea was first officially tabled by the Dehaene-Group in October 1999.[17] In 2000, the Robert Schuman Centre of the European University Institute (EUI) produced a Draft Basic Treaty, on the mandate of the European Commission;[18] this was followed by the Second Report examining the modalities of facilitating the amendment procedures.[19] Most political and academic actors subscribed to this division, focusing rather on potential amendment mechanisms.

The opinions diverged as to whether unanimity should be retained: the need for qualified majority voting was more readily accepted for the non-constitutional part, on the condition that the European Parliament would be involved through the assent procedure.[20] The amendments to the

[17] 'The Institutional Implications of Enlargement', Report by R Weizsäcker, J–L Dehaene, D Simon, delivered to the European Commission on 18 October 1999, Brussels, http://europa.eu.int/ igc2000/repoct99_en.pdf.

[18] 'A Basic Treaty for the European Union — A Study of the Reorganisation of the Treaties', European University Institute, Robert Schuman Centre, 15 May 2000, www.iue.it/RSC/Treaties.html.

[19] 'Reforming the Treaties' Amendment Procedures; Second Report on the Reorganising of the European Union Treaties', European University Institute, Robert Schuman Centre, 31.07.2000, www.iue.it/RSC/Treaties.html.

[20] For example, amendment by (super)-qualified majority or unanimity of the Council and a special majority in the European Parliament has been recommended by the 'Dehaene

constitutional part should according to many still remain subject to a unanimous decision of an intergovernmental conference and be ratified by all Member States.[21] However, besides the danger of blockage resulting from the potential unsuccessful referendums as demonstrated above, a number of other problems have been highlighted. The Second EUI Report pointed out that the IGC solutions often come down to the lowest common denominator and there is therefore a frequent need for new IGCs; exceptions have to be formulated for individual Member States in a non-transparent manner; and, ultimately, the unanimity requirement for amending the treaties is rare in international organisations, as well as in the constitutions of the federal states.

The following alternative mechanisms have been proposed. The EUI Report recommended a super-qualified majority of 4/5 or 9/10 of the Member States representing 4/5 of the population, with a blocking majority of at least 2 states. In this case, the minorities should be given an institutional guarantee, by increasing the influence of the Commission, European Parliament and possibly the European Court of Justice, who would guarantee the collective European interest, and an opt-out clause, which would apply to the substantive scope of competences and intensity of instruments in action but not to the organisational structure and decision-making. In addition, the EUI Report recommended considering a wider use of the autonomous amendment procedure by the EU institutions for issues of a technical nature and the introduction of the 'negative ratification' borrowed from international law — a treaty would enter into force unless a notification of disagreement is submitted. It also recommended the use of the Convention model and reforming the Intergovernmental Conference for amending the Treaties, in order to bring together the representatives of EU institutions, national governments, parliaments and civil society. The national parliaments should be involved in the preparation of the amendment rather than leaving them with a *fait accompli*, in order to facilitate the ratification process and to increase the legitimacy of the treaties.

Amongst other proposals, Mr Giscard d'Estaing, the president of the Convention, has on several occasions called for holding an EU-wide referendum. The Commission's draft for a constitutional treaty, known as

Group', above n 17, and in 'Thinking Enlarged. The Accession Countries and the Future of the European Union — A Strategy for Reform by the Villa Faber Group on the Future of the EU', Bertelsmann Foundation and Center for Applied Policy Research, October 2001, www.europa.eu.int/futurum/conothbis_en.htm#att [hereinafter the 'Villa Faber Group'].

[21] Amongst academic studies, see 'Dehaene group' (above n 17), 'Villa Faber Group' (above n 20), and Art 102 in 'A Basic Treaty for the European Union. Draft Version for the Reorganisation of the Treaties', Bertelsmann Group for Policy Research at the Center for Applied Policy Research, May 2000, www.cap.uni-muenchen.de/.

'Penelope' has proposed the controversial secession-clause, under which a non-ratifying country would have to leave the Union. The 'Faber Group', recognising that the ratification process is fragile, has recommended designing mechanisms to attach specific costs to the repeated rejection of a new treaty, and constructive mechanisms to accommodate the concerns of dissenters. There are also proposals for creating special bodies for amendment of the secondary treaty and to make more frequent recourse to the mechanisms of enhanced cooperation and flexibility.

The line of argument of this chapter also leads to two recommendations concerning the imminent constitutional amendments in the Central and Eastern European Candidate Countries. First, the draft amendments should be addressed to the European Union rather than 'international organisations',[22] as the latter would reduce the room for interpretation when it would come to accommodating major integration steps undertaken by the future treaties in the constitutions. The 'international organisations' approach would be more likely to lead to constitutional amendments, with all the potential procedural complications discussed above. Second, in order to reduce the danger of paralysing the EU treaty amendment procedure, as well as to avoid obstructing the countries' participation internally, it is advisable that the draft amendments would avoid the referendum clauses for ratifying the successive EU treaties after membership and consider instead facilitating the referendum procedures.

V. THE IMPACT OF REFERENDUMS ON CEE POSITIONS IN THE CONVENTION

The complications with referendums in CEE Candidate Countries also indirectly influenced the EU Future Debate by predetermining the Eastern countries' interest for incremental integration concerning the reforms prepared within the Convention. Due to insufficient turnout rates and euro-sceptic public opinion, it was difficult to 'sell' the EU in the accession referendums as it is, and 'selling' a federal union was therefore even harder, considering the historically conditioned anti-federalist sentiments of the CEE populations.

The possibility of an 'incorrect' referendum result was seen as a real danger in the preparations for accession referendums: several CEE Candidate Countries made efforts to find constitutional

[22] The 'international organisation' approach is taken in the Polish 1997 Constitution and the Czech constitutional amendments of 2001, as well as in the initial draft amendments of Latvia, Lithuania, Slovakia and Hungarian draft constitution of 1997 — these were replaced in some at a later stage with a direct reference to the EU. See for details and references Albi, 2003, above n 2.

interpretations to circumvent the referendum or to lower the turnout requirements. For instance, the draft constitutional amendments of the Latvian Working Group suggested reducing the turnout requirement for EU accession from 50 per cent to half of the participants of the previous parliamentary elections.[23] In Estonia, the former President suggested that the referendum should take place after a few years of EU-experience, on whether the people want to secede from the Union.[24] In Lithuania, where so far seven referendums have been held, the Working Group on the EU-related constitutional amendments stated that EU accession does not require a referendum, since the EU forms a traditional international organisation and does not impinge upon Lithuania's independence.[25] Its Rapporteur has later mentioned that a majority with 50 per cent turnout would be difficult to achieve,[26] while, understandably, none of the Lithuanian reporters have mentioned the 3/4 approval of the whole electorate, required for amending Article 1. In Poland, the Government has expressed concern about the referendum with a view to the slippage of EU-support and consistently low election turnouts.[27] In the Czech Republic, the referendum law underwent a prolonged inter-chamber odyssey as the Government has been concerned about the feasibility of achieving the 50 per cent turnout.[28]

The fact that the future EU treaties have to be ultimately accepted by the people in referendums has usually been overlooked by those commentators who have not seen a case for a CEE coalition concerning the issues of the Future Debate. For instance, many commentators have pointed out that the history of voting patterns in the EU shows that coalitions are formed on an issue-driven basis, rather than new versus old or small versus big.[29] This is expected to continue after the enlargement into the Central and Eastern countries, because their size, level of

[23] 'The Theoretical Foundation of the Amendments to *Satversme* proposed by the Working Group', Ministry of Justice of the Republic of Latvia, Riga, 23 November 2001.

[24] H Roonemaa, 'Meri: rahvas võiks aastate pärast hääletada euroliidust välja astumist' [Meri: the people could vote on secession from the EU after a few years], in *Eesti Päevaleht*, 5 May 2001.

[25] 'Republic of Lithuania Constitutional Law on the Amendment of Articles 136 and 138 of the Constitution of the Republic of Lithuania. Draft of the Working Group established under the Seimas Chancellery', in *Stojimas I Europos Sajunga Ir Konstitucija. Seminaro Medziaga 29–30.06.1999* (Vilnius, Eugrimas, 2000), 141ff.

[26] Vadapalas, above n 14 at 351.

[27] G Blazyca, M Kolkiewicz, 'Poland and the EU: Internal Disputes, Domestic Politics and Accession' (1999) 15 *Journal of Communist Studies and Transition Politics* at 141.

[28] 'Czech Senate approves Bill on EU accession referendum', reported by CTK; *RFE/RL Newsline*, 5, (124), Part II, 29 June 2001.

[29] H Wallace, 'The Future of Europe Debate: Opportunities for British Policy', ESRC Policy Paper *One Europe or Several?* No 05/01, 2001, www.one-europe.ac.uk/pdf/p5wallace.pdf, p 27; H Grabbe, 'What Comes After Nice?' Policy Brief of Centre for European Reform, 2001, www.cer.org.uk/n5publicatio/nicetreatyfinal3.pdf (except as concerns institutional matters); 'Villa Faber Group', above n 20 at 44–5.

development and communist history would be outweighed by the facts that amongst them, there are 'more free traders ... and those that are more protectionist; there are protestant and catholic; there are southern and nearly 'northern' countries; there are also small and big ones'.[30] Further, it has been argued that the Candidates have not formed a unified group in the first sessions of bickering over the Convention's procedural rules and in nominating the Candidates' representative in the Presidium: some see themselves as a group, others perceive drawing a line between the new and old members as artificial and prefer to form issue-based coalitions. Nor has there been much cooperation between the CEE Candidate Countries during the accession negotiations.

However, the initial speeches on the Future of Union by the CEE politicians demonstrated that there is a case for CEE coalitions at least with regard to the fundamental issues of the EU future, partly because the CEE positions needed to keep in mind the ultimate acceptability by the people in referendums. The CEE politicians predominantly did not approve of the visions of a federal Europe, but advocated a looser union of nation-states. For instance, former Prime Minister of Hungary, Victor Orban preferred to see 'a union based on nations' instead of 'a European United States'.[31] The Polish President Aleksander Kwasniewski said that 'a federation of nation-states' could only appear in twenty years' time.[32] Tunne Kelam, Estonia's representative in the Convention and Chairman of the Parliament's Committee of European Affairs, has said that all main Estonian political forces share the view that the EU should continue as 'a union of nation-states'.[33] The Slovenian Foreign Minister Dimitrij Rupel would like to see a 'United Nations of Europe' or 'Nation States of Europe';[34] the Romanian Prime Minister Adrian Nastase recommended looking for 'an in-between formula' for the EU polity.[35] The approach of 'union of nation-states' also found expression in the CEE politicians' support for 'a constitutional treaty', with an emphasis on *treaty*.[36] This

[30] Speech delivered by R. Martikonis, Deputy Minister of Foreign Affairs of Lithuania, at colloquium 'The Finalité of European Union: Ideas and Concepts of the Candidate Countries', Centre for European Integration Studies, Bonn, 16–17 November 2001, www.europa.eu.int/ futurum/documents/speech/sp171101_en.pdf.

[31] Interview with V Orban in *La libre Belgique*, 11 July 2001.

[32] A Kwasniewski, 'Enlarged EU: Moving Towards a Political Union', speech delivered at the Stockholm School of Economics, 10 May 2001, www.europa.eu.int/futurum/documents/speech/sp100501_en.htm.

[33] T Kelam, speech delivered at the *Riigikogu* (Estonia's Parliament) session of 11 April 2002.

[34] D Rupel, 'Contribution to the Debate on the Future of the Union', 2001, www.europa.eu.int/futurum/documents/other/oth030701_en.pdf 7, 8.

[35] A Nastase, 'The Future European Union: A Romanian Vision', speech delivered at the Belgian Royal Institute for International Relations, 26.06. 2001, http://domino.kappa.ro/mae/dosare.nsf/IntegrareEng/F7578294EF2ADD20C2256AA7002F3C49?OpenDocument.

[36] Kwasniewski, above n 32; J Buzek (former Prime Minister of Poland), speech delivered at the Belgian Royal Institute of International Affairs, 26 June 2001; 'Initial Position of the Republic of Bulgaria on the Debate on the Future of the European Union', report by the

would provide an 'intermediate' step for accommodating the need for simplification of the EU treaties, as a constitution would be associated by many with the core of a sovereign state. In the domain of institutional architecture, the approach of 'union of nation-states' correlated to the supported of CEE politicians for incremental strengthening of the Community institutions, instead of an 'institutional revolution'. They predominantly supported a gradual strengthening of the Commission and the widening of the powers of the European Parliament; some mentioned that the Community institutions have in the past proved to protect small states, to benefit the less developed countries, to promote common European interest and to form an engine for integration. The speeches insisted on increasing legitimacy and accountability by enhancing the role of the national parliaments, their control over governments and interweaving the national parliaments more closely with the European Parliament.[37]

The few open federalists amongst the top politicians of Slovakia, the Czech Republic and Estonia were usually in disaccord with general domestic political attitudes, at least in the two latter countries whose populations have consistently been famous for their lowest support rates towards the EU. In the Czech Republic, there has been a clash of visions between, on the one hand, pro-federal former President Vaclav Havel[38] and former Prime Minister Milos Zeman,[39] and, on the other hand, the leader of a strong opposition party, former Prime Minister and now President of the Republic, Vaclav Klaus, whose inclination to the British way and support for 'a union of sovereign nation states'[40] has been shared, for instance, by most Czech local politicians.[41] In Estonia, the

Ministry of Foreign Affairs of Bulgaria, February 2002, www.europa.eu.int/futurum/documents/bulgarie0202_en.pdf; Nastase, above n 35; M Geoana (Foreign Minister of Romania), 'Contribution to the Debate on the Future of the Union', 2001, www.europa.eu.int/futurum/documents/speech/sp090901_en.htm; I Berzins (Foreign Minister of Latvia), 'Contribution "The European Union — the way it is and the way we want it to be"', 31 May 2001, www.europa.eu.int/futurum/documents/press/pr310501_en.htm; M Dzurinda, 'The Debate on the European Constitution — A Slovak View', speech delivered by at Humboldt University, Berlin, 19 February 2002.

[37] See for a detailed account of the speeches A Albi, 'Referendums in Eastern Europe: The Effects on Reforming the EU Treaties and on the Candidate Countries' Positions in the Convention', European University Institute, Robert Schuman Centre Working Paper No 2002/65.

[38] See report of Havel's speeches in P Bugge, 'Czech Perceptions of the Perspective of EU Membership: Havel vs Klaus', European University Institute, Robert Schuman Centre Working Paper No 2000/10.

[39] M Zeman, 'Contribution to the Debate on the Future of Europe', 14 June 2001, www.europa.eu.int/futurum/documents/contrib/cont140601_en.htm.

[40] Bugge, above n 38, at 27–8, 34.

[41] C Perron, 'Views of Czech Local Politicians on European Integration', European University Institute, Robert Schuman Centre Working Paper No 2000/39 at 17.

pro-federal speech delivered in the Berlin Humboldt University by the former Foreign Minister Toomas-Hendrik Ilves,[42] although in strictly personal capacity, was much disliked by the Estonian public and it has cost him his place as the Parliament's representative in the Convention. The current Foreign Minister Kristiina Ojuland has made it clear that she does not support the ideas of an EU constitution, a bicameral European Parliament or direct election of the Commission President, which according to her would belong to the 'sphere of dreams'.[43] The federalist views of the Slovak top politicians[44] had higher domestic credibility due to high EU-support among the Slovak population.

At the academic level, CEE studies on the Future Debate are still being developed, but the few that existed at the time of writing equally predicted the adoption of an 'intermediate' approach. A study on the CEE Countries' representatives in Brussels showed their support for a piecemeal integration rather than federalism; they took a pragmatic, incremental approach, as the issue of sovereignty and national independence remained sensitive.[45] The 'Faber Group', composed of academic and professional experts both from the Member and Candidate states, suggested that most CEE countries are likely to be against a federal EU, because they are unitary states or have experience with authoritarian tendencies with federations.[46] Another study on the CEE countries' experience with federations showed that they have not been adequately conditioned by history to embrace federalism, particularly because of the unequal status of different peoples within federations, such as the Hungarians and Romanians during the Habsburg Empire, the non-Serb population in Yugoslavia and the Slovaks in Czechoslovakia.[47] In addition, given their newly acquired sovereignty, people are uneasy about the federal visions of Europe.[48] As I have discussed elsewhere,[49] CEE legal theory has so far depicted the EU

[42] TH Ilves, 'Constructing a New Europe', speech delivered at Humboldt University, Berlin, 5 February 2001.

[43] Reported in '*Euroopa tulevik ootab Eesti poliitikutelt kiireid otsuseid*'. *Eesti Päevaleht*, 28 January 2002.

[44] Dzurinda, above n 36; E Kukan (Slovak former Foreign Minister), 'Slovakia's Vision of the Future Functioning of the European Union', speech delivered by on the second special briefing to meet the new Member States, European Policy Center, 2002, www.theepc.be/documents/.

[45] A Krok-Paszkowska, J Zielonka, 'The EU's Next Big Enlargement: Empirical Data on the Candidates' Perceptions', European University Institute, Robert Schuman Centre Working Paper No 2000/54.

[46] 'Villa Faber Group', above n 20 at 7.

[47] V Mastny, 'The Historical Experience of Federalism in East Central Europe', (2000) 1 *East European Politics and Societies*, 96, as cited in J Motoc 'Europe and its Teleology: Is there a Central-Eastern Vision?' in C Joerges, Y Meny, J Weiler (eds), *What Kind of Constitution for What Kind of Polity?* (Cambridge, MA, Robert Schuman Centre of the European University Institute and Harvard Law School, 2001) at 188–9.

[48] Also Motoc, above n 47, 2001, at 189.

[49] Albi, 2003, above n 2.

prevalently as an 'international organisation', possibly in order to create a psychologically neutral bridge to the countries' move from complete constitutional silence on international organisations towards membership of a deeply integrated supranational organisation, and joining a federal union instead could be too much to absorb. For instance, the Estonian Constitutional Expert Commission has stated that its draft EU-amendments do not permit Estonia's participation in a federal Union, which would emerge if an EU constitution or a bicameral European Parliament were introduced.[50]

VI. CONCLUSION

This chapter has discussed the implications of the constitutional amendment and referendum procedures of the future Central and Eastern European Member States on reforming the EU treaties. Highlighting the procedural and practical obstacles of the 'national constitutional procedures' in Central and Eastern Europe, the chapter sets forth arguments in support of the revision of the EU treaty amendment procedure, which has been a highly sensitive issue on the Convention's agenda. It points out that besides the remarkable increase of the number of Member States, the accession of CEE countries involves further strains on the current system of unanimity and national ratification of new treaty amendments, and may thus lead to a genuine paralysis in the amendment process. For instance, the CEE countries have a tradition of frequent recourse to referendums, while majority of recent referendums have been invalid due to high minimum turnout requirements. These complications concerning referendums also predetermine the central and eastern countries' interest for an incremental integration with a view to the Debate on the Future of the Union, as a federal Union was perceived as a risk to the results of the accession referendums.

[50] *Võimalik liitumine Euroopa Liiduga ja selle õiguslik tähendus Eesti riigiõiguse seisukohalt.* [Potential accession to the European Union and its legal consequences in the light of Estonian constitutional law.] The Report of the Constitutional Expert Commission, 1998.

5

The Accession Treaty and its Transitional Arrangements: A Twilight Zone for the New Members of the Union

KIRSTYN INGLIS*

I. INTRODUCTION

THE ACCESSION OF ten new Member States to the European Union on 1 May 2004[1] will not end the pre-accession strategy. The pre-accession strategy that was developed for the upcoming enlargement will continue to apply for many years to come. Bulgaria, Romania and Turkey are waiting in the wings under the pre-accession strategy, and the Stabilisation and Association Agreements (SAAs) governing relations between the EU and the south east European countries may be included in the pre-accession strategy.[2]

For the purposes of the imminent eastwards enlargement, the pre-accession strategy, from very early on,[3] envisaged the use of limited transitional arrangements to enable the candidates to become full members of the Union without reaching full compliance with and implementation of the entire acquis. Such transitional arrangements are now contained in the Treaty of Accession to the European Union signed in Athens on 16 April 2003 between the Member States of the European Union and ten of the candidate countries (Czech Republic, Estonia, Cyprus, Latvia,

* European Institute, University of Ghent, Belgium. This study was prepared under the auspices of the project 'Pre-accession and accession: a legal appraisal of the EU enlargement strategy', funded by the Flemish Scientific Research Fund (Fonds voor Wetenschappelijk Onderzoek).

[1] See Art 2 Treaty of Accession.

[2] Bulgaria, Romania and Turkey are official Candidates. For Bulgaria and Romania the date for accession is 2007, while negotiations have still to be opened with Turkey. SAAs have been signed with Macedonia and Croatia and both have applied for membership.

[3] See Agenda 2000, COM(1997)2000.

Lithuania, Hungary, Malta, Poland, Slovenia and the Slovak Republic).[4] Also, various instruments of the pre-accession strategy will continue to apply to the future new Members even after their accession.

The use of transitional arrangements in accession treaties is not new. Indeed, transitional arrangements were incorporated into the accession treaties for all previous enlargements.[5] But this enlargement cannot be compared to any previous enlargement. The number and diversity of candidates is one factor in this difference, as is the fact that the Union itself has increased in complexity over the past ten years since the Copenhagen European Council first launched the accession process in 1993.[6] Given the ongoing Union projects, including further revision of the Treaties and the Debate on the Future of Europe, enlargement can be expected to have a cumulative effect on the complexity of the Union. Flexibility in the means of co-operation and integration of the Member States, allowing for differentiation between groups of Member States, is not new to the Union.[7] The result includes notably, Schengen and the introduction of the Euro, in which certain Member States do not participate. An in-depth discussion on flexibility and differentiation would be losing sight of the purpose of this chapter. However, it is relevant that the Accession Treaty introduces new forms of flexibility mechanisms through an extensive network of transitional arrangements and these mechanisms in some cases differentiate between the treatment of new Member States, on the one hand, and the Fifteen on the other. The system of pre-determined and additional transitional measures and transitional safeguard clauses that is planned for the first three years in the post-accession period will undoubtedly contribute to the overall complexity of the Union and the functioning of the acquis in the aftermath of enlargement.

A. The Purpose of Transitional Arrangements in the Accession Treaty

While it is not surprising that the Accession Treaty for this coming enlargement also contains transitional arrangements, it is easier to identify their purpose than to classify the legal nature of the measures. Section II below takes a more detailed look at the substance of the relevant provisions. The

[4] Hereinafter 'the Accession Treaty', OJ 2003 L236/1.

[5] See F Hoffmeister, 'Changing Requirements for Membership' in A Ott and K Inglis (eds), *Handbook on European Enlargement* (The Hague, TMC Asser Press, 2000), 87.

[6] The 1993 Copenhagen European Council began the reorientation of the Europe Agreements as accession vehicles, see M Maresceau, 'Association, partnership, pre-accession and accession', in M Maresceau (ed), *Enlarging the European Union* (London, Longman, 1997), 3.

[7] Thanks to Andrea Ott for her insights on the subject of flexibility and differentiation. See also A Ott, 'The Principle of Flexibility in an enlarged European Union', European University Institute Working Paper, forthcoming.

aim is to enable the continued application of the Union's pre-accession conditionality in the first years after accession to ensure the integrity of the acquis in an enlarged Union, avoiding rifts between the twenty-five Member States, in particular any protectionist backlash against the new Member States. While generally speaking a transitional period of three years can be said to apply, this three-year time frame emerges from an analysis of all the transitional arrangements. To qualify this last statement however, the transitional arrangements that were agreed by the candidates and the Union at the 2002 Copenhagen European Council vary in time scale and do not follow a three-year rule. If a transitional arrangement was fixed in December 2002, it may allow a derogation until 2017 for example, or require conformity with the acquis by the end of 2005.

B. Pre-Determined and Additional Transitional Measures and Transitional Safeguard Clauses

Before going any further, it is important to classify the various types of transitional arrangement, contained in the Part Four of the Accession Treaty on 'Temporary Provisions'. Title I of Part Four contains 'transitional measures' while 'other' temporary provisions are contained in Title II. The transitional measures take the form of temporary technical amendments and/or derogations from the acquis, which are fixed in time and scope. They provide for the interim technical adjustment or amendment of the institutions or pre- and post-accession financial arrangements and set down numerous temporary derogations that delay the entry into force of specific measures of the acquis in the new Member States. Thus, the transitional measures give form and substance to the terms agreed at the Copenhagen European Council in December 2002 or before and can therefore be referred to as ***pre-determined* transitional measures**. Thus, there are various pre-determined transitional measures for the existing Fifteen as well as for the Ten new Member States that delay the full entry into force of the acquis.

The 'other' temporary provisions, however, provide the legal basis for the adoption, upon or after the date of accession, of ***additional* transitional measures**. This category includes the possible introduction of derogations from the acquis for the Common Agricultural Policy and veterinary and phytosanitary rules. The content or time frame of such measures cannot as yet be known of course (although they should not exceed three years in duration),[8] given the overhaul of the Common Agricultural Policy and the continuing evolution of the agri-food law acquis.

Also under the title of 'other' temporary provisions are the temporary safeguard measures in respect of the Internal Market, the Justice and

[8] Subject to only limited possibilities for extension, see further below.

Home Affairs[9] acquis and a general economic safeguard clause.[9a] The general economic safeguard clause for the benefit of the acceding and existing Member States alike is the same clause that was used in the Accession Treaty for the last enlargement[10] and can be found in the Accession Treaty (Article 37 Act of Accession) but runs for three years as opposed to one year, as in the case of last enlargement.[11] Although the safeguard clause for Justice and Home Affairs provides that safeguard measures take the form of 'temporary suspension of the application of the relevant provisions and decisions in the relations between a new Member State and any other Member State or Member States', there is no specification as such of the type of measures other than that they should be 'appropriate'. Safeguard measures should not apply beyond three years from the date of accession. As such, they can be correctly referred to as **transitional safeguard clauses** and the measures taken thereunder as **temporary safeguard measures**.

C. The Example of Temporary Arrangements Used in Previous Accession Treaties

The enlargements of 1973 and of 1995 bringing in the UK, Ireland and Denmark first and then Austria, Finland and Sweden, involved a general transitional period of four years beginning 1 January 1973 and 1 January 1995, the date of accession in the case of the former and the latter respectively. The 1982 accession of Greece also involved a general four-year transition period. For Portugal and Spain the overall timeframe was seven years. As regards the UK, Ireland and Denmark, the purpose of the transition was to reduce progressively and eventually eliminate, tariff barriers and quota systems and to adapt the Common Agricultural Policy and the same applied to Greece.[12] For Portugal and Spain these arrangements covered the customs union. For the last enlargement to take in Austria, Finland and Sweden, there was no generally established

[9] Legally speaking, as a result of the Amsterdam Treaty, the title of Justice and Home Affairs acquis is no longer correct and is used here and throughout the remainder of this chapter solely for ease of reference. The scope of application of the safeguard clause concerns 'framework decisions or any other relevant commitments, instruments of co-operation and decisions relating to mutual recognition in the area of criminal law under Title VI of the EU Treaty and Directives and Regulations relating to mutual recognition in civil matters under Title IV of the EC Treaty'.

[9a] Safeguard measures are also envisaged in respect of workes. However, these are framed within the context of the pre-determined arrangements in the country annexes concerning the movement of workers.

[10] Art 152, Act of Accession for Austria, Finland and Sweden (OJ 1994 C241).

[11] See Ott, above n 7.

[12] Resolution 1980/703, OJ 1980 C346/29, Resolution 1980/688, OJ 1980 C346/28, Resolution 1979/399, OJ 1979 C289/51.

transitional period due to the fact that these countries had already been closely involved with the Union in the far-reaching economic and legal approximation framework of the European Economic Area Agreement, although there had been a generally applicable transitional economic safeguard clause of one year's duration.[13]

Exceptionally, however, a special fisheries regime applied to the UK until 1983. For Greece an exceptional pre-determined transitional period for free movement of workers applied for seven years from the date of accession. A ten-year pre-determined transitional period applied to Spain and Portugal in respect of the free movement of workers[14] as well as for the common agricultural policy and fisheries. Exceptional pre-determined transitional arrangements were incorporated in the Accession Treaties with Austria, Finland and Sweden, for certain environment related and sanitary standards, and a special fisheries regime was also granted to Finland and Sweden while Austria secured a derogation for transit traffic.

D. Distinguishing Features of the Transitional Arrangements in the Accession Treaty

Six observations are immediately striking when comparing this Accession Treaty to the previous accession treaties. First, throughout the period of enhanced pre-accession, the new Member States have been under an obligation to transpose and implement the entirety of the acquis without exception, even in those chapters of the acquis where certain existing Member States do not participate.[15] In those chapters of the acquis where pre-determined transitional measures in the form of derogations from the acquis have already been agreed, the new Member States are under an obligation to continue in their efforts, according to fixed results and time-limits and failing which, the new Member States will fall prey to the transitional safeguard clauses.

Second, measures adopted under the transitional safeguard clauses will be at the European Commission's disposal to ensure compliance with, as well as implementation of, the new Members' pre-accession commitments. These measures will apply to the future new Members in addition to the typical Treaty obligations applicable to any (existing) Member State. For the Internal Market and for the Justice and Home Affairs acquis

[13] See Art 152 Act of Accession Austria, Finland and Sweden.
[14] See Declarations by the EEC on Spanish and Portuguese workers taking up aid employment in the then Member States (OJ 1985 L302/492) and Joint Declarations on workers already established (OJ 1985 L302/480) or on the free movement of workers (OJ 1985 L302/480).
[15] For example, EMU and the Schengen acquis.

and Justice and Home Affairs. All fifteen Member States participated in drafting the Amsterdam Treaty and the Nice Treaty, which amended and revised the Treaties and, of course, the introduction of the Euro. The worries of the existing fifteen Member States and the EU institutions as concerns the repercussions for the acquis and the functioning of the Union in the immediate aftermath of eastwards enlargement have led to the new mechanisms to safeguard the interests of the Fifteen.

This complexity was reflected in the pre-accession process that began following the 1993 Copenhagen European Council and is now also to be seen in the system of transitional arrangements and related temporary provisions of the Accession Treaty and accompanying Act of Accession, dealt with further below. It must be remembered that some of the candidates had been focusing their efforts on accession from before 1993, their aspirations already borne out in the preambles to the earliest Europe Agreements. Certainly, since the launch of the enhanced pre-accession strategy set out in the European Commission's Agenda 2000 document of 1997, the candidates' preparations for accession have been fully accession driven. The main thrust of all Community and other international funding and technical assistance has been focusing singly on the adoption of the acquis in its entirety as well as the building-up of the administrative capacity necessary to apply and enforce it, and to keep up with its evolution. Additional post-accession assistance is also provided to the candidates temporarily and a number of predetermined transitional measures will apply to the institutions of an enlarged Union pending, notably, the first elections of the European Parliament and the appointments of the Commissioners as well as the Council voting majorities.

The Treaty of Accession 'establish(es) by common agreement the conditions of admission and the adjustments to be made to the Treaties on which the European Union is founded.'[20] The provisions contained in its accompanying Act Concerning the Conditions of Accession, hereinafter the Act of Accession, 'form an integral part of this Treaty' of Accession.[21] Without labouring the ratification process,[22] the General Affairs Council 'formally decided'[23] on the admission of the ten new Member States on 14 April 2003 before the final signature of the Accession Treaty by all twenty-five of the countries concerned on 16 April 2003 in Athens. Having been ratified, it will enter into force on 1 May 2004. While the new Member States will be bound, from the date of accession,[24] by the original Treaties

[20] Sixth recital to the Treaty of Accession.
[21] Art 1(2) Treaty of Accession.
[22] See Maresceau, above n 6 at 15–21; see also Hoffmeister, above n 5 at 99–102.
[23] See IP 8220/03 (Presse 105).
[24] Art 54 Act of Accession.

and the acts adopted by the institutions and the European Central Bank before accession,[25] Article 10 of the Act of Accession acts as a general legal basis for derogations therefrom, 'as a transitional measure'.[26] It is also expressly provided that these transitional provisions will not affect the status in law of the acts they derogate from and that the procedures for amending those acts will continue to apply.[27]

As mentioned at I.B above, Title I of Part Four of the Act of Accession, entitled 'Temporary provisions' and containing Articles 24 to 42, sets out a variety of transitional arrangements of application to the new Member States.[28]

A. Pre-Determined Transitional Measures to Smooth the Path for Participation of the New Members States in the Budget, Institutions and Financial Instruments

Articles 25–36 of the Act of Accession deal specifically with:

— the amendment of or adjustment to the Community's own resources system and the budget and the new Members' participation therein;[29]

— institutional matters during the period between accession on 1 May 2004 and the time of the first elections of the Commission or Parliament and the weighting of country votes in Council — see also Title I of Part Five of the Act of Accession;[30]

[25] Art 2 Act of Accession.

[26] Art 10 Act of Accession reads: 'The application of the original Treaties and acts adopted by the institutions shall, as a transitional measure, be subject to the derogations provided for in this Act.'

[27] Art 8 Act of Accession.

[28] Art 22 Act of Accession, contained in Part Three on Permanent provisions, refers to Annex IV which does not contain derogations from the acquis but rather provides specific guidelines on applying the acquis in the fields of free movement of capital (tax laws), company law (the supplementary protection certificate), competition policy (state aid provisions), agriculture (public stocks and carry over stocks and aid to agriculture), customs union (Common Customs Code and proof of origin, allowing for the continued validity of stocks or goods in transport subject, inter alia to proof of origin under the Europe Agreement Protocols or equivalent agreements between the new Member States themselves).

[29] Arts 27, 28, 29, 30 & 31 Act of Accession detail certain transitional measures relating to the Communities' own resources system, the participation of the new Members in the budget, the receipt by the new Members of the special lump-sum cash flow facility and the participation of the new Members in the Research Fund for Coal and Steel.

[30] Arts 25 and 26 Act of Accession specify the temporary situation as regards the European Parliament and the Council voting majorities in line with the provisions of the Nice Treaty (specify provisions), which should be read in conjunction with Arts 11 and 12 Act of Accession. There are no temporary provisions applicable to the Commission, the Committee of the Regions or the European Court of Justice.

— the changeover of the new Members from eligibility under the pre-accession instruments[31] to eligibility for financing from the structural funds (or the Agricultural Guarantee and Guidance Fund), including the continuation of certain pre-accession financing in the immediate transition period after accession;[32]
— introducing the new Transition Facility to further finance the strengthening of and developing administrative capacity and the continued implementation and enforcement of EC law as well as to foster best practice among peers;[33]
— the creation of the new Schengen Facility to provide financing to address the main shortcoming in the new Members' ability to meet the requirements of the Schengen acquis and to operate the new Schengen Information System-SIS.[34]

In the very first Part of the Act of Accession, on 'Principles', a number of seemingly transitional arrangements are also relevant to the smooth insertion of the new Member States in the period immediately preceding accession. While not strictly speaking a transitional measure, Article 4 of

[31] Art 32 Act of Accession cuts off the entitlement of the new Members to the PHARE, CBC, ISPA and SAPARD funds (and Cyprus and Malta will also be cut off from their pre-accession funding instruments) — as of 31 December 2003. They will be treated as any other Member State, as of 1 January 2004 for the purposes of participating in Community agencies and programmes. From that time, the rules set out in the Draft Act of Accession will apply (unless of course the candidates do not actually accede for whatever reason). Art 33, Act of Accession, concerns the implementation of contracts and payments for pre-accession assistance, which will be managed in the new Member States (subject to special ex-ante control of the relevant body by the European Commission). Generally speaking, pre-accession assistance must be programmed within the year preceding accession (ie by 1 May 2003). Basically, individual legal commitments and payments undertaken in accordance the pre-accession financial instruments, will continue to be met according to the rules of the pre-accession instruments but with the money being charged to the relevant Community budget heading. This situation will continue until all programmes and projects have been closed. Finally, Art 33(4) of the Act of Accession makes special provision for the use of ISPA funds for the purposes of maintaining the necessary statutory staff in the new Member States for fifteen months after the date of accession. This is important because 'officials assigned to posts in the new Member States before accession and who are required to remain in service in those States after the date of accession shall benefit, as an exception, from the same financial and material conditions as were applied to the Commission before accession — in accordance with Annex X to the Staff Regulations of Officials and the Conditions of Employment of Other Servants of the European Communities (Reg 259/68, as amended). Certain ISPA funds will be used together with the Community Budget (part B — 'Support expenditure for operation').
[32] Art 32(5) Act of Accession enables the Commission to adopt additional measures to facilitate the transition from the pre-accession funding — see also Art 2(3) Accession Treaty.
[33] Art 34 Act of Accession provides for certain temporary financial assistance to be given the new Member States in the form of a 'Transition Facility': EUR 200 million for 2004, EUR 120 million for 2005, EUR 60 for 2006.
[34] See Art 35 Act of Accession.

the Act of Accession provides that the candidates will participate as a Member State in the Economic and Monetary Union from the date of accession but will be subject to the derogation applicable under Article 122 EC, alongside Denmark and the UK.

While also not strictly speaking a transitional arrangement, Article 3 of the Act of Accession makes clear that the new Member States will be party to all those measures of the Schengen acquis that are listed in the 'Schengen Protocol' and contained in Annex I to the Act of Accession together with any acts that are adopted before the date of accession. However, Article 3(2) Act of Accession expressly excludes the *application* of the Schengen acquis in the new Member States on the date of accession. The possibility of additional transitional measures relevant to the Schengen acquis are considered below in the context of Justice and Home Affairs acquis.

Finally, certain other arrangements are made for external agreements or conventions,[35] thus for example, the new Members will accede to the Cotonou Agreement[36] upon signature of the Act of Accession but agree to accede to the EEA Agreement.[37] Also, the new Members will be entitled to maintain fisheries agreements that they have concluded with third countries but on a provisional basis only — that is until their expiry — and subject to those agreements being managed by the EC.[38]

B. Pre-Determined Transitional Arrangements Concerning Internal Market and Sectoral Policies

Turning to those pre-determined transitional measures in the form of derogations from the acquis, the relevant provision is found in Article 24 of the Act of Accession. Certain pre-determined transitional arrangements provide for derogations from the acquis applicable to the Fifteen and the new Members. The Commission has been keen to reserve the possibility, where appropriate, to propose transitional measures in the interests of the Union'.[39] The Fifteen are entitled to derogations from Article 39 EC and the first paragraph of Article 49 EC in respect of the

[35] Art 6(1)–(12) Act of Accession.
[36] Art 6(4) Act of Accession.
[37] There have been delays in the negotiations of the terms for the accession of the candidate countries to the EEA agreement, in particular because of Poland's concerns over the fish quotas and their management. Consequently, the agreement was not ready for signature alongside the Accession Treaty on 16 March 2003. See news report of euobserver.com, 10 April 2003.
[38] Art 6(9) Act of Accession.
[39] Enlargement Strategy Paper, Report on progress towards accession by each of the candidate countries (for 2000) http://www.europa.eu.int/comm/enlargement/report_11_00/index.htm.

eight new Members from central and eastern Europe but not with regards to Cyprus and Malta.[40] The derogations can be summarised as follows:

- a two year period during which national measures will be applied by current Member States to new Member States, with an option for the Fifteen to continue these measures for a further three years and potentially even seven years provided there are serious disturbances of the labour market in one of the current Member States;
- review after the expiry of the two year period and further reviews at the request of a Member State;
- provision for safeguards to be taken by the Fifteen Member States for up to seven years from the date of accession.

Additionally, the transitional arrangement includes a standstill clause preventing the Fifteen from restricting their markets during the transitional arrangements and preference must given by the Fifteen to the nationals of the new Member States over third country labour. Moreover, those nationals from the new Member States will be protected provided they have been legally working in the Fifteen for the 12 months prior to accession but they will only be protected in the country where they have been legally resident, not in another of the fifteen Member States. However, any of the Fifteen may apply to relax such national measures including full labour market access and may at any time decide to fully apply the rules of Regulation 1612/68. Only Austria and Germany have secured specific 'flanking measures' to address serious disturbances in certain specified sectors of their labour markets,[41] measures which will necessarily affect the EU rules on establishment and services. In practice, all fifteen current Member States have already expressed the intention to restrict the freedom of movement to nationals of the new Member States as of the date of accession.[42]

Turning to the chapters on free movement of services and free movement of capital, there are also transitional arrangements that will apply to the Fifteen and the new Member States concerning investor compensation

[40] See for example Annex XII, 2.1.–2.14 Act of Accession, 876–878.
[41] Namely construction, industrial cleaning and interior decorators in Germany and in Austria, horticultural services, the cutting, shaping and finishing of stone, the manufacture of metal structures and parts thereof, construction, security activities, industrial cleaning, home nursing and social work and activities without accommodations. See Annex XII, 2.13 Act of Accession.
[42] A search on the EUobserver website gives examples: www.euobserver.com/index.phtml?aid=6886, www.euobserver.com/index.phtml?aid=8703, www.euobserver.com/index.phtml?aid=9016. Thanks to Atilla Borsos on Hungarian papers.

schemes and the establishment of Polish branches of investment firms in the Union.[43] All of the new Member States will apply transitional arrangements for the acquisition of secondary residences and/or agricultural land.[44]

By far the bulk of the pre-determined transitional arrangements, however, exclusively concern the new Member States. Article 24 Act of Accession,[45] referring to Annexes V through to XIV, provides for technical adaptations to various laws in order to apply the transitional arrangements correctly to each of the candidates. Each Annex relates to a different new Member State and, as was the procedure with previous enlargements, specifies the derogations from all those Community acts in line with the transitional arrangements agreed at the December 2002 Copenhagen European Council. The transitional arrangements do not relate to the entirety of a piece of legislation and the exact nature of the derogation is specified in the relevant country annex — the derogations for each of the new Member States are not the same. A survey of all transitional arrangements is too ambitious for a contribution of this size. However, certain comments on the various transitional arrangements contained in the ten country annexes should be mentioned here. Taking an example from the Annex XII for Poland, this will mean that Poland will be entitled to maintain certain existing national certificates for medical devices or authorisations for pharmaceuticals until December 2005 or 2008 respectively, contrary to the terms of the relevant Directives. However, other Member States, including the new Member States, will not be obliged to recognise those authorisations or certificates and may therefore prevent the products concerned from being placed on their markets.[46] Also, for example, Poland is the only new Member that will have a derogation in respect of medical devices but Cyprus, Lithuania, Malta and Slovenia have similar derogations in respect of pharmaceuticals, although different time-limits apply.

Transitional arrangements apply in the following fifteen chapters (out of a total of thirty-one chapters) of the acquis: free movement of goods; freedom of movement of persons; freedom to provide services; free movement of capital; company law; competition policy; agriculture; fisheries; transport policy; taxation; employment and social policy; energy; telecommunications, IT and postal services; culture and audio-visual policy, and environment. In some cases, the derogations are minimal and are relatively short. For example, Malta may allow certain collective agreements on working time to remain in force until 31 December 2004, otherwise in

[43] See Annex XII, 3.1. Act of Accession.
[44] See for example Annex XII, 4.1.–4.2. Act of Accession.
[45] Art 54 Act of Accession expressly allows for the application of the time-limits set out in Annexes V–XIV.
[46] See Annex XII, 1.1.–1.5. Act of Accession, 875.

contravention of Directive 93/104/EC. The derogations in the chapter on the free movement of goods are also minimal.[47] Other derogations are far longer in duration and will involve considerable continued efforts, including financial, such as in the case of the environment acquis where Poland[48] will benefit from a derogation in respect of large combustion plants until 2017.[49] And Poland has been granted limited derogations from the state aid acquis to support necessary investments in meeting the environment acquis.[50]

The transitional arrangements referred to in Article 24 Act of Accession and worked out in the ten country annexes, enumerate the content of the European Commission's Guide to the Negotiations,[51] published almost immediately after the 'closure' of the negotiations in December 2002. In no circumstances may the enforcement of the new Member States' national rules during the transitional periods referred to in the annexes lead to border controls between the Member States.[52] Due to the fact that the acquis is constantly evolving, the candidates are approximating to a moving target and the references of the acquis legislation may well change between now and the date of accession. A generally applicable provision contained in Article 55 of the Act of Accession[53] allows, at the request of a new Member, additional 'temporary derogations' to be added to those agreed in December 2002 but only in respect of new acquis measures adopted between 1 November 2002[54] and the date of signature of the Accession Treaty. Such 'temporary derogations' in the sense of Article 55 of the Act of Accession, therefore, are not additional transitional arrangements.[55] From

[47] And relate only to licensing of medical equipment and the marketing authorisations for pharmaceutical products as described earlier in the text, concerning Malta, Cyprus, Poland and Slovenia.
[48] See Annex XII, 13.A.–E. Act of Accession, 3810–44.
[49] *Ibid.*
[50] Annex XII, 5.1.(a)(II)(bb) and 5.2. Act of Accession, 879–880.
[51] See http://europa.eu.int/comm/enlargement/negotiations/chapters/negotiations-guide.pdf
[52] Art 40 Act of Accession reads: 'In order not to hamper the proper functioning of the internal market, the enforcement of the new Member States' national rules during the transitional periods referred to in Annexes V to XIV shall not lead to border controls between Member States.' Same as Art 153 Act of Accession for Austria, Finland and Sweden, mentioned above n 10.
[53] Art 55 Act of Accession reads: 'At the duly substantiated request of one of the new Member States, the Council, acting unanimously on a proposal from the Commission, may, before 1 May 2004, take measures consisting of temporary derogations from acts of the institutions adopted between November 2002 and the date of the signature of the Treaty of Accession.'
[54] Being just after the 2002 Commission Country Reports that formed the basis for the December negotiations, where the transitional arrangements were agreed upon. These country reports can be found on http://europa.eu.int/comm/enlargement/report2002/#report2002 The 2003 Reports can be found on the same page.
[55] As regards the CAP, by reference to Art 23 of the Act of Accession, Art 2(3) of the Accession Treaty also provides that the Act of Accession may be modified by unanimous

the wording of Article 2(3) of the Treaty of Accession, the institutions of the Union may indeed adopt other 'measures' between the dates of signature of the Accession Treaty and its entry into force in 2004, which measures will enter into force as of the date of accession.

However, this paragraph does not refer to any possibility of additional 'derogations' from or 'transitional' arrangements in respect of the acquis. It refers to the possibility of further implementing the annexes containing the general transitional arrangements (Article 56 Act of Accession)[56] and also of amending the Annexes that set out the transitional arrangements (Article 57 Act of Accession) for each new Member. The wording of Article 57 of the Act of Accession enables the Council or, where appropriate, the Commission, to make additional 'necessary adaptations' to the acquis, including measures that pre-date the agreement last December on the Accession Treaty. Clearly, however, the intention is only to allow the adaptation of the relevant provisions to take account of evolutions in the acquis before accession rather than to add further derogations to the country annexes.[57]

C. Possible Additional Transitional Measures

Article 41 specifically provides for new 'transitional measures' to be introduced for the common organisation of agricultural markets (COMs), again subject to a three year duration beginning on the date of accession, which will enable the reforms to the COMs to continue in the EC, reforms that the Ten will be expected to implement upon accession.[58] And Article 42, Act of Accession[59] allows for the adoption of transitional measures to

decision of the Council in order to incorporate any amendments to the Common Agricultural Policy in the time between signature and ratification of the Treaty of Accession. Art 23 Act of Accession reads: 'The Council, acting unanimously on a proposal from the Commission and after consulting the European Parliament, may make the adaptations to the provisions of this Act relating to the common agricultural policy which may prove necessary as a result of a modification in Community rules. Such adaptation may be made before the date of accession.'

[56] Referring to Arts 20–22 and Annexes II, II and IV Act of Accession.

[57] By reference to Art 57 Act of Accession, which stipulates: '(1) Where acts of the institutions prior to accession require adaptation by reason of accession, and the necessary adaptations have not been provided for in this Act or Annexes, those adaptations shall be made in accordance with the procedure laid down in paragraph 2. (2) The Council acting by qualified majority on a proposal from the Commission, or the Commission, according to which of these two institutions adopted the original acts, shall to this end draw up the necessary texts.'

[58] The procedure for the adoption of such measures is specified in the second paragraph of Art 41.

[59] Also referred to in Art 2(3) Accession Treaty.

facilitate transition in the application of the Community veterinary and phytosanitary rules, again for a three-year period.[60]

While the new Member States will be subject to the same mechanisms as the Fifteen for checking the implementation of the veterinary and phytosanitary rules, for the first three following years the European Commission will be able to introduce additional transitional arrangements for the new Member States if they fail to meet the veterinary and phytosanitary rules. This concerns temporary derogations from the acquis (coupled with restrictions on the placing on the market of the Ten's products of course) rather than safeguard measures. For Poland, the derogations from the acquis on health and production and marketing of meat, milk, fishery products etc., basically prevent such Polish products from being placed on the EC market and require that they bear special markings. Given the drastic food scares that the Community has experienced since the BSE crisis, this provision seems well justified, especially given the tendency of Member States to institute national protective measures that are blatant obstructions to intra-Community trade on grounds of health and consumer protection.[61]

Something of a double standard seems to arise here. Article 42 introduces an additional legal basis for the different treatment of the new Member States from the existing Member States. The Fifteen are no angels in this field of the acquis. Many cases have been brought by the Commission against the Fifteen for serious hygiene and other violations of fundamental Community laws. Take for example Directive 64/433/EEC on health conditions for the production and marketing of fresh meat produce. Specified Polish meat producing establishments are excluded from marketing their produce in the EU under the very same Directive.[62] However, the Commission has had to bring France before the ECJ for refusing to comply with an Food and Veterinary Office (FVO) report requiring that it withdraw health approval for an abattoir that failed to meet the requirements of the same Directive. The UK has also been condemned for infringements by certain of its poultry abattoirs.[63] Recently, Greece was forced to close a number of slaughterhouses which the FVO found to be of 'extremely poor structural and hygienic standards and expressed very serious concerns on veterinary supervision'.[64] Moreover, the Member States have not proved exemplary in implementing

[60] See for example Annex XII.6.I & II, Accession Treaty.

[61] French measures to prevent British beef from being placed on the market in France are one example, and Swedish measures requiring the prior notification of arrivals of agri-food products from other Member States is another.

[62] See Annex XII.6.B.I. Act of Accession.

[63] See *Nineteenth Annual Report on Monitoring the application of Community Law*, COM(2002) 324 at 67.

[64] See DG(SANCO)/8660/2002, FVO mission of 26 November to 6 December 2002, 14.

judgments of the ECJ against them for failing to implement the same veterinary and phytosanitary laws for which the new Members' have pre-determined transitional arrangements excluding their produce from the market.[65]

D. Transitional Safeguard Measures to Continue the Pre-Accession Momentum in the Post-Accession Transitional Period

Between the signature of the Accession Treaty and its entry into force on 1 May 2004, the candidates have considerable work to do but it is clear that no further transitional arrangements can be added to the country annexes contained in the Act of Accession. Temporary safeguard measures will apply in the first three years after accession to ensure the continued efforts of the new Members towards meeting their pre-accession commitments.

In its Opinion of 19 February 2003, the Commission delivered 'its *favourable opinion* on the accession to the European Union' [italics added] of the Ten. However, no mention is made of the readiness of the Ten. While in the fifth recital the Commission found the Ten to 'fulfil the political criteria for membership and that they will have fulfilled the economic and acquis criteria and will be ready for membership from the beginning of 2004',[66] in the eleventh recital the Commission specifically noted the need for 'vigorous' action by the candidates 'in the context of the political and economic criteria for membership and in relationship to the adoption, implementation and enforcement of the acquis'. This eleventh recital is entirely new to previous Commission Opinions, and refers to the fact that the candidates must continue to make substantial efforts *after* their accession.

This gives a hint as to the extent of the pre-accession priorities and actions that must continue to direct the actions of the new Member States even after their accession. A vast programme of work faces the candidates, as can be seen from the Commission's reports of October 2002.[67] The transitional arrangements fixed in December 2002 appear minimal by comparison. It was clear from the Commission's Agenda 2000 document of 1997,[68] that while transitional arrangements were inevitable, they were to be the exception rather than the rule and to be avoided insofar as feasibly possible. Obvious central themes underlying this approach were the

[65] See *Eighteenth Annual Report on Monitoring the application of Community Law*, COM(2001) 309, Annex V.
[66] It made this recommendation on the basis of its 2002 Strategy Report, COM(2002)700.
[67] See the Commission's ten country reports, above n 54.
[68] See Agenda 2000, above n 3 at 56.

indivisibility of the acquis and a concern to avoid a protectionist backlash against the new Member States, and the consequent disunity that this would involve.

In its Enlargement Strategy Paper for 2000,[69] the Commission framed its approach: transitional arrangements would be exceptional,

> 'limited in time and scope, and accompanied by a plan with clearly defined stages for application of the acquis. They must not involve amendments to the rules or policies of the Union, disrupt their proper functioning, or lead to significant distortions of competition. In this connection, account must be taken of the interests of the Union, the applicant country and the other applicant states'.

Recapping on the 2000 enlargement strategy paper, the Commission went on to note that 'for those areas linked to the extension of the single market, regulatory measures could be implemented quickly. Any transition periods should therefore be few and short. For those areas of the acquis where considerable adaptations are necessary and which require substantial effort, including important financial outlays in areas such as environment, energy and infrastructure, transition arrangements could be spread over a definite period of time, provided candidates can demonstrate that alignment is under way and that they are committed to detailed and realistic plans for alignment, including the necessary investments.'

Each request for a pre-determined transitional measure was assessed on a case by case basis, taking account of that country's interests and the likely impact of each request on the functioning of the Union and the interests of the other candidates. That one country was given a transitional arrangement was not taken as a precedent for the other countries and nor was the fact that transitional measures had been granted in a previous accession. Requests for transitional arrangements were divided into three types:

— *Acceptable:* being transitional measures of a technical nature that pose no significant problem.[70] Acceptance of this type of request helped to advance negotiations in certain chapters from early on the negotiations.
— *Negotiable:* being those requests with a more significant impact, in terms of competition or the internal market, or in time or

[69] Enlargement Strategy Paper, Report on progress towards accession by each of the candidate countries (for 2000), 225–28; see http://www.europa.eu.int/comm/enlargement/report_11_00/index.htm

[70] The Commission had, since September 2000, been examining favourably requests for transitional measures that were limited in time and scope, and were considered not to have a significant impact on competition or the functioning of the internal market.

space. Such transitional measures were acceptable subject to set conditions and a time-limit. Account was taken of their relationship to other transitional arrangements or areas of the acquis without transitional measures or of the country's commitment to well-defined plans for implementation and investment. Necessarily, implications for competition and the single market were a decisive factor in the final grant of the transitional arrangement, as were effects on the economy, health, safety, the environment, consumers, citizens, other common policies and the Community budget.

— *Unacceptable:* being requests for transitional measures posing fundamental problems.

To see what this means in practice, let us take the example of the environment acquis, second only to the agriculture chapter in terms of the number and extent of transitional arrangements. It is useful to note that the Internal Market acquis has not been addressed as a chapter in its own right neither in the accession negotiations nor in the Commission's reports. The Internal Market acquis has always been addressed in the context of the thirty-one chapters of the acquis.

For Poland, transitional arrangements in the environment acquis are fewer in number than had originally been intended. Applying its approach set out in the 2001 Strategy Paper, the Commission, in its Guide to the Negotiations,[71] highlighted the fact that transitional measures have not been granted on: the transposition of legislation (as opposed to implementation); framework legislation (air, waste, water, Environmental Impact Assessment, access to information); nature protection (habitat, birds); essentials of the Internal Market (all product-related legislation); the compliance of all new installations with the acquis. The thrust of the transitional arrangements are to allow the new Member States the time to attract the often massive infrastructure investment required for implementing a Directive or to introduce new institutions structures and systems for the enforcement and monitoring of legislation.[72]

[71] Above n 49 at 57.

[72] See Annex XII, 13.A–E., Act of Accession. Examples of transitional arrangements for environmental rules: *Directive 99/32 relating to a reduction in the sulphur content of certain liquid fuels* (until 31st December 2006): the most challenging task for both this Directive and the VOC Directive is the introduction of a new institutional structure and systems for the monitoring and enforcement of the legislation. In the case of Poland, in the negotiations it was shown that the application of regular limits would raise specific technical and economic problems. Moreover, this Directive is linked to other Directives, notably in the case of Poland, the large combustion plants Directive. The large combustion plants Directive will also be subject to a transitional arrangement, allowing time to attract the necessary investments. Thus, this derogation should help to draw in the crucial investment and financing required but the derogation must not bring about any negative effects on the

1. The Extent of the Pre-Accession Commitments Outstanding

Much of the future new Members' pre-accession commitments are excluded from pre-determined transitional measures. Reading the programme of work to be achieved by the new Members in the Commission's 2002 country reports,[73] it is clear that 'improvement' must indeed be 'vigorous' in a number of areas, particularly in building administrative and judicial capacity, before the end of April 2004.

As concerns the environment chapter, keeping in mind that there can be no deviation from compliance and implementation as pointed out earlier, by 30 April 2004 Poland must (a summary):

— complete transposition in practically all areas, adopt ministerial regulations and put them into practice. Laws are lacking or remain to be transposed for: air quality directives; water-related directives; chemicals; Integrated Pollution Prevention and Control (IPPC); nature protection; some waste directives (packaging waste, landfills)

— improve implementation for waste management, water quality, industrial pollution control, nature protection, chemicals.

— improve environmental integration into the definition and implementation of all other sectoral policies so as to promote sustainable development.

— improve administrative capacity for implementing the environmental acquis through additional staff resources, making the voivodships and counties fully operational and completing the creation of the national and 16 regional Environmental Impact Assessment Commissions.

— increase environmental staff (and further their training) in regional and district authorities and ensure that the available staff resources are allocated in a way that reflects the new and wider tasks arising from EC environment acquis, notably the IPPC Directive.

— launch integrated permits by end 2002 — a significant challenge for the regional and local authorities as some 70 per cent of the

market in gas oil. *Directive 94/63 on volatile organic compound emissions from storage and distribution of petrol* (until 31st December 2005): again, the most challenging task for both this Directive and the VOC Directive is the introduction of a new institutional structure and systems for the monitoring and enforcement of the legislation. It also involves local actors in the candidate countries. Operators of petrol terminals, service stations and petrol transports are also involved in the implementation of technical and management requirements to minimise vapour losses from the handling of petrol.

[73] Above n 54.

installations covered by the IPPC Directive will have to be dealt with at district level.[74]

— establish far-reaching co-operation between regional and local authorities to maintain appropriate expertise.
— improve environmental planning and programming[75]
— improve monitoring capacity[76]
— improve environmental inspectorates[77]
— to agree on improvement programmes for fines and enforcement with the environmental authorities — an important incentive to operators and a source of finance to authorities
— improve investments.[78]

In the environment chapter, considerable financing is necessary for the full adoption and compliance by the candidates with the environmental acquis.[79] Initial estimates were that EUR 120 billion was needed for the CEECs alone. The compliance-costing Reports from the Commission in April 1997[80] and another for Cyprus in June 1999[81] provide more detail regarding the order of magnitude of the capital and recurring costs

[74] To do this, there is an urgent need for training staff at regional and district level in issuing integrated permits, notably as regards process-issues and technology; some staff increases; clear guidelines from central authorities on how to implement the new laws; the newly established Centre for 'Best Available techniques' needs of more staff.

[75] While the situation is improving, and deadlines have been set to establish plans and programmes required under the acquis (preparation of programmes for air quality, the national waste management plan) — however, regional and district plans still need to be improved.

[76] For air, the monitoring capacity needs to be strengthened, notably as regards particulates (PM10); for water, monitoring at the tap of drinking water needs to be extended and all laboratories must be able to measure the full set of parameters under the drinking water directive; modern laboratory equipment is lacking; more efficient pooling of laboratory facilities in regional centres is necessary to meet the requirements of EU directives at lower costs.

[77] Although well established and well staffed, they need a transfer of staff from laboratories to monitoring and inspection in some cases, the frequency of inspections also needs to be improved, in particular for small and medium-sized installations. Nonetheless, large installations are sufficiently inspected and voivodship inspectorates have a good basis for planning and carrying out inspections and for ensuring follow-up to non-compliance.

[78] Investments are already significant but more effort is needed to establish comprehensive investment strategies to improve investment efficiency by focusing the available resources on implementing the requirements of the EC acquis; to introduce a more strategic approach to environmental investments with clear investment planning and listing of priorities; considerable investments need to be secured, also in the medium-term, to ensure the implementation of the environment acquis

[79] Recently reported estimates for Poland's full environmental compliance amounted to EUR 40 billion — being the entire Polish annual budget, see EUobserver of 28 March 2003 reporting on the conference 'Environment Protection and European Integration', held in Warsaw on 29 March 2003. See also K Inglis, 'Candidate countries and the environment', in Ott & Inglis, above n 5, 672.

[80] http://www.europa.eu.int/comm/environment/enlarg/compcos.pdf.

[81] An estimated EUR 1,117.7 to EUR 1,263.5 million is required (infrastructure and capital) for Cyprus to comply with the acquis. The full report can be found at http://www.europa.eu.int/comm/environment/enlarg/cocyp.pdf

associated with meeting the acquis in the various environmental sectoral areas. However, it has also been clear from the outset of the Reports that estimating the actual costs is a venture fraught with uncertainties. It was clear that the EC will not provide the majority of funding that is necessary. Scarcity of financial and other resources threaten the implementation necessary for eventual accession. Poland alone has secured a complementary transitional arrangement for state aid regulations but only for aid related to the environment transitional arrangements and only for the time frame of those same derogations.[82] While Poland has the largest number of transitional arrangements, all of the new Member States also have transitional arrangements for the environment acquis and also for legislation that involves long-term investment and restructuring.

Consequently, the new Member States are still in the thick of their pre-accession obligations. A comparison between the Commission country reports of October 2002[83] with the Guide to the Negotiations Chapter by Chapter,[84] shows that they have a considerable approximation and capacity building programme to fulfil in order to meet their commitments undertaken at the December 2002 European Council. In a few areas of the acquis, some are still in the very early process of approximation and, as at November 2003, *all* of the Ten give rise to serious concerns not only in terms of mere transposition of legislation but particularly in terms of implementation and the administrative and judicial capacity to enforce it. It has been apparent since the pre-accession strategy has been enhanced that transitional arrangements were unavoidable if the political momentum of accession was to be maintained.[85] One cannot help but notice the

[82] The transitional arrangements concerning state aid provide specified derogations under Arts 87–9 EC, relate to state aid for environmental protection standards for which a transitional period has been granted for the duration of the environmental transitional arrangement. Such state aid is limited to the regional ceiling with a 15% supplement for SMEs; a 30% aid intensity will be allowed until end 2010 for IPPC installations entitled to transitional arrangements; a 30% aid intensity is accepted until 31 October 2007 for IPPC related investment that is *not* covered by a transitional arrangement under the environment chapter, and large combustion plants that are subject to transitional arrangements will be entitled to state aid intensity of 50%.

[83] Above n 52.

[84] Above n 49.

[85] Take for example the view of the British House of Lords Select committee on the matter '(i)f there is a political wish among existing Member States to accelerate enlargement, they must face the crucial question of whether applicants should be allowed to join before they have not only adopted, but also implemented, the whole of the acquis *communautaire*. There is no point in pretending that this question will not arise. Member States must come to grips with the fact that the price of accelerated enlargement may well be the acceptance of what would amount to a two tier EU membership for several years to come. We think this is a price which the European Union can and should pay, though we emphasise that such a decision should not be allowed to remove the pressure for new Members to play their full part as soon as possible.' See 21st Report 1998–99 of House of Lords Select Committee on the European Communities, Enlargement of the EU: Progress and Problems, HL Paper 118, paras 33 and 169 at 11 and 36 respectively.

divergence in rhetoric of the different Commissioners on this point. While on the one hand Commissioner Verheugen has been careful to emphasise the readiness of the Ten,[86] other Commissioners have been more cautious, less convinced even, in their predictions.[87]

2. *Legal Instruments to Ensure the New Members Meet Their Pre-Accession Commitments*

So what will happen if full compliance with the programme of work set out in the Commission's country reports of October 2002,[88] has not been completed by the date of accession? The considerable efforts are required of the candidate in the run-up to accession remain under the conditionality of the Pre-accession Strategy — the ultimate incentive of accession. Where is the incentive to continue with the pre-accession commitments?

The need for additional means of maintaining the incentive for and pressure on the Ten to continue in their efforts after the date of accession had been envisaged from early on. The pre-accession strategy was characterised by its inclusive yet differentiating approach to the candidate countries[89] and the Accession Treaty continues this inclusive/differentiating approach. A strong conditionality was attached to the bilateral relationship between the Union and each of the Ten. The ultimate incentive of accession that has propelled the accession efforts of the candidates and has been rooted in the full focus of all Community as well as international technical assistance and financing, will no longer be an objective on the date of accession. So far, the pre-accession strategy has culminated in the agreement between the EU and the Ten upon an Accession Treaty that contains general, inclusive temporary provisions and specific, differentiating transitional arrangements applicable to the candidates individually. In order to keep up the momentum in the efforts of the new Member States' actions in line with the Commission's country reports of October 2002 and the subsequent Commission warning letters of February and May 2003,[90] the Accession Treaty contains a number of innovative provisions, which are designed to continue the conditionality of the pre-accession period and it is this that the

[86] See Press Release IP/03/1498 of 5 November 2003.
[87] See for example the speech of Commissioner Fischler of 4 November 2003, SPEECH/03/515 on CAP reform and EU Enlargement: 'huge efforts will still be required to ensure the common agricultural policy does work properly in the new Member States: thousands of public employees in the accession countries have to learn how to implement Community law in practice. Programmes will have to be created, agencies developed, tenders organised, controls developed and discussions held. The course has been set therefor; we are on track but not yet moving at full speed'.
[88] Above n 52.
[89] See M Maresceau, 'Pre-accession', in M Cremona (ed), *Enlargement of the European Union* (Oxford, OUP, 2003), 10. See also Inglis, above n 16.
[90] See Commission Press Release IP/03/1498.

Commission was referring to in the eleventh recital of its Opinion of February 2003, mentioned earlier.

3. *Transitional Safeguard Clauses*

During the first years after accession, the European Commission will continue to play its pre-accession strategy role in evaluating the Ten's progress in meeting their commitments for the adoption and implementation of the acquis. To this end it will avail of new tools to ensure that the Ten do not fall back in terms of meeting their pre-accession commitments. The considerable monitoring and reporting role of the European Commission throughout the pre-accession strategy will continue in the three years following accession.[91] This will continue the inclusive approach towards all the new Member States as well as the differentiating approach in accordance with their respective progress. However, Article 2(3) of the Accession Treaty is also relevant here: it refers to 'measures' which include[92] those 'appropriate measures' that are at the disposal of the Commission and Council in the event of continued failure by the Ten to comply with their pre-accession commitments. How the temporary safeguard measures introduced in the draft Accession Treaties will be used in the post-accession phase remains to be seen. They are also in addition to the safeguard clauses provided for in Articles 30[93] and 95(10) EC.[94]

The specific instruments to keep the transitional arrangements on track in the years following accession are contained in Articles 38 and 39 of the Act of Accession. Article 38 relates to pre-accession commitments concerning the Internal Market under the EC Treaty and enables the Commission to take 'appropriate measures' against new Member States that have failed to implement their commitments made during the accession negotiations.[95] As for the Justice and Home Affairs dimension,

[91] See for example the Commission Report submitted to the 2002 Seville European Council on the specific action plans in the field of Justice and Home Affairs, and on the follow-up of the future new Members' commitments.

[92] By reference to Arts 38 and 39 Act of Accession.

[93] Art 30 EC sets out an exception to the rule that national measures which amount to quantitative restrictions on imports or measures having equivalent effect and are illegal, under Art 28 EC. The exception applies to measures taken on the grounds of 'public morality, public policy or public security; the protection of health and life of animals or plants; the protection of national treasures possessing artistic, historic or archeaological value; or the protection of industrial and commercial property'.

[94] Art 95(1) EC is the general legal basis for Internal Market measures and Art 95(10) EC contains specific safeguard clauses to be incorporated into Internal Market measures on the same grounds as those listed in Art 30 EC.

[95] Art 38 (1) Act of Accession reads: '(i)f a new Member State has failed to implement commitments undertaken in the context of the accession negotiations, causing serious breach of the functioning of the internal market, including any commitments in all sectoral policies

Article 39 provides for different safeguard measures. These are to deal with matters concerning mutual recognition in criminal law and regulations on mutual recognition in civil matters. Where a new Member State demonstrates 'serious shortcomings or any imminent risk of such shortcomings in transposition, implementation or application of laws or other instruments or commitments or decisions', the Commission will be able to take 'appropriate measures' against that Member during the first three years of their membership.[96] The Commission has expressly declared[97] that it will hear the views of Member States directly affected by such measures and will duly take into account these view and positions.

a) Temporary Safeguard Measures for the Internal Market The Commission may take 'appropriate measures' under Article 38 Act of Accession, if one of the new Member States fails to meet their commitments under the accession negotiations. Such a failure must however, 'cause serious breach of the functioning of the internal market, including commitments.'[98] This safeguard clause may be invoked before accession on the basis of the Commission's monitoring findings but will enter into force on the first day of accession. Only the Commission may adopt measures under the safeguard-clause, although any Member State including the new Members may make a request that they be adopted.

Preference will be given to measures that least disturb the functioning of the common market. The principles of proportionality and non-discrimination are explicitly incorporated into the formulation of safeguard measures under Article 38 Act of Accession, and those measures must also not act as disguised restrictions on trade. In terms of duration, they must, first, 'be maintained no longer than strictly necessary, and, in any case,

which concern economic activities with cross-border effect, or an imminent risk of such breach the Commission may, until the end of the period of up to three years after the date of entry into force of this Act, upon motivated request of a Member State or on its own initiative, take appropriate measures. Measures shall be proportional and priority shall be given to measures, which disturb least the functioning of the internal market and, where appropriate, to the application of the existing sectoral safeguard mechanisms. Such safeguard measures shall not be invoked as a means of arbitrary discrimination or a disguised restriction on trade between Member States. The safeguard clause may be invoked even before accession on the basis of the monitoring findings and enter into force as of the first day of accession. The measures shall be maintained no longer than strictly necessary, and, in any case, will be lifted when the relevant commitment is implemented. They may however be applied beyond the period specified in the above paragraph as long as the relevant commitments have not been fulfilled. In response to progress made by the new Member States concerned in fulfilling its commitments, the Commission may adapt the measures as appropriate. The Commission will inform the Council in good time before revoking safeguard measures, and it will take duly into account any observations of the Council in this respect.'

[96] The modalities are spelled out in Art 39(2) Act of Accession.
[97] Declaration 43 to the Final Act.
[98] Art 38(1) Act of Accession.

will be lifted when the relevant commitment is implemented' and second, the Commission is restricted to instituting these safeguard measures within the first three years of the date of accession. However, where such measures are in place before the end of the three-year period, the Commission will be able to continue their application should the new Member State not have met the commitments to which the safeguard measures apply. Once in place, the Council must be informed 'in good time' before the Commission may revoke the measures, and it must take the Council's observations into account — although the Commission will be able to adapt the safeguard measures in line with the new Member State's progress in meeting its commitments. Thus, the Internal Market safeguard clause gives broad discretion to the Commission together with seemingly far-reaching powers to sanction action or inaction by the new Members under their pre-determined transitional measures and under their December 2002 commitments to be ready for membership on 1 May 2004. In an attempt to introduce some legal certainty into the use of this clause, six of the new Members have jointly declared[99] that they understand

> 'the notion 'has failed to implement commitments undertaken in the context of the accession negotiations' only [to cover] the obligations that are arising from the original Treaties ... under the conditions laid down in the Act of Accession and the obligations defined in this Act'

and that therefore, they 'understand that the Commission will consider application of Article 38 only in cases of alleged violations of the obligations' arising from the original Treaties. The Commission has given no such commitment.[100]

No safeguard measures are foreseen in respect of horizontal and sectoral policies as such, unless of course the Internal Market is affected. Therefore in areas including environment or social policies, safeguard measures will not be appropriate. Much will depend on the Commission's programming of the Community post-accession assistance to keep up the momentum of continued reforms in these areas.

As for the environment acquis proper (measures based on Article 175 EC), Member States are able to adopt stricter national environmental standards than those of the acquis. However, should such measures

[99] Joint Declaration 22 to the Final Act. The countries concerned are the Czech Republic, Estonia, Lithuania, Poland, Slovenia and the Slovak Republic. They have also expressly declared, in paras 2 and 3, that Art 38 is without prejudice to jurisdiction of the Court of Justice and insofar as any sanctions might be concerned and that they must be heard before measures are taken against them.

[100] See Declaration 43 to the Final Act.

affect the Internal Market acquis, a notification and evaluation procedure applies under Article 95 EC, potentially allowing the Commission to refuse to legalise those proposed higher national standards. For the last enlargement, the new Members Austria, Finland and Sweden were traditionally pusher countries for environment measures both at national and international level. They were granted a number of four year environment derogations — some being Internal Market measures based on Article 95 — to enable them to maintain higher standards than the other Member States. At the end of the four years, these derogations were to fall and the acquis would apply to all the Member States alike.[101] The intention was to allow the other twelve Member States to reach the same higher standard. With the entry into force of the Amsterdam Treaty, these three countries were then only able to introduce higher standards by means of the Articles 30 or 95 procedures in environmental provisions that affected the Internal Market. However, rather than raising the generally higher Community standards for these laws, certain innovations of the Amsterdam Treaty[102] have tended to be used to enable Austria, Finland and Sweden to maintain their higher standards. But the overall raising of the Community standard to the higher level has been slower than anticipated.

Therefore, those Member States seeking higher environmental standards are held back at national and international level by the common denominator. Much responsibility falls on the European Commission to keep up the efforts of the new Member States in meeting their pre-accession commitments, if the Community common denominator for environmental standards is not to be diluted upon eastwards enlargement. The Commission will not have the Article 38 Act of Accession safeguard clause at its disposal for the environment acquis, although it will be able to rely on Article 38 for the Internal Market environment measures.

b) Temporary Safeguard Measures for Justice and Home Affairs As for mutual recognition in criminal law and regulations on mutual recognition in civil matters (Title VI EU and Title IV EC), Article 39 of the Act of Accession provides for the '*temporary suspension* of the application of relevant provisions and decisions in the relations between a new Member State and any other Member State or Member States, without prejudice to the continuation of close judicial co-operation' [italics added]. But Article 39 only mentions 'serious shortcomings or any imminent risks of

[101] See Arts 69, 84 and 112 Act of Accession for Austria, Finland and Sweden (above n 10) and Annexes VIII, X and XII.

[102] See Art 95(5) EC *et seq*, which allowed for national measures based on new scientific evidence relating to the protection of the environment on grounds of a problem specific to that Member State, subject to notification and procedural requirements.

such shortcomings in the transposition, state of implementation, or the application of the laws concerned *in a new Member State*' [italics added].[103]

The JHA chapter of the acquis also houses the areas of judicial co-operation in civil and criminal matters. No transitional arrangements as such were agreed at the December 2002 Copenhagen European Council in the field of Justice and Home Affairs, although various Council and Presidency Conclusions have singled out administrative and judicial capacity for special attention.[104] The justification for this safeguard clause stems from the sensitive internal security issues that this chapter of the acquis raises for the Member States. It is a matter of confidence in the capacity of the future new Members' courts and judicial systems. The October 2002 country reports all highlighted the need for reinforced administrative and judicial capacity as do the 2003 reports.[105] From a study by the Open Society Institute on the EU Accession Monitoring Programme dedicated to Judicial Capacity in the candidate countries, it is clear that all of the new Member States still have much to do in order to improve their judiciary.[106] Certainly the lack of independence in the concept of adjudication as a result of the communist period justified the intensive efforts of the new Member States over the past fifteen years. However, a number of problems remain in spite of the impressive progress made.

The Fifteen have been forthright on the need for strong judicial systems as a matter of priority. These concerns were demonstrated in the Commission's Guide to the Negotiations:

> 'Negotiations on the Justice and Home Affairs acquis are not about transition periods ...rather, it has been necessary to find ways to build confidence, among Member States, in the candidate countries' capacity to implement the acquis. On issues such as border control, illegal migration, drugs trafficking and money laundering, organised crime, police and judicial co-operation, data protection and the mutual recognition of court judgments, there is a need to ensure that candidate countries are equipped to meet adequate and acceptable standards of implementation. It is important that candidate countries' administrative capacity is up to these standards by the date of accession. Furthermore, the establishment of an independent,

[103] 'If there are serious shortcomings or any imminent risks of such shortcomings in the transposition, state of implementation, or the application of the framework decisions or any other relevant commitments, instruments of co-operation and decision relating to mutual recognition in the area of criminal law under Title VI of the EU Treaty and Directives and Regulations relating to mutual recognition in civil matters under Title IV of the EC Treaty in a new Member State.'

[104] See for example the 2002 Seville Presidency Conclusions, Conclusion 20, or the Council Conclusions of 10 June 2002.

[105] Above n 54. See also the 2002 Strategy Paper, SEC(2002) 1400–12.

[106] Open Society Institute, *Monitoring the EU Accession Process: Judicial Capacity* (2002) http://www.eumap.org/reports/2002/content/70/

reliable and efficient judiciary and police organisation are also of paramount importance.'[107]

The matter of establishing and reinforcing mutual trust is certainly attracting increasing attention for the moment and in addition to the European Commission's Green Paper on Procedural Safeguards, work is also beginning on a mutual evaluation system for the reinforcement of mutual trust.[108] The Open Society Institute report also pushes for EU standards for the Fifteen and the new Members, advocating such 'common minimums' as 'expressions of the political commitments made in the Copenhagen criteria and consequently continuing obligations on all members.'[109]

Like the transitional safeguard clause relating to the Internal Market, these 'appropriate measures' may be instituted in respect of the new Member States only, and they are at the Commission's disposal, either by its own initiative or at the request of Member State, but the Member States (including the new Member States) must be consulted before their adoption. Again, these measures are limited to the three-year period beginning on the date of accession, may be adapted according to the new Member State's progress in remedying the shortcomings, should be maintained no longer than is strictly necessary, must be lifted once the shortcomings have been remedied and may be extended for as long as the shortcomings persist, even after expiry of the three-year period. Finally, the Council must be informed in good time before the measures are to be revoked and the Council's observations must be duly taken into account. Unlike the provision for temporary safeguard measures under Article 38 of the Act of Accession, the Member States must be consulted before such measures are adopted or before they are adapted and there is no reference to the principles of proportionality or non-discrimination.

The Schengen acquis was mentioned briefly above. It is relevant that the new Member States will all have transposed the Schengen acquis by the date of accession but unlike with the transitional arrangements contained in the Temporary Provisions of the Act of Accession, there is no specified time limit set down for the application of the Schengen acquis to begin in the new Member States.[110] The procedure for extending the

[107] See Commission Guide to the Negotiations, above n 49, 73.
[108] Presented by Isabelle Jegouzo, JHA Counsellor, Permanent Representation of France to the EU at a conference organised by the Université Libre de Bruxelles, held in Brussels on 17 and 18 March 2003.
[109] Above n 99 at 20.
[110] According to Art 3(2) Act of Accession: 'Those provisions of the Schengen acquis as integrated into the framework of the European Union and the acts building upon it or otherwise related to it not referred to in para 1, while binding on the new Member States from the date of accession, shall only apply in a new Member State pursuant to a Council decision to that effect after verification in accordance with the applicable Schengen evaluation procedures

application of the Schengen acquis to the new Member States is set down in that same paragraph and allows for the individual inclusion of each of the new Member States subject to the evaluation procedure and the unanimous decision in Council of the existing Member States and the new Member State concerned.[111] Thus, it is a two-stage procedure to allow enlargement to go ahead and for the completion of full Schengen implementation subject to the regular evaluation and reporting of the Schengen Evaluation Group. Only a Decision of the participating Schengen Member States will lift border controls for the new Member States. The new Schengen Facility will go some way to helping the new Member States to fully implement the Schengen acquis, including the SIS 2. After all, SIS 2, which will eventually link all twenty-five Member States technically, will only become operational by end 2005 and the Schengen evaluation process itself will take some time. Basically the new Member States will have to meet all the provisions which are not directly linked to the lifting of internal border controls.

4. *Emergency Protection for a Given Sector of the Economy*

Also in the category of transitional safeguards are protective measures, designed to protect against the serious deterioration of a given sector of the economy or the serious deterioration in the economic situation of a given area. These measures are incorporated into the Accession Treaty in Article 37 Act of Accession.[112] They may involve derogations from the EC

that the necessary conditions for the application of all parts of the acquis concerned have been met in that new Member State and after consulting the European Parliament.

The Council shall take its decision acting with the unanimity of its members representing the Governments of the Member States in respect of which the provisions referred to in the present paragraph have already been put into effect and of the representative of the Government of the Member State in respect of which those provisions are to be put into effect. The members of the Council representing the Governments of Ireland and of the United Kingdom of Great Britain and Northern Ireland shall take part in such a decision insofar as it relates to the provisions of the Schengen acquis and the acts building upon it or otherwise related to it in which these Member States participate.'

[111] The UK and Ireland will participate in the unanimous Council decision only as regards those provisions of the Schengen acquis that they participate in.

[112] Art 37 Act of Accession: '(1) If, until the end of a period of up to three years after accession, difficulties arise which are serious and liable to persist in any sector of the economy or which bring about serious deterioration in the economic situation of a given area, a new Member State may apply for authorisation to take protective measures in order to rectify the situation and adjust the sector concerned to the economy of the common market. In the same circumstances, any present Member State may apply for authorisation to take protective measures with regard to one or more of the new Member States. (2) Upon request by the State concerned, the Commission shall, by emergency procedure, determine the protective measures which it considers necessary, specifying the conditions and modalities in which they are to be put into effect. In the event of serious economic difficulties and at the express request of the Member State concerned, the Commission shall act within five working days

Treaty or derogations from the Act of Accession but are restricted to the first three years following accession. The Fifteen and the new Member States alike will be able to apply to the Commission for protective measures, subject to certain conditions. Serious difficulties must arise and be liable to persist in a sector of the economy or those serious difficulties must bring about a serious deterioration in the economic situation of a given area. The protective measures taken must be necessary and must aim to rectify the situation, adjust the sector to the economy of the common market — this will determine the extent and the timeframe of any derogation that is granted. Preference will be given to measures that least disturb the functioning of the common market and they may not involve frontier controls. The applicable procedure is an emergency procedure carried out by the Commission at the request of the Member State seeking the protective measures. It is clear from the European Commission's declaration on the safeguard clauses[113] that the Commission is already contemplating economic safeguard measures in respect of the agriculture sector. Due to the specific problems facing Poland — having a considerable agriculture sector and being excluded from full participation in the CAP upon accession — the Commission intends to include measures under this safeguard clause to monitor trade flows between Poland and other Member States.

III. CONCLUSIONS

Providing a system of transitional arrangements in the Accession Treaty is unavoidable for practical reasons. The derogations from the acquis that are fixed in the individual country annexes to the Accession Treaty are tightly framed and have been limited to technical problems of implementation of the acquis and to those areas where considerable lead times are required in order to comply or to attract the necessary large scale infrastructure investment. As a rule, transposition of the acquis has not been the subject of transitional arrangements.

It is clear from the European Commission's monitoring findings published in October 2002 and again in November 2003, that much remains

of the receipt of the request accompanied by the relevant background information. The measures thus decided on shall be applicable forthwith, shall take account of the interests of all parties concerned and shall not entail frontier controls. (3) The measures authorised under para 2 may involve derogations from the rules of the EC Treaty and from this Act to such an extent and for such periods as are strictly necessary in order to attain the objectives referred to in paragraph 1. Priority shall be given to such measures as will least disturb the functioning of the common market.'

[113] See Declaration 43 of the Final Act.

to be done by the new Members before 1 May 2004 and the Union is eager to ensure that compliance, implementation and enforcement does not wane in the first years after their accession. The three-year long transition period that will follow the date of accession gives the impression that the new Members will be suspended in a sort of twilight zone, somewhere between the pre-accession strategy and membership on a par with the Fifteen.

The transitional arrangements are no longer negotiable and the new temporary safeguard measures will prevent any relaxation of this rule. A major part of the challenge for the new Member States in the time between the signature and the entry into force of the Accession Treaty, will be reaching the required level of administrative and judicial capacity. To some extent, the target will continue to move in the first years after actual accession with the introduction of additional transitional measures foreseen in the field of the Common Agricultural Policy and veterinary and phytosanitary rules. For the rest, the boundaries of the transitional arrangements have been set. The new forms of temporary safeguard measure contained in the Accession Treaty will supplement the pre-determined transitional arrangements and will be crucial to maintaining the progress in the administrative and judicial capacity as well as the continued evolution of the acquis communautaire in an enlarged Union.

Setting a tangible date for accession and sticking to it has been necessary to maintain the enthusiasm of the candidates for enlargement and their enormous pre-accession efforts. The system of transitional arrangements extends the conditionality that characterised the pre-accession strategy, to the post-accession period. The nature and extent of the temporary safeguard measures is not yet fully apparent but, being inevitable, they will introduce new targets and priorities for action by the Ten on the very first day of accession. It can, however, be said that the overall system of transitional arrangements in the Accession Treaty will maintain the flexibility in the approach to the Fifteen that also characterised the pre-accession strategy. While on the one hand, the Accession Treaty is all inclusive, in that it attempts to treat all the new Members on the same legal footing, it will also enable the continued differentiation in the treatment of the Ten new Member States in line with their progress under their respective pre-accession commitments agreed in December 2002.

The major difference between the pre-accession and the post-accession scenarios will be the fact that the temporary safeguard clauses will take the place of the incentive of accession as the means to ensure compliance by the future new Members with their pre-accession commitments. As concerns the Internal Market and the Justice and Home Affairs acquis in particular, the rationale behind the introduction of the transitional safeguard clauses clearly stems from concerns about the continued functioning of an enlarged Union, the evolution of the acquis communautaire and the need for instilling trust between the old and new Member States. Moreover, the use of the safeguard measures to further only the efforts of the Ten in the fields of the Internal Market and Justice and Home Affairs gives the impression that these areas of the acquis are to be prioritised over other horizontal and sectoral policies of the Union and undermines the notion of the indivisibility of the acquis. Most remarkable, however, is that the two new forms of safeguard clause in the Accession Treaty introduce a new form of legal differentiation into the Union's accession treaty format, to allow the treatment of the new Member States differently from the existing Member States in order to ensure that they continue to comply with the constantly moving target that is the ever evolving acquis communautaire, irrespective of whether the existing Members are in full compliance. The temporary safeguard measures provide the means for different and potentially discriminatory treatment of the Ten compared to the Fifteen for the purposes of compliance with and implementation of certain chapters of the acquis. In other words, the Accession Treaty introduces legal bases to delay the full implementation of the principle of solidarity of the enlarged European Union.

6

A Spectre is Haunting Europe… Free Movement of Persons and the Eastern Enlargement

MICHAEL DOUGAN*

I. INTRODUCTION

THE EUROPEAN COUNCIL meeting in Copenhagen in December 2002 formally concluded accession negotiations with ten candidate countries — welcoming a 'balanced outcome' deemed to provide a solid basis for the smooth integration of the new Member States, and to ensure the continued functioning of the Internal Market. The Treaty of Accession was signed in Athens in April 2003, paving the way for the national ratifications that allowed the enlargement to proceed on 1 May 2004.[1]

Free movement of persons, and especially of workers, was one of the few areas in which the EU (rather than the candidate countries) negotiated transitional provisions deviating from the guiding principle that the *acquis communautaire* should become fully applicable from the moment of accession. The basic problem as regards free movement within the context of enlargement is the scale of income differences between existing Member States and the CEECs; coupled with the slow rate of actual/expected

* University of Liverpool. This chapter is based on papers delivered at the Cambridge Enlargement Conference in July 2002, and at the University of Nottingham in November 2002. I am very grateful to participants at both events for their comments, to Eleanor Spaventa for her valuable suggestions, and to Harriet Barseghian Marsh at the Enlargement Information Centre (Brussels) for her kind assistance.

[1] Presidency Conclusions of the Copenhagen European Council (12–13 December 2002). Treaty of Accession 2003 (and related documents), OJ 2003 L236 and C227E (23 September 2003). The ten countries are: Cyprus, the Czech Republic, Estonia, Hungary, Latvia, Lithuania, Malta, Poland, the Slovak Republic and Slovenia. The Copenhagen Conclusions envisage the accession of Romania and Bulgaria in 2007. A decision on whether to open formal accession negotiations with Turkey will be taken in December 2004.

economic convergence at least for the foreseeable future.[2] This situation is popularly perceived to create a powerful push-pull dynamic, entailing three potentially adverse consequences for the existing Member States: that enlargement might lead to large-scale benefit migration towards western countries which have established relatively generous welfare systems; that a massive influx of workers from the CEECs would seriously disrupt labour markets in the existing Member States; and that differences between wages and other compliances costs might lead to social dumping in favour of undertakings operating from the CEECs.

This chapter will offer some observations on the legal context within which such fears seem likely to be addressed.

II. LIMITING BENEFIT MIGRATION TOWARDS WESTERN STATES

The first spectre which has haunted the popular imagination of many Western Europeans is that enlargement might lead to large-scale benefit migration towards existing Member States which have established relatively generous welfare systems.

At first sight, the post-accession regime on free movement for CEEC nationals effectively neutralises any such danger. The transitional arrange-ments envisage that freedom of establishment will be complete from the time of accession.[3] CEEC nationals who are able to rely on Article 43 EC thanks to their active participation in the economic life of the host society are entitled to equal treatment as regards social advantages;[4] and their right of residency should not be called into question by the fact that they are or become in some way financially dependent upon assistance offered by the host state.[5] Free movement of services will also be complete from the time of accession — subject to safeguard measures concerning posted workers, negotiated by Germany and Austria, for the protection of domestic labour markets related to certain sensitive

[2] Note the additional problems posed by accession of the CEECs to the Area of Freedom, Justice and Security, as regards the integrity of the enlarged EU's new external boundaries. Further, J Monar, 'Enlarging the Area of Freedom, Security and Justice: Problems of Diversity and EU Instruments and Strategies' (2000) 3 *Cambridge Yearbook of European Legal Stuides* 301; K Pollet, 'The European Union and Migratory Pressure from the Mediterranean and Central and Eastern Europe' in M Maresceau and E Lannon (eds), *The EU's Enlargement and Mediterranean Strategies: A Comparative Analysis* (Basingstoke, Palgrave-Macmillan, 2001).

[3] Subject to certain temporary restrictions on the free movement of capital negotiated by several candidate countries, eg transitional periods restricting the acquisition of secondary residences and agricultural and forestry land by foreigners.

[4] Eg Case 197/84 *Steinhauser* [1985] ECR 1819; Case C–168/91 *Konstantinidis* [1993] ECR I–1191.

[5] Eg Case 305/87 *Commission v Greece* [1989] ECR 1461; Case C–337/97 *Meeusen* [1999] ECR I–3289; Case C–299/01 *Commission v Luxembourg* [2002] ECR I–5899.

industries.[6] CEEC nationals who are able to rely on Article 49 EC will again be entitled to equal treatment as regards social advantages.[7] In appropriate circumstances, this can include equal treatment as regards public benefits: for example, where social provision is merely incidental to the claimant's effective exercise of rights to provide or receive economic services, and does not represent the primary objective of the claimant's presence in the host state.[8] The transitional arrangements further envisage that Directives 90/364, 90/365 and 93/96 shall also take full effect upon accession — creating rights to free movement and residency for the benefit of individuals who satisfy the twin requirements of possessing sufficient resources,[9] and having comprehensive medical insurance.[10] In all cases, the Community regime for the cross-border coordination of social security benefits will become fully applicable — assisting many individuals to meet the qualifying criteria contained in the Residency Directives, for example, by facilitating the exportation of pension payments to support retired CEEC nationals who move to another Member State.[11]

To this extent, the agreement reached between the EU and the candidate countries seems to have restricted migration opportunities only to those who will qualify as either economically active in an appropriate capacity, or financially independent within the meaning of the Residency Directives. The documentation publicly available at the time of writing does not suggest that Article 18 EC, purporting to establish a general right of free movement and residency for all Union citizens, detained the diplomats for long. Even if such complacency could be justified when negotiations on free movement of persons were provisionally closed — by the widespread assumption that Article 18 merely codified the privileges

[6] On the German / Austrian safeguards, see Section IV (below). Free movement of services may also be affected by transitional restrictions on free movement of capital.

[7] Eg Case 63/86 *Commission v Italy* [1988] ECR 29; Case C–45/93 *Commission v Spain* [1994] ECR I–911; Case C–274/96 *Bickel and Franz* [1998] ECR I–7637; Case C–388/01 *Commission v Italy* [2003] ECR I–721.

[8] Eg Case 186/87 *Cowan v Trésor public* [1989] ECR 195. Cf. P Craig and G de Búrca, *EU Law: Text, Cases, and Materials* 3rd edition (OUP, 2002), 812–14. Further: A-P van der Mei, *Free Movement of Persons Within the European Community* (Oxford, Hart Publishing, 2003).

[9] Dir 90/365 and Dir 90/364: claimant must have sufficient resources to avoid becoming burden on state's social assistance. Dir 93/96: student need only assure national authorities he/she has sufficient resources to avoid becoming burden on state.

[10] Dir 90/364, OJ 1990 L180/26; Dir 90/365, OJ 1990 L180/28; Dir 93/96, OJ 1993 L317/59. Again, free movement for these citizens may be affected by transitional restrictions on free movement of capital.

[11] Last consolidated text published at OJ 1997 L28/1; more recent consolidated text available at <www.europa.eu.int/eur-lex/en/consleg/index1.html>. Note that a new coordination regime may soon be adopted by Council and Parliament on the basis of Commission proposal for a Council Regulation on coordination of social security systems, COM(98) 779 Final.

already conferred under other provisions of Community law — it now needs to be re-evaluated in the light of developments in the caselaw. In *Grzelczyk*, the Court held that Union citizenship is destined to be the fundamental status of nationals of the Member States.[12] Moreover, in *Baumbast*, the Court affirmed that Article 18(1) EC confers on individuals rights which are enforceable by them and which the national courts must protect.[13] Nevertheless, the judgment in *Kaba* had already established that, since Article 18(1) expressly refers to the limitations laid down under primary and secondary Community law, the citizen's right to free movement and residence cannot be considered unconditional.[14] This raised the question: how far do these limitations include the requirements of financial independence contained in the three Residency Directives; and therefore how far might Union citizenship act as a green light for free movement into the most generous welfare states by individuals who are neither economically active nor capable of supporting themselves?

In its judgments in *Grzelczyk* and *Baumbast*, the Court confirmed that the limitations and conditions referred to in Article 18(1) EC indeed include the requirements of sufficient resources and health insurance laid down by the three Residency Directives. However, the Court in *Baumbast* continued to decide that these limitations and conditions are themselves based on the idea that the citizen's right of residence can be subordinated to the legitimate interests of the Member States; and in particular, to the idea contained in the preamble to each of the three directives that citizens must not become an unreasonable burden upon the public finances of the host state. But those limitations and conditions must be applied in compliance with the general principles of Community law — including the principle of proportionality. This might well justify upholding the Article 18 right to residency, despite the fact that the claimant in some way fails to comply fully with the black-letter of the relevant directive — provided only that the claimant does not actually become an unreasonable financial burden upon the host society.

Grzelczyk illustrates (though more in hindsight than in the explicit reasoning of the judgment itself) the application of the principle of proportionality to the requirement of 'sufficient resources' set out in the Residency Directives. Here, a French student sought to supplement his income during the final year of his university course in Belgium by claiming the host state's minimum subsistence allowance. The Court held that the requirement of sufficient resources contained in Directive 93/96 should itself be read subject to a principle of limited financial solidarity

[12] Case C–184/99 *Grzelczyk* [2001] ECR I–6193, para 31.
[13] Case C–413/99 *Baumbast* [2002] ECR I–7091, para 86.
[14] Case C–356/98 *Kaba* [2000] ECR I–2623. Also: Case C–466/00 *Kaba II* [2003] ECR I–2219.

between Community and own nationals — particularly as regards temporary difficulties, and especially if the claimant's financial position changes for reasons beyond his control. However, under no circumstances could this justify the migrant Union citizen becoming an unreasonable burden on the public finances of the host state. In that event, the host state was still entitled to consider that the claimant no longer fulfilled the conditions of his right to residence, and therefore to take appropriate steps to withdraw (or refuse to renew) his residence permit.[15]

Baumbast illustrates the application of the principle of proportionality to the 'health insurance' requirement imposed by the three Residency Directives. Here, a German national lived in the UK with his family. He had already worked in the UK for several years, but was now employed by a German company to work outside the EU. The claimant and his family were self-sufficient and did not draw on British social security benefits. They also had comprehensive health insurance in Germany, and travelled there to receive medical treatment when necessary. However, the claimant's application for renewal of his residence permit was rejected on the grounds that he lacked sickness insurance in respect of emergency treatment within the UK. The Court held that to deny the claimant a right of residency under Article 18 EC would be a disproportionate application of the requirement of 'health insurance' contained in Directive 90/364, going beyond what was necessary to protect the host state's legitimate interests.[16]

Grzelczyk and *Baumbast* thus represent a culmination of two trends in the caselaw on free movement of persons and Union citizenship. The first trend is the Court's increasing emphasis on free movement as an individual right — not conferred merely for the economic benefit of the Single Market, but inherent in the wider process of European integration. This trend was already apparent from judgments in which the Court recognised rights to residence and equal treatment for migrant students for the purpose of pursuing vocational training in another Member State;[17] and more recently, in which the Court constructed under the auspices of Article 49 EC a right to seek healthcare abroad at the expense of the home state's insurance system.[18] Article 18 EC

[15] Case C–184/99 *Grzelczyk* [2001] ECR I–6193, paras 38–46. Annotated by A Iliopoulou and H Toner, (2002) 39 *CMLRev* 609. Further: A P van der Mei, 'Freedom of Movement and Financial Aid for Students: Some Reflections on *Grzelczyk* and *Pinedo Amoris*' (2001) 3 *European Journal of Social Security* 181; G Jacqueson, 'Union Citizenship and the Court of Justice: Something New Under the Sun?' (2002) 27 *ELRev* 260.

[16] Case C–413/99 *Baumbast* [2002] ECR I–7091, paras 90–94. Further: M Dougan and E Spaventa, 'Educating Rudy and the non-English Patient: A Double-Bill on Residency Rights Under Article 18EC' (2003) 28 *ELRev* 699.

[17] In particular: Case 293/83 *Gravier* [1985] ECR 593; Case C–357/89 *Raulin* [1992] ECR I–1027.

[18] In particular: Case C–158/96 *Kohll* [1998] ECR I–1935; Case C–157/99 *Smits and Peerbooms* [2001] ECR I–5473.

furnishes a coherent reference point for these developments — together with a perhaps more convincing, and potentially more far-reaching, legal basis. The second trend is the location of these individualised rights to free movement within a wider framework of social solidarity defining also the Union citizen's responsibilities vis-à-vis the Member State in which he or she contemplates taking up residence. In particular, the practical content of Article 18 EC is constrained ultimately by the Community's limited re-distributive competences in the sphere of social protection: the EU cannot simply grant full rights of residency to all its citizens because it cannot foot the consequent welfare bill in respect of individuals whose links with the host state fail to satisfy the latter's own understanding of its civil obligations.[19] The supranational model of citizenship embodied in Article 18 therefore remains tied to disparate national understandings of social solidarity — and its limits. Thus, migrant students are entitled to equal treatment as regards tuition fees and limited social security benefits, but may still be discriminated against in the provision of maintenance grants.[20] Similarly, patients may properly be refused authorisation to seek hospital treatment abroad where such healthcare is available without unreasonable delay at home.[21] And Article 18 EC will be employed by the Court to effect only a limited reallocation of the welfare responsibilities envisaged by the Member States when they agreed to adopt the three Residency Directives.

Enlargement is therefore taking place at a particularly exciting point in the evolution of free movement law.

CEEC nationals who fall within the non-economically active but financially independent bracket of the citizenship provisions will enjoy migration rights which are no longer conditional upon meeting the specific conditions set out in the three Residency Directives. The key criterion is that CEEC nationals do not become an unreasonable burden upon the public finances of the host state: the requirements of health insurance and sufficient resources act as a starting point in this regard; but their application is subject to the principle of proportionality to ensure that the Member States do not exceed what is necessary for the protection of their legitimate interests. Within these limits, it seems that

[19] Further, eg G Majone, 'The European Community Between Social Policy and Social Regulation' (1993) 31 *JCMS* 153; M Rhodes, 'Defending the Social Contract: The EU Between Global Constraints and Domestic Imperatives' in D Hine and H Kassim (eds), *Beyond the Market: The EU and National Social Policy* (London, Routledge, 1998); T Faist, 'Social Citizenship in the European Union: Nested Membership' (2001) 39 *JCMS* 37.

[20] In particular: Case 39/86 *Lair* [1988] ECR 3161; Case 197/86 *Brown* [1988] ECR 3205; Case C–184/99 *Grzelczyk* [2001] ECR I–6193.

[21] In particular: Case C-157/99 *Smits and Peerbooms* [2001] ECR I–5473. Cf. Case C–385/99 *Müller-Fauré* [2003] ECR I–4509; Case C–56/01 *Inizan* (Judgment of 23 October 2003).

CEEC nationals of (almost) independent means will enjoy rights to equal treatment within the host state under Article 12 EC as regards all matters falling within the material scope of the Treaty. This will include non-discrimination in the availability of social advantages in general,[22] and of welfare benefits in particular.[23] Moreover, free movement rights for such CEEC nationals have become individualised, not only in the sense of detached from the economic imperatives of the Single Market, but also to the extent that Member States cannot rely on blanket rules and irrebutable presumptions to calculate when any given person has outstayed their welcome.[24]

Of course, many questions remain about the full scope of the citizenship rights being haphazardly elaborated by the Court. For example, the judgment in *Baumbast* conspicuously refrained from addressing the legal status of the protected family members of migrant citizens (say) as regards access to employment or rights to education within the host state.[25] Uncertainties will surely arise when assessing whether any given migrant citizen has become an 'unreasonable financial burden' upon the host society: would the Baumbast family have been treated any differently had they claimed limited public payments such as child-raising benefits (as opposed to general allowances such as income support); or if they had only recently moved to the Member State (without having ever worked there, or resided for any significant period of time)? But in any case, given that these caselaw developments largely post-date the provisional closure of the accession negotiations on free movement of persons, the Member States might have cause to feel that the goalposts have shifted subtly but significantly. In particular, with the prospect of around 100 million new Union citizens enjoying rights to free movement, residency and equal treatment even on these terms, Eastern enlargement clearly has greater *cumulative* financial implications for the existing Member States than they believed they had assumed.

Beyond this, however, the Court seems to have adopted the position that Article 18 EC confers meaningful rights to residency only upon people who are (in a broad sense) either economically active or financially

[22] Eg Case C–274/96 *Bickel and Franz* [1998] ECR I–7637; Case C–148/02 *Garcia Avello* (Judgment of 2 October 2003).

[23] Eg Case C–85/96 *María Martínez Sala* [1998] ECR I–2691. In both cases, save where discriminatory treatment is expressly authorised by the Treaty or (in appropriate circumstances) objectively justified under the case law.

[24] Compare the emphasis placed on the individual patient's personal circumstances in Case C–157/99 *Smits and Peerbooms* [2001] ECR I–5473; Case C–385/99 *Müller-Fauré* [2003] ECR I–4509; Case C–56/01 *Inizan* (Judgment of 23 October 2003).

[25] Case C–413/99 *Baumbast* [2002] ECR I–7091, para 95. Cf. AG Geelhoed at paras 116–23 Opinion (5 July 2001).

independent — and thus excludes those remaining categories of Union citizen dependent to any further extent upon the Member State's public resources (whether through disability, old age or poverty). Coupled with the transitional arrangements on free movement of workers,[26] which might otherwise have accommodated automatic rights of residency for low-pay employees who are or become dependent upon public assistance from the host state,[27] there seems little prospect that the application of Article 18 EC within the context of the Eastern enlargement will lead to a flood of welfare tourists into the West against the will of the existing Member States. Conceptions of social solidarity in providing for the least wealthy members of society remain firmly tied to the responsibilities of the nation state, rather than the supranational process of European integration.[28]

Yet even here, two potentially more complicated situations are worth bearing in mind. First, the Court has confirmed that all Union citizens enjoy a directly effective right to residency under Article 18. Even where the Member State is entitled to enforce the limitations and conditions applicable to exercise of that right to residency, its conduct remains subject to judicial review, in particular, to ensure compliance with the general principles of Community law. Although the Court did not say so expressly in *Baumbast*, these general principles should include the protection of fundamental rights.[29] This might provide some limited protection even for CEEC nationals who are unable to claim entitlement to residency *qua* self-employed person under the terms of Article 43 EC, or *qua* financially independent person under the rough cover of the Residency Directives, ie by arguing that expulsion would infringe the right to private and family life as protected under Article 8 ECHR.[30] For example: if the claimant has lived in the host state for a significant period of time, perhaps with his/her family and children, such that the claimant has few remaining personal ties to the country of origin, and the host state has become his/her home for all purposes save nationality, expulsion might be held to strike an unfair balance between the legitimate interests of the Member State and the private rights of the individual.[31]

[26] Discussed in Section III (below).

[27] In particular: Case 53/81 *Levin* [1982] ECR 1035; Case 139/85 *Kempf* [1986] ECR 1741.

[28] Save insofar as affected, eg by the open method of coordination on the modernisation of social protection flowing from the Lisbon European Council (23–4 March 2000).

[29] In particular: Case 11/70 *Internationale Handelsgesellschaft* [1970] ECR 1125; Opinion 2/94 *(Accession by the Communities to the Convention for the Protection of Human Rights and Fundamental Freedoms)* [1996] ECR I–1759. Eg Case C–260/89 *ERT* [1991] ECR I–2925; Case C–23/93 *TV10* [1994] ECR I–4795.

[30] Consider, eg Case C–60/00 *Carpenter* [2002] ECR I–6279; Case C–109/01 *Akrich* (Judgment of 23 September 2003).

[31] Consider, eg *B v Secretary of State for the Home Department* [2000] 2 CMLR 1086.

If this analysis is correct, it means that certain CEEC nationals could enjoy an enforceable right of residency under Article 18 EC — despite not otherwise qualifying as economically active or financially independent. Being lawfully resident as a matter of Community law, such claimants would be entitled under Article 12 EC to protection against discrimination on grounds of nationality as regards access to social advantages in general, and to welfare benefits such as subsistence allowances in particular.[32] In this regard, one could also mention the Commission's 2001/2003 proposal for an umbrella directive on free movement for Union citizens.[33] One of the most important innovations of this initiative is the recognition for Community nationals, after four years of lawful and continuous residence within any Member State, of 'permanent resident' status. The aim of this innovation is to realise the moral and social imperative — inherent in the creation of Union citizenship — of achieving the complete integration of long-term residents (short only of granting nationality itself). Thus, permanent residents would no longer need to satisfy any conditions relating to economic activity or financial independence; would be entitled to full equal treatment as regards all matters falling within the scope of the Treaty; and could no longer be expelled even on public policy, security or health grounds.[34] If this proposal is adopted either before or during the currency of the transitional period, then clearly Union citizenship would have an even more significant impact upon the social integration at least of long-term resident CEEC nationals.[35]

Secondly, it appears that the Accession Treaty's transitional restrictions on free movement for workers (discussed in Section III) will not extend to CEEC nationals who arrive in an existing Member State in search of gainful employment.[36] Such workseekers will enjoy rights to free movement and lawful residency under Article 39 EC as construed by the Court in *Antonissen*, ie for a reasonable period of time, and even longer if the individual proves he/she is still looking for work and has genuine chances of becoming engaged.[37] Of course, national restrictions

[32] Eg Case C–85/96 *María Martínez Sala* [1998] ECR I–2691.

[33] Commission proposal for a Directive on the rights of Union citizens and their family members to move and reside freely within the territory of the Member States, COM(2001) 257 Final; revised proposal, COM (2003) 199 Final.

[34] In particular, Chapter IV of the proposed directive. It is envisaged that certain categories of individual could acquire permanent resident status under more generous conditions. However, permanent resident status could be withdrawn after four years' absence from the host state.

[35] On 22 September 2003, the Council reached political agreement on the proposed directive, subject to certain amendments, including raising the threshold for acquiring permanent residence from four to five years. (f. Dir 2003/109 concerning the status of third-country nationals who are long-term residents, OJ 2004 L16/44).

[36] European Commission.

[37] Case C–292/89, Free Movement for Persons: A Practical Guide for an Enlarged European Union (Brussels, European Commission, 2002). *Antonissen* [1991] ECR I–745.

upon CEEC nationals participating in the domestic labour market, adopted pursuant to the transitional regime, may be relevant or even decisive when appraising the claimant's chances of finding lawful employment, for example, where the host state's work permit quota has already been filled.[38] But for those CEEC nationals able to rely on Article 39 EC *qua* migrant workseeker, it is arguable that the recent caselaw on Union citizenship has enhanced their previously unfavourable position under Community law, by extending rights of equal treatment beyond mere access to employment so as to embrace also social advantages.[39] Thus, during the period in which a CEEC national is legitimately searching for work within an existing Member State, he/she might be entitled to challenge restrictions on the availability of appropriate subsistence benefits — certainly where the host state is guilty of direct discrimination, and perhaps also as regards indirect discrimination which cannot be objectively justified by legitimate public interest concerns.[40] The extent to which Member States may indirectly discriminate against migrant workseekers relying on their status as Union citizens, through requirements such as 'habitual residence' within the national territory as a precondition for claiming income support, is now pending before the Court in *Collins*. The Advocate General believes such restrictions are compatible with Article 12 EC. Indeed, one suspects that for Community law to insist on CEEC (or even other) workseekers enjoying unlimited access to social protection benefits would sorely test the generosity of many welfare states, and for that reason alone might persuade the Court to suppress this aspect of the fledgling legal framework underpinning novel expectations of social solidarity between Union citizens.[41]

III. INSULATING THE NATIONAL LABOUR MARKETS

The second main fear to arise from the prospect of the Eastern enlargement is that the free movement of workers would lead CEEC nationals to swamp the labour markets of existing Member States.

[38] Once the CEEC workseeker does find suitable employment, he/she will become subject to the transitional regime discussed in Section III (below).
[39] Further: M Dougan, 'Free Movement: The Workseeker as Citizen' (2001) 4 *Cambridge Yearbook of European Legal Studies* 93.
[40] Contrast: Case C–85/96 *María Martínez Sala* [1998] ECR I–2691; with Case C–224/98 *D'Hoop* [2002] ECR I–6191.
[41] Case C–138/02 *Collins* (Opinion of 10 July 2003; Judgment pending). Note that some existing Member States are already considering imposing further limits to the benefits which might otherwise become available to migrant CEEC workseekers. See: 'Denmark restricts labour access before enlargement' (3 December 2003) at www.euobserver.com; 'Benefits Hedge Against New EU Workers' in *The Guardian* (3 February 2004). Consider, in this regard, the idea of some legitimate connection between migrant Community national

A. The Background Debate

On the one hand, neo-liberal economists stress the benefits of having income differences between different components of the Single Market, and permitting the free interplay of market forces to attain the most efficient equilibrium between supply and demand on the labour market.[42] Even less extreme theorists point out the potential benefits of migration from the CEECs: for example, to fill key labour shortages and skills bottlenecks within the existing Member States; and to maintain labour supply, and government revenues, in the face of demographic change (especially ageing populations) in Western Europe.[43]

On the other hand, it seems that policymakers' chief worry is rather social and political in character, in terms of public acceptance of the enlargement process itself. In particular, there are popular fears that a massive influx of workers from the CEECs would push down wages within existing Member States through a glut in the supply side of the labour market — increasing levels of unemployment within the host state, and with it the gross costs of social protection and welfare assistance. Ultimately, the worry is that *worries about* unrestrained free movement could threaten civil solidarity — particularly in these volatile days of Haid(er, Le Pen and Pym Fortuyn.[44]

Attempts to predict the actual impact of free movement of CEEC workers upon the existing Member States generally acknowledge their own fallibility.[45] Most investigations emphasise regional income differentials as the key variable in determining the probable scale of international labour migration. Nevertheless, experience with the Spanish and Portuguese accessions suggests that mass immigration is not a realistic probability.[46] This is especially true given the daunting practical obstacles

and host society as stressed by the Court in Case C–224/98 *D'Hoop* [2002] ECR I–6191 and Case C–257/00 *Givane* [2003] ECR I–345. Consider also the discussion of links between residence and access to subsidised public services in Case C–388/01 *Commission v Italy* [2003] ECR I–721.

[42] Further: V Curzon Price, 'Reintegrating Europe: Economic Aspects' in V Curzon Price, A Landau and R Whitman (eds), *The Enlargement of the European Union: Issues and Strategies* (London, Routledge, 1999).

[43] Consider, eg Commission, *The Free Movement of Workers in the Context of Enlargement* (Information Note: 6 March 2001); Commission Action Plan For Skills and Mobility, COM(2002) 72.

[44] Commission, *The Free Movement of Workers in the Context of Enlargement* (Information Note: 6 March 2001), esp. p 17. Consider the findings of Flash Eurobarometer 132/2, *Enlargement of the European Union: Results and Comments* (November 2002).

[45] For an evaluation, see H Fassmann and R Münz, 'EU Enlargement and Future East-West Migration in Europe' in *Migration Challenges in Central and Eastern Europe* (International Organisation for Migration, 2002). Also: Commission, above n 44, Tables 1 and 3.

[46] Indeed, the transitional periods originally applicable to Spain and Portugal were subsequently reduced from 7 to 6 years (from 10 to 8 years in the case of Luxembourg), when it became clear that fears of mass labour migration had not materialised.

which often inhibit exercise of the legal right to free movement, and make the European labour force significantly less mobile than (for example) the US population: linguistic, cultural and social barriers; as well as the high transaction costs of migration itself.[47] It is reinforced by the fact that economic growth, higher living standards and better employment prospects within the home state could effectively neutralise any incentive to relocate caused by appreciable wage disparities across the enlarged EU.[48]

Recent studies (based on the assumption of full free movement rights from the time of accession) estimate that the total number of CEEC nationals living within the existing Member States would peak at three- to four-million in the years around 2030 — representing just over one per cent of the present EU population. Of these three- to four-million CEEC immigrants, only around 35 per cent would be economically active as workers; the rest would be made up of self-employed persons, the financially independent, and protected family members.[49] In any case, research suggests that one should draw careful distinctions between the *aggregate* and the *regional* impact of free movement, ie whereby the bulk of CEEC immigration would continue to be concentrated in Germany and Austria. In addition, income differences between certain border regions of these two Member States and of the CEECs are among the most pronounced in the world. Concerns are acute that, within this particular geographical context, free movement would actually mean cross-frontier commuting: CEEC nationals could enjoy the benefits of participating on the local labour markets, without having to endure many of the costs associated with transferring residency to another country, thus posing greater risks of economic disruption and social tension.[50] Research suggests that one must also distinguish between the *aggregate* and the *sectoral* impact of free movement, ie whereby CEEC immigrants and frontier workers would be more likely (at least in the initial post-accession period) to compete for low-skill vacancies in the services sector, and for blue-collar vacancies in the manufacturing and construction industries.[51]

[47] Further: Commission, above n 44, Annex 1.
[48] Eg R Langewiesche, 'Enlargement and the Free Movement of Labour' in *European Trade Union Yearbook 1999* (Brussels, European Trade Union Confederation, 2000). Commentators have also noted the historical shift from long-term migration (usually motivated by political factors) to short-term migration (now motivated largely by economic interests) between the CEECs and the EU, eg D Stola 'The Social and Political Context of Migration Between Central Europe and the European Union' in E Guild (ed), *The Legal Framework and Social Consequences of Free Movement of Persons in the European Union* (The Hague, Kluwer Law International, 1998).
[49] In particular: T Boeri and H Brücker *et al*, *The Impact of Eastern Enlargement on Employment and Labour Markets in the EU Member States: Final Report* (European Integration Consortium, Berlin and Milan, 2000).
[50] Further: Commission Communication on the impact of enlargement on regions bordering candidate countries, COM(2001) 437 Final.
[51] Further: Boeri and Brücker, above n 49.

B. The Transitional Arrangements

The overall economic impact of enlargement and free movement on the existing EU states was likely to be limited, but the regional/sectoral impact could have been more significant. In any case, public perceptions (however ignorant) of the risks to domestic labour markets posed by Eastern enlargement could have endangered the successful ratification of the Accession Treaty. For these reasons, in April 2001, the Commission proposed a relatively flexible system of transitional arrangements to deal with the free movement of workers within the context of enlargement.[52] This was endorsed by the Council as the EU common position vis-à-vis all the candidate countries (except Malta and Cyprus).[53] It was accepted (with certain modifications) by all those candidate countries (including Bulgaria and, in December 2003, Romania). For the eight CEECs joining on 1 May 2004, the Accession Treaty therefore establishes a transitional regime as follows.[54]

There will be a basic five-year period after accession during which each existing Member State may continue to apply its own national rules on access to the labour market.[55] These national rules (or bilateral agreements) might mean anywhere between no or full rights to free movement and residency for CEEC nationals for the purposes of taking up employment within any given Member State (whether as immigrant or frontier workers). However, CEEC nationals admitted to the labour market of an existing Member State for an uninterrupted period of at least twelve months, whether at the time of accession or during the transitional regime, will acquire a secure right of access to the labour market of that Member State (though not any right to free movement *qua* worker across the rest of the EU).[56] Declarations annexed to the Final Act exhort the existing Member States to liberalise their immigration rules as soon as possible, and encourage them to improve labour market access even before accession actually takes place. Such exhortations have largely fallen on deaf ears. It seems that thirteen of the fifteen existing Member

[52] See Press Release IP/01/561 (11 April 2001).

[53] Maltese nationals will not be subject to any transitional restrictions on free movement vis-à-vis the existing Member States, but Malta has negotiated a special seven-year safeguard clause to cope with fears about the impact of accession upon its own labour market. No transitional provisions will apply as regards free movement of workers between Cyprus and the existing Member States.

[54] This description is based on Part 1: Freedom of Movement for Persons, Annex V: List Referred to in Article 24 of the Act of Accession (Czech Republic), Act of Accession. Identical provisions are contained in the Annexes concerning the other affected CEECs.

[55] Through the suspension of Arts 1–6 Reg 1612/68, OJ 1968 L257/2 (and corresponding provisions of Dir 68/360, OJ 1968 L257/13).

[56] This limited security of employment will be forfeited if the CEEC national voluntarily leaves the labour market of the relevant Member State.

States intend to impose some limits on the free movement of CEEC workers (only the United Kingdom and Ireland still waiving their right to do so).[57]

This basic transitional regime will be automatically reviewed, for each CEEC, before the end of its second year (by the Council, on the basis of a report by the Commission). However, this review would not affect the right of each existing Member State to continue applying its own national immigration rules for the rest of the basic five-year transitional period — provided that it duly notifies the Commission. Failure to so notify the Commission would mean that free movement for workers from the relevant CEEC comes into operation. At the request of any given CEEC, and following the same procedure, the Commission will initiate an optional second review in respect of that CEEC.

After the basic five-year period has elapsed, full free movement of workers will extend to relations between all Member States — subject to two provisos. First, those existing Member States which are still applying their own immigration rules may continue to do so for a further period of two years, where there are serious disturbances (or the threat thereof) on the domestic labour market, and having again notified the Commission. Secondly, any existing Member State applying the Community *acquis* on free movement of workers (whether having decided to shorten or terminate the transitional regime following a Commission review, or upon the natural expiry of the basic five-year period) may still invoke a safeguard clause, until the end of the seventh year following accession, to cope with exceptional situations. In particular, if the Member State undergoes or foresees disturbances on its labour market that could seriously threaten the standard of living or level of employment in a given region or occupation, it may request the Commission to authorise the total or partial suspension of free movement for workers from the relevant CEEC, until the situation has been restored to normal. This authorisation would be subject to annulment or amendment by the Council (acting by qualified majority vote).[58]

[57] See eg, 'Denmark restricts labour access before enlargement' (3 December 2003) and 'Dutch to restrict worker numbers from new States' (23 January 2004) at www.euobserver. com; and 'Sweden acts to stop influx of EU workers' in *The Guardian* (31 January 2004). One suspects that a 'domino effect' may be at work: the more Member States decided to restrict access to their labour markets, the more the remaining Member States feared *they* would be swamped by CEEC workers, and responded by restricting access to their labour markets too. Consider: 'Norway under pressure to close labour market' (3 February 2004) at www.euobserver.com.

[58] In urgent cases, the Member State may reintroduce national immigration restrictions before notifying the Commission. Cf. the other possibilities discussed in Commission, above n 44. Cf. also the safeguard clause contained in Art 20 Reg 1612/68, OJ 1968 L257/2 (repealed by Reg 2434/92, OJ 1992 L245/1). Note that the Accession Treaty will also contain horizontal safeguard clauses allowing the Commission to respond to unexpected economic disturbances following enlargement. See: Part 4, Title II of the Act of Accession.

The Accession Treaty contains several additional provisions applicable throughout this transitional regime. First, a standstill clause permits the Member States to enact only more generous rights to free movement for CEEC workers — something which the ECJ had already held to be implicit in the imposition of transitional provisions, within the context of the Greek, Portuguese and Spanish accessions.[59] Thus, neither national immigration rules nor ad hoc safeguard measures may result in conditions for the access of CEEC workers to the labour markets of the existing Member States which are more restrictive than those prevailing on the date of signature of the Accession Treaty. Secondly, a preferential treatment clause gives CEEC workers priority over third country nationals as regards access to the national labour markets of the existing Member States, and guarantees for CEEC nationals no less favourable treatment than third country nationals lawfully employed in the domestic territory. Thirdly, there will be a guarantee of non-discrimination on grounds of nationality for CEEC workers lawfully employed within any existing Member State. This reflects the current situation under the Europe Agreements as construed by the Court in the *Pokrzeptowicz-Meyer* case;[60] but will extend to equal treatment not only as regards terms and conditions of employment, but also as regards tax and social advantages, including welfare benefits such as income support and family allowances.[61] As with other categories of Union citizen, migrant CEEC workers will also be entitled to rely on the Community system for the cross-border coordination of social security benefits. Fourthly, as long as an existing Member State applies transitional restrictions to CEEC workers, provision will be made for the staggered introduction of employment rights for family members within its territory. Following the model set by the Spanish and Portuguese enlargements, rights to employment will automatically be granted to the protected family members of CEEC workers already lawfully resident in the host state at the

[59] Eg Case 77/82 *Peskeloglou* [1983] ECR 1085; Case C–3/87 *Agegate* [1989] ECR 4459. Though note the definitional issues discussed in Case C–302/97 *Konle* [1999] ECR I–3099; Case C–355/97 *Bergdorf* [1999] ECR I–4977.

[60] Case C–162/00 *Pokrzeptowicz-Meyer* [2002] ECR I–1049. Also: Case C–438/00 *Deutscher Handballbund* [2003] ECR I–4135.

[61] Indeed, anything not expressly excluded by the Accession Treaty will become subject to the general principle of equal treatment contained in Art 12 EC (as elaborated by Art 39 EC and measures such as Reg 1612/68): eg Case 305/87 *Commission v Greece* [1989] ECR 1461; Case 9/88 *Lopes da Veiga* [1989] ECR 2989. Also: Case C–122/96 *Saldanha* [1997] ECR I–5325; Case C–195/98 *Österreichischer Gewerkschaftsbund* [2000] ECR I–10497; Case C–290/00 *Duchon* [2002] ECR I–3567. However, even those existing Member States which do not restrict access to their labour markets *per se* are coming under (tabloid) pressure to restrict access to welfare benefits by lawfully resident CEEC workers. Consider eg, 'Benefits Hedge Against New EU Workers' in *The Guardian* (3 February 2004). Such restrictions will be difficult to justify if directly discriminatory, less so if indirectly discriminatory. See further: Section II (above).

moment of accession;[62] whereas rights to employment would progressively be extended to the protected family members of CEEC workers subsequently arriving in the host state.[63]

Finally, the principle of reciprocity will apply: if an existing Member State adopts restrictive measures against workers from a CEEC, the latter may adopt equivalent measures against the former's nationals. Moreover, if any existing Member State suspends the free movement of workers from a given CEEC, the latter would become entitled to invoke the ad hoc safeguard clause against all other new Member States — thereby enhancing the perception that it is a fully-fledged partner in the expanded Union, able to respond (if necessary) to serious labour market disturbances caused by intra-CEEC migration.[64] Otherwise, however, there will be full free movement of persons in accordance with the *acquis communautaire* as between the new Member States from the moment of accession.

As an acceptable compromise between the competing constituencies of interest represented at the accession negotiations, this proposed regime clearly has several merits, not least in meeting the demand for flexibility identified by the Commission in its initial policy assessments. Those Member States which want or need to import workers from the CEECs can do so on a bilateral basis; those Member States which face threats to the stability of their regional or sectoral labour markets can address them. In any case, the facility of a double review during the first five years after enlargement helps overcome some of the uncertainties associated with attempts to predict the cross-border movement of workers. It has been argued that transitional restrictions on labour migration will, incidentally, help avert the threat of a damaging 'brain (or skills) drain' from the CEECs — stabilising the pool of human resources essential for continuing economic growth in the new Member States.[65] Moreover, by the time the legal restrictions and safeguards contained in the Accession Treaty will have finally expired around 2011 (assuming enlargement proceeds as planned in 2004), research suggests that demographic change in the CEECs caused by falling fertility and rising mortality rates, coupled with further

[62] Unless the CEEC worker was admitted to the host state's labour market for a period of less than 12 months.

[63] After 18 months' residency, or 3 years from accession (whichever is earlier). Cp. Arts 57 and 217 Accession Treaty with Spain and Portugal, OJ 1985 L302/9. Cf. the less generous provisions contained in Art 45 Accession Treaty with Greece, OJ 1979 L291/9. Note the situation where a CEEC worker lawfully resident in an existing Member State dies before the accession of his / her home state to the EU, but is survived by family members who later attempt to rely on Reg 1612/68; cf. Case C–131/96 *Romero* [1997] ECR I–3659 (as regards the Spanish accession).

[64] This facility would not apply to relations between the CEECs and Malta or Cyprus.

[65] Eg speech by Odile Quintin at *The Impact of Enlargement on the Labour Markets of the European Union* (seminar organised by the Commission, Brussels, 15 March 2001). Cf. critical comments on this argument by Curzon Price, above n 42.

economic convergence with the existing Member States, will have placed a natural limit on the potential for any large-scale labour emigration — addressing criticisms that the transitional provisions have merely postponed the inevitable problems associated with free movement in an enlarged EU.[66]

In any case, several legal issues should immediately spring to mind from this basic transitional regime. For example, to have less extensive protection as regards one fundamental freedom than the others requires a careful delimitation of the threshold criteria for relying on the various Treaty provisions, the broad outlines of which have already been established by the ECJ. In particular, the relationship between employment and establishment will become crucial in determining whether an individual is subject to the transitional measures on workers, or entitled to full free movement for the self-employed.[67] Similarly, the relationship between workers and services will become crucial in determining whether a CEEC national posted to one of the existing Member States by his/her employer is subject to the transitional measures on workers, or to the rules on (almost) full free movement of services.[68]

Other problems will arise with the concept of serious disturbances on the labour market (as the basis for Member State restrictions on free movement for workers imposed systematically beyond the basic five-year transitional period, or authorised under the ad hoc safeguard clause before expiry of the overall seven-year transitional regime). In particular, how might the Court react to a legal challenge brought by a disgruntled CEEC national? The Court generally accepted without question the rationale behind transitional restrictions on free movement within the context of the Greek, Spanish and Portuguese enlargements, ie so as to prevent disturbances on the domestic labour markets 'as a result of immediate and substantial movements of workers following accession'.[69] Such a passive reaction was understandable when faced with primary Treaty

[66] Eg Fassmann and Münz, above n 45. Cf. critical comments on the Commission's proposed transitional arrangements by H Brücker, 'The Impact of Eastern Enlargement on EU Labour Markets' in ZEI Policy Paper B12 2001, Centre for European Integration Studies, Rheinische Friedrich-Wilhelms-Universität, Bonn.

[67] As elaborated by the ECJ in judgments such as Case C–3/87 *Agegate* [1989] ECR 4459 under the EC Treaty, and Case C–268/99 *Jany* [2001] ECR I–8615 under the Europe Agreements.

[68] As addressed by the ECJ in judgments such as Case C–113/89 *Rush Portuguesa* [1990] ECR I–1417, and Case C–43/93 *Vander Elst* [1994] ECR I–3803. Further: Section IV (below).

[69] Case 77/82 *Peskeloglou* [1983] ECR 1085, para 12 (and the Opinion of AG Slynn at p 1098); Case 9/88 *Lopes da Veiga* [1989] ECR 2989, para 10 (and the Opinion of AG Darmon at para 10); Case C–113/89 *Rush Portuguesa* [1990] ECR I–1417, para 13 (and the Opinion of AG van Gerven at para 12). Also: AG Darmon in Case C–171/91 *Tsiotras* [1993] ECR I–2925, para 17 Opinion. Though, of course, derogations from fundamental Treaty freedoms contained in accession instruments are always strictly construed, eg Case C-233/97 *KappAhl Oy* [1998] ECR I–8069.

provisions themselves immune from judicial review; but it is unlikely to be replicated as regards the legality of inferior measures adopted by the Member States. Nevertheless, it is unclear whether the Court would in this context apply the standard of judicial review appropriate to restrictions on a fundamental freedom (including a detailed proportionality assessment, and requiring objective evidence to support the Member State's claims);[70] or that appropriate to national decisions involving complex economic and policy considerations (limited to manifest absurdity or bad faith amounting to misuse of power).[71] The latter option might seem particularly likely as regards ad hoc safeguard measures authorised by the Commission under political supervision by the Council.[72]

C. Impact of Union Citizenship on the Transitional Provisions

However, this chapter will concentrate on the legal issues arising from the transitional arrangements on free movement of workers through the potential impact of Union citizenship.

The transitional arrangements envisage that Member States may impose restrictions on immigration for employment purposes, and may discriminate on grounds of nationality as regards access to domestic labour markets. But Article 18 EC, broadening significantly the potential availability of rights to free movement and residency, make these restrictions — and the consequences of their infringement — more difficult to police.[73]

In particular, the existence of potentially simultaneous rights of residency for purposes other than employment raises questions about the legal status of a CEEC national who has unlawfully participated on the national labour market; but also satisfies the criterion of being economically active (in a self-employed capacity) or financially independent (in the broad sense of having sufficiently sufficient resources and sufficiently comprehensive medical insurance) — and thus still qualifies for a right to residence under Article 18 EC (via Article 43 EC or the Residency Directives respectively). What punitive steps might the host state take?

[70] Consider, eg Case 40/82 *'Newcastle Disease'* [1982] ECR 2793; Case 178/84 *'German Beer'* [1987] ECR 1227.

[71] Consider, eg Case C–120/97 *Upjohn v Licensing Authority* [1999] ECR I–223.

[72] Consider recently, eg Case T–70/99 *Alpharma* [2002] ECR II–3495; Case T–74/00 *Artegodan* [2002] ECR II–4945.

[73] Indeed, it has been argued that a generalised right to circulate freely within the EU, coupled with significant restrictions on the right lawfully to engage in employment, might facilitate a black market in CEEC labour: R Langewiesche and M Lubyova, 'Migration, Mobility and the Free Movement of Persons: An Issue for Current and Future EU Members' in European Trade Union Institute, *Enlargement as a Trade Union Issue*, Transfer 3/2000.

The dilemma here is to balance the desire to enforce any free movement rights under Community law which the claimant is prima facie entitled to enjoy, against the reluctance to condone breaches of national law, especially in a way that might undermine the effectiveness of the transitional provisions on workers. This is especially true bearing in mind that the claimant may be using funds and contacts acquired through unlawful employment within the host state to support his/her alternative claim to residency rights.[74] It is possible to identify several potential responses.

First, without questioning the claimant's prima facie entitlement to residency under some legitimate legal basis, the Member State could try to expel the claimant from its national territory by reference to the express Treaty derogations on public policy.[75] However, one could query whether unlawful participation in employment would be enough in itself to meet the strict criteria developed by the Court: there must be a genuine and sufficiently serious threat to a fundamental interest of society (not just a breach of the law);[76] and expulsion must be justified by reference to the claimant's personal conduct (not as a general preventative or deterrent measure).[77] One suspects that only a few very flagrant cases of unlawful employment would satisfy these rigorous criteria.

Secondly, one might be tempted to cross-refer to the abuse of rights doctrine developed by the Court in its recent Europe Agreement judgments, whereby the Member State was able to justify removing an individual from its national territory after discovering his/her irregular status under domestic immigration rules, even though the claimant satisfied the substantive criteria for claiming a right of establishment under Community law.[78] However, the legal framework of the Europe Agreements is entirely different from the legal framework of the Accession Treaty. In particular, freedom of establishment under the Europe Agreements remains subject to national rules on entering and staying within the territory. This entitles the Member State to impose

[74] As the ECJ pointed out in analogous circumstances in Case C–63/99 *Gloszczuk* [2001] ECR I–6369, paras 72–4; Case C–235/99 *Kondova* [2001] ECR I–6427, paras 78–9.

[75] Art 39(3) EC on workers, Art 46(1) EC on establishment, Art 55 EC on services. These derogations apply also to Union citizens relying on the three Residency Directives; and indeed on Art 18 EC, eg Case C–348/96 *Calfa* [1999] ECR I–11; Case C–357/98 *Yiadom* [2000] ECR I–9265; Case C–100/01 *Olazabal* [2002] ECR I–10981.

[76] Eg Case 36/75 *Rutili* [1975] ECR 1219; Case 30/77 *Bouchereau* [1977] ECR 1999.

[77] Eg Case 67/74 *Bonsignore* [1975] ECR 297; Case C–348/96 *Calfa* [1999] ECR I–11.

[78] In particular: Case C–63/99 *Gloszczuk* [2001] ECR I–6369; Case C–235/99 *Kondova* [2001] ECR I–6427. Cf. the different factual situation involved in Case C–257/99 *Barkoci and Malik* [2001] ECR I–6557, all annotated by Hillion, (2003) 40 *CMLRev* 465. Further: A Ott, 'The Rights of Self-Employed CEEC Citizens in the Member States Under the Europe Agreements' Issue 8–2000/01 *The European Legal Forum* 497; S Peers, 'The Right of Establishment for Nationals of Central and Eastern European Countries' (2002) 16 *Immigration, Asylum and Nationality Law* 19; B Bogusz, 'Regulating the Right of Establishment for Accession State Nationals' (2002) 27 *ELRev* 472.

prior controls on all immigration, even for the purposes of taking up legitimate self-employed activities, provided such controls do not nullify or impair the benefits accruing to individuals under the Europe Agreements.[79] According to the ECJ, the Member State's power to expel fraudulent CEEC nationals was a necessary manifestation of this domestic discretion, which might otherwise have been deprived of its effectiveness.[80] By contrast, freedom of establishment (or for Union citizens) under the Accession Treaty will not be subject to any comparable reservation in favour of national immigration rules, and the Member States will not be competent to impose any such prior controls upon the entry of CEEC nationals for the purposes of taking up residency rights under Article 43 (or Article 18) EC. The Member State could not expel CEEC nationals who have fraudulently participated on the domestic labour market in the exercise of a national discretion which does not exist; and the Europe Agreement caselaw on establishment thus seems to be of limited relevance in the post-accession era.[81]

Thirdly, the Member State could attempt to rely instead upon the abuse of rights doctrine developed under Community law itself, whereby the Court recognises the competence of Member States to take action against Community nationals seeking to rely on Treaty provisions for abusive purposes.[82] This doctrine might well catch the situation, for example, of a CEEC national who claims residency as a student or financially independent person, but is in fact using this as a mere cover to engage in unlawful employment. Such a claimant would find him/herself taken outside the protection offered by Community law, just as if they had no legal basis to claim free movement or residency rights at all, entitling the host state to

[79] Eg Arts 44 and 58 Association Agreement between the European Community and Poland, OJ 1993 L348/1. On free movement under the Europe Agreements generally: M Cremona, 'Movement of Persons, Establishment and Services' in M Maresceau (ed), *Enlarging the European Union: Relations Between the EU and Central and Eastern Europe* (Longman, 1997); W Weiss, 'The Chapter II on Establishment in the Europe Agreements' (2001) 6 *European Foreign Affairs Review* 243; E Guild, *Immigration Law in the European Community* (Kluwer Law International, 2001) Ch. 6. On the Europe Agreements in the wider context of free movement rights for third country nationals: H Staples, *The Legal Status of Third Country Nationals Resident in the European Union* (Kluwer Law International, 1999); N–F Sola, 'Different European Union Approaches to Immigration' (2001) 25 *Polish Yearbook of International Law* 241.

[80] In particular: Case C–63/99 *Gloszczuk* [2001] ECR I–6369, esp. paras 68–85; Case C–235/99 *Kondova* [2001] ECR I–6427, esp. paras 73–90. Cf. the more generous approach adopted in Case C–257/99 *Barkoci and Malik* [2001] ECR I–6557, esp. paras 70–74.

[81] Similar reservations apply as regards free movement under the Association Agreement with Turkey as construed by the Court, eg in Case C–37/98 *Savas* [2000] ECR I–2927. However, this body of jurisprudence might be more relevant to the situation of a CEEC national who claims a secure right to employment within an existing Member State, on the basis of having been admitted to its labour market for at least 12 months, but had procured such admission through fraudulent means: consider, eg Case C–285/95 *Kol* [1997] ECR I–3069.

[82] Generally, eg Case C–367/96 *Kefalas* [1998] ECR I–2843; Case C–212/97 *Centros* [1999] ECR I–1459, esp. para 24.

expel without having to satisfy the express Treaty derogations on public policy.[83] However, this doctrine probably would not catch the situation of a CEEC national who may well have engaged in unlawful employment, but was not abusing other rights to free movement (say, as a genuinely self-employed person) under Community law; or indeed who is now seeking to rely upon fresh rights to free movement (say, as a genuine student) under the Treaty. Such a claimant could not be said to be taking advantage of *these* provisions of Community law for abusive purposes.

In this situation, the host state might have to accept that the claimant enjoys a right to residency under legitimate provisions of Community law, and rest content with the competence to impose proportionate and non-discriminatory sanctions for having contravened the domestic prohibition on engaging in employment.[84] Such an outcome might in any case seem consonant with the *Baumbast* principle, that action to protect the Member State's legitimate interests should not go beyond what is necessary, having regard to the Union citizen's rights under Article 18 EC. In any case, this remains the only realistic solution where (for example) the CEEC national resides in Poland but commutes to Germany to engage in unlawful employment there — precisely the sort of situation which tallies with the Commission's research on the regional impact of post-enlargement migration patterns.

In other words, the influence of Union citizenship means that, in many cases, the Member State's sanctions against illegal participation by CEEC nationals in the domestic labour market are less likely to lie in the traditional tools of immigration law (expulsion of the unlawful worker from the host territory), than in criminal or administrative penalties (as regards which the true burden of compliance will often fall as much on the employer as on the employee).

Where the CEEC national has engaged unlawfully upon the host state's labour market, but does not otherwise satisfy the criterion of being economically active under the terms of Article 43 EC or financially independent under the umbrella of the Residency Directives (since unlawful employment provided the claimant's sole or primary source of income), the caselaw on Article 18 EC suggests that the Member State is not limited to the adoption of proportionate and non-discriminatory sanctions for having breached its labour restrictions. It is also entitled to protect its legitimate interests against Union citizens becoming an unreasonable burden upon the public purse, by revoking the claimant's residence permit (if any), and

[83] Consider analogous observations in judgments such as Case 39/86 *Lair* [1988] ECR 3161, esp. para 43. Also: Case 33/74 *van Binsbergen* [1974] ECR 1299; Case 205/84 *Commission v Germany* [1986] ECR 3755; Case C–23/93 *TV10* [1994] ECR I–4795.

[84] Eg Case 48/75 *Royer* [1976] ECR 497; Case 118/75 *Watson and Belmann* [1976] ECR 1185; Case C–24/97 *Commission v Germany* [1998] ECR I–2133; Case C-378/97 *Wijsenbeek* [1999] ECR I–6207; Case C–459/99 *MRAX* [2002] ECR I–6591.

removing the claimant from the national territory. However, as we saw before, all Union citizens now enjoy a directly effective right to residency under Article 18 EC, and even where the Member State is entitled to take steps to enforce the limitations and conditions applicable to exercise of that right to residency, its conduct remains subject to judicial review, in particular, to guarantee compliance with the general principles of Community law. Insofar as this includes the protection of fundamental rights (such as Article 8 ECHR on private and family life), certain CEEC nationals may enjoy an enforceable right of residency within the host state under Article 18 EC despite the fact that they have participated unlawfully on the domestic labour market, and are unable to claim entitlement to free movement *qua* economically active or financially independent person.[85] Being lawfully resident within the host state as a matter of Community law, such claimants would (again) be entitled under Article 12 EC to protection against discrimination on grounds of nationality as regards welfare benefits such as subsistence support. This might present the host state with a dilemma, ie of cutting off its nose to spite its face, by effectively paying for someone not to work. In such circumstances, Union citizenship combined with healthy common sense might impose a de facto limitation on the Member State's competence to exclude CEEC nationals from the domestic employment market during the post-accession transitional period: better that the claimant works and pays for him/herself, than that the taxpayer subsidies compulsory garden leave from the labour force.

In any event, it is worth recalling that Community law already confers upon certain CEEC nationals a right to employment within the Member States, and these provisions will continue to apply post-enlargement. For example, if the CEEC national is the spouse of a Community worker holding the nationality of one of the existing Member States and resident in the territory of another existing Member State under Article 39 EC, then that CEEC national is entitled to equal treatment as regards access to and conditions of employment under Article 11 Regulation 1612/68, ie *qua* spouse and regardless of his/her own nationality.[86]

IV. SOCIAL DUMPING AND REGULATORY COMPETITION

The final main fear arising from the free movement of persons within the context of the Eastern enlargement is that differences in direct labour costs such as wages, indirect labour costs such as working time and

[85] Cf. Commission Green Paper on a Community return policy on illegal residents, COM(2002) 175 Final; Commission Communication on a Community return policy on illegal residents, COM(2002) 564 Final.
[86] Reg 1612/68, OJ 1968 L257/2.

safety standards, and other compliance costs such as environmental protection legislation, will encourage a process of social dumping within the enlarged EU.[87]

For example, the free movement of services might allow CEEC undertakings to offer cheap competition to domestic undertakings within the existing Member States — encouraging Western businesses and consumers to contract from Eastern undertakings whose lower prices depend upon depressed wages and poorer standards of labour regulation. Similarly, it is feared that the free movement of capital and freedom of establishment might divert foreign direct investment away from the existing high-cost Member States towards the new low-cost CEECs. Anecdotal evidence abounds: for example, in October 2002, manufacturing company Black & Decker announced significant job losses at its factory in north-east England, so as to relocate to the Czech Republic, citing lower labour costs as a key factor in this decision.[88] Indeed, in November 2002, Ernst & Young's European Investment Monitor released data to show that, whereas new investment projects in the existing Member States declined by around 15 per cent in the first six months of 2002 as compared to the first six months of 2001, new investment projects in central and eastern Europe (though including not only the CEECs accepted for accession, but also countries such as Romania and Russia) rose by over 50 per cent during the same period.[89] But as ever, the empirical debate on this issue is far from straightforward. For example, other economists argue that recent foreign direct investment flows from the EU to the CEECs have been driven largely by market access, and do not adversely impact upon employment or wages in the existing Member States. Only a relatively small proportion of foreign direct investment is driven by low-wage costs, often related to cross-border labour specialisation whereby CEEC workers perform labour-intensive activities while Western employees concentrate on other aspects of the undertaking's production processes. This type of foreign direct investment might have limited sectoral effects on wages and employment in existing Member States, particularly in industries dominated by unskilled labour.[90]

[87] For an overview of this debate, and extensive references: M Dougan, 'Vive la Différence? Exploring the Legal Framework for Reflexive Harmonisation Within the Single European Market' in P Zumbansen and R Miller (eds), *Annual of German and European Law* (Oxford, Berghahn Books, 2004).
[88] 'Black & Decker Cuts 1000 Jobs' in *The Guardian* (4 October 2002).
[89] Ernst & Young, *European Investment Monitor: A Six-Month View: January-June 2002* (20 November 2002).
[90] Boeri and Brücker, above n 49. Cf. A Henriot and A Inotai, 'Economic Interpenetration Between the European Union and the Central and Eastern European Countries' (1997) 2 *European Foreign Affairs Review* 167. Note also that productivity in the CEECs is lower than in the existing Member States, reducing the economic incentive to engage in social dumping: see, eg H Grabbe, *Profiting from EU Enlargement* (London, Centre for European Reform, 2001).

Nevertheless, the argument continues, the actual or perceived phenomenon of social dumping via the free movement provisions might in turn stimulate a process of regulatory competition, whereby the existing Member States are forced to respond by lowering their own wages, labour standards and other compliance costs, in an attempt to protect domestic industry from allegedly unfair competition, and to attract or maintain inward investment.[91] Or at the very least, it might emasculate the bargaining power of trade unions and social democratic governments vis-à-vis industry representatives in the process of industrial negotiations and legislative reform.[92]

As a matter of principle, neo-liberal economic theory claims that regulatory competition should in fact encourage the Member States to converge around a legislative regime which regulates the Common Market in optimal fashion.[93] But market failures, such as significant imbalances in the relative mobility of individual workers and consumers as compared to economic undertakings and capital, distort this theoretical model.[94] In any case, the Union has already decided to encourage economic growth based on a model of high pay/high productivity, whereby decent standards of social protection for workers and citizens are understood not as a burden on efficiency, but as a positive and valuable input into the market process.[95] Moreover, the Union is also keen to make a strong political statement about what type of European integration is being pursued, combining the quest for strong economic growth with the maintenance of high standards of employment or environmental protection viewed as autonomous policy values in their own right.[96] For these reasons, Community law is believed to have a justified vocation in limiting even the risk of harmful competition between legal orders.

[91] Eg S Deakin and F Wilkinson 'Rights vs. Efficiency? The Economic Case for Transnational Labour Standards' (1994) 23 *Industrial Law Journal* 289; A Lo Faro, *Regulating Social Europe: Realty and Myth of Collective Bargaining in the EC Legal Order* (Oxford, Hart Publishing, 2000) Ch. 2.

[92] Eg W Streeck, 'Neo-Voluntarism: A New European Social Policy Regime?' (1995) 1 *ELJ* 31.

[93] Further: R Van den Bergh, 'Subsidiarity as an Economic Demarcation Principle and the Emergence of European Private Law' (1998) 5 *Maastricht Journal of European and Comparative Law* 129; J Smits 'A European Private Law as a Mixed Legal System: Towards a Ius Commune through the Free Movement of Legal Rules' (1998) 5 *Maastricht Journal of European and Comparative Law* 328; A Ogus, 'Competition Between National Legal Systems: A Contribution of Economic Analysis to Comparative Law' (1999) 48 *ICLQ* 405.

[94] Further: S O'Leary, 'The Free Movement of Persons and Services' in P Craig and G de Búrca (eds), *The Evolution of EU Law* (Oxford, OUP, 1999).

[95] Eg Presidency Conclusions of the Lisbon European Council (23–4 March 2000); and of the Nice European Council (7–9 December 2000). Also: Commission, Concerted Strategy for Modernising Social Protection, COM(1999) 347 Final; Commission, Social Policy Agenda, COM(2000) 379 Final.

[96] Consider, in particular, Charter of Fundamental Rights of the European Union, OJ 2000 C364/1.

Fears of free movement being used to engage in social dumping exist in relations between the current Member States.[97] In many areas, the assumed solution to this alleged problem has been harmonisation at the Community level, so as to guarantee through centralised norms the sorts of social standards valued by the Union, and to pre-empt the Member States from taking unilateral action to undermine these standards for the sake of gaining some short-sighted competitive advantage.[98] Within the context of the forthcoming Eastern enlargement, this perhaps helps to explain some of the emphasis placed upon full adoption and effective implementation of the *acquis communautaire* before accession takes place, so as to allay the worries of existing Member States that competition within the widened Single Market might otherwise be distorted by social dumping and deregulatory pressures.[99]

Particularly as regards employment rights, Community legislation tends to be minimum rather than fully pre-emptive in nature — leaving Member States free to adopt higher standards of protection than the (sometimes modest) common norm.[100] Moreover, the ECJ has sanctioned the extension of more stringent domestic labour standards adopted by any given Member State to foreign service providers entering the national territory with their own employees under Article 49 EC. For example, the Working Time Directive provides that workers must enjoy a certain number of paid holidays per year; but Article 15 preserves the Member State's right to apply more favourable rules for the protection of the health and safety of workers.[101] The Court held in *Finalarte* that construction companies established in the United Kingdom and Portugal who sent their workers to Germany to provide services could be required to respect the

[97] Though the theoretical and empirical debate remains contested: consider, eg D Goodhart, 'Social Dumping Within the EU' in D Hine and H Kassim (eds), *Beyond the Market: the EU and National Social Policy* (Routledge, 1998); S Deakin, 'Two Types of Regulatory Competition: Competitive Federalism Versus Reflexive Harmonisation. A Law and Economics Perspective on *Centros*' (1999) 2 *Cambridge Yearbook of European Legal Studies* 231; C Barnard, 'Social Dumping and the Race to the Bottom: Some Lessons For the European Union From Delaware?' (2000) 25 *ELRev* 57.

[98] Eg K Van Wezel Stone, 'Labour in the Global Economy: Four Approaches to Transnational Labour Regulation' in W Bratton, J McCahery, S Picciotto and C Scott (eds), *International Regulatory Competition and Coordination: Perspectives on Economic Regulation in Europe and the United States* (Clarendon Press, 1996).

[99] Consider, eg speech by Commissioner Frits Bolkestein, 'Enlargement and Its Impact on Internal Market Freedoms' (The Hague, 10 October 2000). It has also been argued that alignment with Community employment legislation during the pre-accession process protected CEEC nationals against the state-sanctioned deterioration of labour standards as a means of attracting foreign investment, eg C de la Porte, 'Enjeux et Perspectives de la Dimension Sociale de L'Élargissement' (2001) full text available at http://socialsecurity.fgov.be/bib/frames/fr/rbss_1_2001_porte_b.htm.

[100] Further: M Dougan, 'Minimum Harmonization and the Internal Market' (2000) 37 *CMLRev* 853.

[101] Dir 93/104, OJ 1993 L307/18.

longer holiday entitlements enshrined in German law, even though this constituted an obstacle to free movement in prima facie breach of Article 49 EC.[102] Directive 96/71 has made compulsory such assimilation of posted workers into the labour legislation of the host state, even where their employer satisfies the minimum conditions established by Community secondary legislation and imposed by their state of origin.[103] This legal framework further cushions the existing Member States against allegedly unfair competition from the lower cost CEECs.[104]

But there is a counter-argument — based upon the premise that the best safeguard against social dumping lies not in legal regulation but in the rapid economic development of the CEECs — that the EU's harmonised standards of labour and environmental protection, evolved in and designed for Western Europe, will inhibit growth among the CEECs for whom they represent a luxury rather than a social expectation, and therefore prolong the threat of regulatory competition even further.[105] In any case, one should recall that the Community enjoys only limited competence to pursue harmonisation, especially as regards significant compliance costs such as employees' wages. Article 137 EC specifically rules out any harmonisation of national wages within the context of the Community's competence over social policy. Similarly, Article 95 EC on harmonisation for the purposes of completing the Internal Market does not apply to employment matters.[106]

The existing Member States will thus have to rely on alternative methods of averting social dumping in favour of CEECs inspired by wage differences across the enlarged Union. In the current state of Community law, these secondary safeguards focus primarily upon the posting of workers under Article 49 EC.

For example, even in the absence of any Community harmonising legislation, the primary Treaty rules on free movement of services still permit Member States to require payment of their own minimum wage to employees temporarily posted within the national territory by foreign service providers.[107] The Court observed in *Portugaia Construções* that the

[102] Cases C–49, 50, 52–54 and 68–71/98 *Finalarte* [2001] ECR I–7831.
[103] Dir 96/71, OJ 1997 L18/01.
[104] Cf. O Deinert, 'Posting of Workers to Germany: Previous Evolutions and New Influences Throughout EU Legislation Proposals' (2000) 16 *International Journal of Comparative Labour Law and Industrial Relations* 217. Cf. also the implications, particularly as regards measures adopted under Arts 94 and 95 EC, of Case C–376/98 *Germany v Parliament and Council* [2000] ECR I–8419, and Case C–491/01 *British American Tobacco* [2002] ECR I–11453. Further: M Dougan, above n 87.
[105] Eg Curzon Price, above n 42.
[106] Note also the amendments to Art 157 EC by the Treaty of Nice. Further: B Ryan, 'Pay, Trade Union Rights and European Community Law' (1997) 13 *International Journal of Comparative Labour Law and Industrial Relations* 305.
[107] Eg Cases 62 and 63/81 *Seco* [1982] ECR 223; Case C–43/93 *Vander Elst* [1994] ECR I–3803; Case C–272/94 *Guiot* [1996] ECR I–1905.

objective of reducing allegedly unfair competitive advantages enjoyed by businesses established in countries with lower wage costs was, in itself, incapable of constituting a valid imperative requirement due to its protectionist economic nature.[108] However, the earlier judgment in *Arblade and Leloup* had already accepted that hindrances to free movement under Article 49 EC caused by the imposition of the host state's minimum wage could be justified in principle by the public interest in protecting workers.[109] Indeed, provided the objective effect of the national rules is to confer genuine benefits upon posted employees, the Member State's subjective intention of preventing social dumping will not be fatal to the process of objective justification.[110] Again, Directive 96/71 has now transformed the principle of compliance with the host state's minimum wage into a binding obligation — at least insofar as such wages have been laid down by law, regulation or administrative provision; or by collective agreements or arbitral awards which have been declared universally applicable and relate specifically to the building industry — a provision intended specifically to address German concerns about the award of construction contracts to undertakings established in low-pay Member States.[111]

However, these alternatives to centralised legislative harmonisation in the field of wages are not necessarily watertight guarantees against social dumping. For example, the Court in *Mazzoleni* observed that requiring undertakings operating in frontier regions, whose employees might be posted across the border on a regular basis and for short periods of time, to comply in all cases with the host state's minimum wage could breach the principle of proportionality: it might entail onerous administrative burdens for the individual service provider by necessitating hour-by-hour wages calculations; and could lead to the payment of different wages to employees carrying out identical work — threatening good working relations within the particular undertaking, and the cohesion of collective labour agreements within the Member State of establishment.[112] Moreover, the impact of the Member State's discretion/duty to extend its minimum wage to all employees operating within its national territory is limited in practice by the fact that most domestic workers are already paid more than that basic level of remuneration — thus ensuring that differences

[108] Case C–164/99 *Portugaia Construções* [2002] ECR I–787.
[109] Cases C–369/96 and C–376/96 *Arblade and Leloup* [1999] ECR I–8453.
[110] Cases C–49, 50, 52–54 and 68–71/98 *Finalarte* [2001] ECR I–7831; Case C–164/99 *Portugaia Construções* [2002] ECR I–787.
[111] Further: P Davies, 'Posted Workers: Single Market or Protection of National Labour Law Systems?' (1997) 34 *CMLRev* 571; 'The Posted Workers Directive and the EC Treaty' (2002) 31 *Industrial Law Journal* 298. Also R Gieser, 'Posting: Social Protection of Workers vs. Fundamental Freedoms?' (2003) 40 *CMLRev* 143.
[112] Case C–165/98 *Mazzoleni* [2001] ECR I–2189.

in labour-related compliance costs may be reduced, but are certainly not equalised even within the host state.[113] In any case, the protection offered by both Article 49 EC and Directive 96/71 presupposes that the Member State is prepared, of its own free will, to ignore any economic pressure to reduce its minimum wage generated by the perceived threat of unfair competition from cheaper foreign labour. Without the formal competence to harmonise wages, Community law can only accommodate rather than compel Member State resistance to inequitable social dumping. Finally, the safeguards contained in Article 49 EC and Directive 96/71 may thus seem precarious enough even as regards the particular phenomenon of posted workers — but they are powerless to control the broader economic forces which compel Member States to sacrifice social standards so as to help domestic undertakings compete *qua* service providers in other EU countries, and to attract higher levels of foreign direct investment into the national territory.

Against this background, one can perhaps understand the German and Austrian insistence on including safeguard measures in the Accession Treaty as regards serious disturbances (or the threat thereof) on the labour markets related to specific sensitive services, which could arise from the transfrontier posting of CEEC workers: construction and industrial cleaning in the case of Germany; also sectors such as home nursing and security activities in the case of Austria. This is where the Commission has identified the greatest risk that enlargement will have adverse economic consequences (both at a regional and a sectoral level). It is also where neither the Treaty rules on free movement of services nor Directive 96/71 on posted workers, as construed by the Court, seem entirely sympathetic to concerns about social dumping and its adverse policy consequences. A minimalist option for achieving the legitimate aims of the relevant Member States might have been simply to sanction Germany and Austria to require payment of their national minimum wage to all workers posted from the CEECs, despite the judgment in *Mazzoleni*. By such means, CEEC firms which could compete on the basis of the German and Austrian social models — offering efficient services without compromising domestic welfare standards — would have been permitted to do so, to the benefit of both existing and newly acceded components of the Single Market, through increased competition and economic growth.

However, social dumping caused by differences in wages and other employment costs is not the only problem raised by posted workers within the context of the Eastern enlargement. Although the Court has distinguished carefully between the *legal classification* of posted workers under Article 49 EC on the one hand, and of immigrant or frontier workers

[113] Eg S Simitis, 'Dismantling or Strengthening Labour Law: The Case of the European Court of Justice' (1996) 2 *ELJ* 156.

under Article 39 EC on the other hand,[114] it seems that posting could *in practice* have regional and sectoral effects not dissimilar to direct participation on the labour market of the host state. Imagine, for example, that significant numbers of CEEC nationals are sent to Bavaria to perform construction services on behalf of their employers in the Czech Republic: Article 39 EC is inapplicable because such workers are not engaged upon the German labour market; but the impact upon German workers now excluded from economic activity in the building sector poses problems under Article 49 EC equivalent to those which inspired the transitional restrictions on the free movement of CEEC workers-proper. One can therefore concede that more extensive safeguard clauses — sanctioning the imposition of outright restrictions on the posting of workers — might be justified by the need to respond more flexibly to any adverse effect upon particularly vulnerable labour markets caused by the large-scale transfer of contracts to CEEC undertakings, even under the protected conditions offered by Article 49 EC and Directive 96/71. Thus, for as long as Germany and Austria apply transitional restrictions on the general free movement of workers under Article 39 EC, they will also be permitted to derogate from Article 49 EC insofar as it would otherwise permit the temporary posting of such workers from the relevant CEEC. Nevertheless, given that the adoption of these additional safeguard measures will require only simple ex ante notification to the Commission, one hopes that ex post scrutiny before the Court will not be limited to the censure of manifest absurdity; but should extend to verifying whether objective evidence exists of a serious disturbance (or threat thereof) within the employment sectors specified in the Accession Treaty — such that ad hoc flanking measures on posted workers will genuinely contribute to the integrity of the main transitional provisions on labour migration.[115]

V. CONCLUSIONS

A mixture of pandering to popular misconceptions and addressing genuine policy concerns has driven the EU's approach to the free movement of persons within the context of the Eastern enlargement — but this approach in turn has implications which reverberate deeper than guaranteeing emergency treatment for Polish playboys, reprimanding illegal Czech workers, or reassuring nervous German trade unions.

[114] In particular: Case C–113/89 *Rush Portuguesa* [1990] ECR I–1417, esp paras 12–17; Case C–43/93 *Vander Elst* [1994] ECR I–3803, para 21.

[115] See Section III (above). Note: the principle of reciprocity will apply in relations between Germany/Austria and the relevant CEEC; and there will be a standstill clause preventing Germany/Austria from adopting any more restrictive provisions on posted CEEC workers than those prevailing at the date of signature of the Accession Treaty.

Of course, transitional arrangements on free movement are nothing new within the context of accession procedures.[116] Indeed, compared to the transitional periods applied to Greece, Spain and Portugal when they joined the Community, the CEECs are to receive relatively generous treatment, given that on this occasion, income differences are more pronounced, and the risk of mass labour migration is correspondingly higher. But what has changed since the enlargements to Greece, Spain and Portugal is the introduction under the Maastricht Treaty of Union citizenship — and there is an argument that this alters the equation dramatically. From a strictly *legal* viewpoint, it might seem relatively straightforward to accommodate differentiated rights to free movement and residency into the framework of Union citizenship: Article 18(1) EC states that the citizen's rights to free movement are to be exercised subject to the conditions and limitations contained in the Treaty. Similarly, the Nice Charter of Fundamental Rights states that the Union citizen's right to free movement is to be defined according to the Treaties.[117] But from a *legal policy* viewpoint, differentiated rights to free movement and residency for Union citizens perhaps pose greater problems.

Consider first the perspective of the newly acceded countries. As the present author understands the historical situation, the practical benefits of citizenship in a socialist state were linked at first to membership of a particular economic class (the dictatorship of the proletariat); and later to membership of the ruling elite (the dictatorship of the Communist party). So, whilst lip-service was paid to the notion of equal treatment for all, the reality was very different — with some citizens enjoying much more extensive rights to free movement within and across the national borders than others.[118] At least in the short-term, will perceptions of Union citizenship, for all its rhetorical vocabulary of equality and inclusion, look much different for many Eastern Europeans? In particular, some commentators have observed that the main losers in the 'great victory' of the market economy in Eastern Europe have been the working classes; yet they are exactly the people who are not being compensated for their sacrifices, by the enjoyment of greater opportunities for economic and personal fulfilment, within the context of the forthcoming EU enlargement.[119] The risk of endangering popular acceptance of enlargement in the West might well have been

[116] Cf. the position as regards the accession of Austria, Finland and Sweden: D Booss and J Forman, 'Enlargement: Legal and Procedural Aspects' (1995) 32 *CMLRev* 95.
[117] Arts 45 and 52 Charter of Fundamental Rights of the European Union, OJ 2000 C364/1.
[118] Further: V Petev, 'Citizenship and *Raison d'État*: The Quest for Identity in Central and Eastern Europe' in M La Torre (ed), *European Citizenship: An Institutional Challenge* (Kluwer Law International, 1998).
[119] Eg M Wyrzykowski, 'Constitutional Changes in the Candidate Countries', paper delivered at the Cambridge Enlargement Conference (12–13 July 2002).

averted by increasing the danger of undermining popular acceptance of accession in the East.[120]

Consider next the perspective of the enlarged EU as a whole. Do the transitional provisions on free movement for CEEC workers really undermine the credibility of an egalitarian model of Union citizenship? The main problem with this critique is that, even as regards nationals of the existing Member States, free movement rights vary according to distinctions drawn by the Treaty itself, under secondary legislation passed by the Community institutions, and through the caselaw of the Court — distinctions based on nationality, economic worth and financial status — whereby (as we have seen) some of the least wealthy and most vulnerable members of society are excluded from rights to free movement and residency across the EU.[121] At worst, the CEEC accessions will further entrench the current practice of differentiated 'fundamental rights' for Union citizens. And the latter is no spectre set to be exorcised after seven years, but a reality likely to persist for the foreseeable future.

[120] Consider, eg Commission Report on explaining Europe's Enlargement, COM(2002) 281 Final; though cf. Press Release IP/02/1682 (15 November 2002). Note also that the CEECs may have accepted transitional restrictions on the free movement of workers as a bargaining tool to secure concessions on issues of more pressing social and economic concern such as free movement of capital: see, eg M Pechstein and P Kubicki, 'The Legal Framework of Accession to the European Union' (2001) 25 *Polish Yearbook of International Law* 197; H Grabbe, *Profiting From EU Enlargement*, Centre for European Reform, London, 2001.

[121] See Section II (above). For another perspective, consider H Stalford, 'The Impact of Enlargement on Free Movement: A Critique of Transitional Periods' (paper presented at the *Third Meeting of the UACES Study Group on EU Migration Law and Policy*, 5 December 2003). Available via www.liv.ac.uk/ewc.

7

The Financial and Budgetary Impact of Enlargement and Accession

ALAN MAYHEW*

I. INTRODUCTION

AT THE END of every European Union accession negotiation, there is a fight about finance. Yet finance is by no means the most important element of the negotiations. Matters affecting the vital interests of new and old members like the free movement of labour or the representation of the new member state in the institutions of the Union are usually far more important in the longer term. But it is easier for politicians to talk to voters about money than about policy.

The budgetary negotiations in this first enlargement to the countries of central and eastern Europe were perhaps more important in that these are relatively poor countries compared to the Union average per capita gross domestic product. They all will have to invest heavily in transport and environmental infrastructure in the coming decades in order to catch up with the standards of the EU-15 and support higher economic growth and development. Assuming responsible macro-economic policy in the new Member States, EU budgetary transfers can speed up this investment process considerably, allowing these countries to catch up with the old Member States in terms of per capita income more quickly.

Higher transfers to the new Member States means of course larger net budgetary contributions for the old Member States (EU-15). This comes at a time when budget deficits are high and rising throughout the EURO-zone and when Member States are making politically controversial cuts in social spending. The fiscal discipline involved in membership of the monetary union and implementation of the Broad Economic Policy Guidelines therefore means that the existing Member States of the Union

* Sussex European Institute, University of Sussex.

are not keen to see their net budgetary position with Brussels deteriorate or even their gross contributions to the budget rise.

This chapter investigates the background to the budget negotiations and the political economy behind them.

II. AGENDA 2000 AND THE BERLIN FINANCIAL FRAMEWORK

The European Commission had been asked by the Madrid European Council of 1995 to report on the impact of enlargement with specific reference to the structural funds and agriculture as well as to give its opinions on the applications for membership of the candidate countries. It was also invited to report on the next financial framework for the period 2000–06. It reported on all these issues in mid-1997, in a series of documents collectively called Agenda 2000.

The Commission proposal was determined by financial prudence and an intention to demonstrate to the existing Member States that the budgetary cost of enlargement would not be as high as most of them would expect. Budgetary prudence was necessary as most Member States were preparing to enter the third stage of monetary union. The attempt to demonstrate that the cost of enlargement would not be exorbitant reflected perhaps the Commission's desire to push ahead quickly with enlargement. It was however also its first proposal for the negotiating position vis-à-vis the candidate countries.

Agenda 2000 assumed that six countries (the 'Luxembourg Group' consisting of the Czech Republic, Cyprus, Estonia, Hungary, Poland and Slovenia) would join the Union in 2002.

In policy terms, the Commission proposed significant reforms to both main areas of budgetary expenditure, the Common Agricultural Policy and the Structural Funds.

In agriculture, Agenda 2000 proposed reforms to policy in several product areas and in the organisation of rural development support. These proposals were intended to take forward the reforms begun in the early nineteen-nineties, in response to the needs of the WTO Uruguay Round. Price reductions in the cereals and beef sectors and to a lesser degree in milk, were to be compensated by increasing direct income subsidies to the farmers affected in the move from price subsidies to income subsidies.

In Agenda 2000 the Commission took a decision with respect to enlargement which was to plague relations and the accession negotiations up to the very end. It was proposed not to pay these direct income subsidies to farmers in the new Member States in the 2000–06 financial framework. The Commission thus proposed a competitive distortion in the internal market, when normally as guardian of the treaties it is supposed to work towards the elimination of such distortions. With direct income subsidies becoming the predominant form of subsidy in the CAP, this allowed a major saving in the resources required for enlargement.[1]

It is true that the Commission proposed some additional funds for rural development in the new Member States, but this brought expenditure on the CAP in the new Member States to only just under EUR two billion in 2002 rising to almost EUR four billion in 2006 compared to annual expenditure in the old Member States of above EUR 40 billion.

The Commission also proposed a reform of the structural funds (including the Cohesion Fund) with a concentration of the available resources on the most needy areas and a graduating out of areas which had per capita GDP above 75 per cent of that in the Union. It further proposed a maximum level of transfers from the structural funds to Member States of four per cent of national GDP. It thus maintained a level of expenditure over the whole period of below 0.46 per cent of the EU's GDP.

The limitation on the level of transfers looked reasonable, partly because a transfer of more than 4 per cent of GDP had never been exceeded in the history of the funds and partly because very large transfers are difficult to manage in the context of a stability-oriented macro-economic policy. But of course the new Member States would be relatively far poorer than even Greece and Ireland when they joined the Union and with massive investment deficits in transport and environmental infra-structure. Four per cent of a very low GDP is also a fairly limited resource for major developments. While there is certainly no danger in the short-run that the new Member States will be capable of using more than this, in the longer run there may be a case for making this limit flexible under certain circumstances.

The Commission therefore proposed structural funds financing for the period 2000–06 for the old Member States which in real terms would decline over the period as regions were progressively excluded from financing. Financing of the new Member States was expected to grow steadily to 2006, at which point it would amount to around a third of the total structural fund spending.

To prepare the candidate countries for accession, Agenda 2000 proposed a doubling of pre-accession aid. This additional financing (EUR 1.5 billion annually) would be spent through a pre-accession structural fund (ISPA) and an agricultural structural improvement fund (SAPARD).

On the own resources side of the budget, the Commission assumed that the new Member States would contribute fully to own resources from the first day of their accession. This became an essential part of the Union's negotiating tactics. By refusing any concession on the own

[1] The proposal not to pay these subsidies was supported by a series of arguments, which did not stand up to even preliminary analysis. It was difficult to explain why such subsidies were good for agriculture in the old Member States but not in the new. If the intention was to reduce and eventually eliminate direct subsidies in the Union as a whole, the position could have been rationalised, but no such intention apparently existed.

resources side of the budget, the candidate countries were constrained to negotiate only on the expenditure side and therefore within the limits of the Berlin Financial Framework

The Berlin European Council meeting in March 1999 modified the Commission's proposals but maintained the main elements with respect to the financing of enlargement (Table 1). Although the economic situation was only just beginning to turn down, the third stage of monetary union had introduced a new discipline and an increased reluctance to see growth in spending through the EU budget.

Maintaining the same assumptions about the date of accession and the number of countries involved, the Berlin European Council reduced the overall level of budgetary financing for the enlarged Union. This was the result of delaying some of the agricultural reforms proposed by the Commission and marginally reducing the available finance to the structural funds.

The Berlin Council reaffirmed that direct income subsidies would not be paid to farmers in the new Member States and that structural funds transfers to all Member States would be limited to four per cent of the recipient country's GDP. It also accepted the Commission's proposals on pre-accession aid. All expenditure on accession (excluding pre-accession aid) was 'ringfenced' in the Berlin financial framework. This implied that expenditure on accession could not be increased by transferring funds from other headings and that any surplus funds from enlargement could not be used for other purposes. It reaffirmed that the new Member States would be expected to contribute fully to own resources from the first day of accession.

The result was that in terms of appropriations for payments the financial framework would remain well below the own resources ceiling of 1.27 per cent of GDP throughout the whole period. Indeed the maximum level of planned spending fell from 1.13 per cent of GNP in 2000 to 1.09 per cent in 2006. Expenditure on enlargement in 2006 was planned to rise to 13.7 per cent of total EU payments.

The agreed financial framework was good news for the old Member States. Enlargement could proceed while at the same time expenditure would remain well under control. The margin below the own resources ceiling remained so large that it could absorb any likely shock such as slower economic growth or unexpected additional expenditure.

The financial framework was inserted in the Inter-Institutional Agreement 2000–06 agreed between the Council, the European Parliament and the Commission.[2] As a legally binding agreement, the financial framework can not be fundamentally changed without the approval of all

[2] Interinstitutional Agreement of 6 May 1999 between the European Parliament, the Council and the Commission on budgetary discipline and improvement of the budgetary procedure, OJ 1999 C172/1.

parties to the Inter-Institutional Agreement, although small adjustments and changes made for technical reasons are allowed, all sides feared the reopening of the Berlin agreement because of the unlikely chance of obtaining the agreement of all parties to a significant change. It became therefore the unbreachable framework within which the enlargement was to take place. By the end even the candidate countries realised that there was no hope of changing the financial framework and they concentrated instead on ensuring that the resources it contained for enlargement were utilised fully.

In the end technical adjustments had to be made to correct the assumptions on which Berlin was based: ten countries will join in May 2004 rather than six in 2002. But the overall financial framework remained unchallenged until the end of the negotiations.

III. THE ACCESSION NEGOTIATIONS

Finance and budget settlements are always the last steps in any enlargement negotiation. This enlargement was no exception to this rule. This meant that neither the Member States of the EU nor its institutions concentrated on the financial aspects of enlargement until towards the end of the negotiations.

However negotiations on some chapters of the acquis had clear financial implications. This was particularly the case in the agricultural chapter.

Table 1: Financial Framework EU-21

EUR million — 1999 prices — Appropriations for commitments	**2000**	**2001**	**2002**	**2003**	**2004**	**2005**	**2006**
1. AGRICULTURE	**40920**	**42800**	**43900**	**43770**	**42760**	**41930**	**41660**
CAP expenditure (excluding rural development)	36620	38480	39570	39430	38410	37570	37290
Rural development and accompanying measures	4300	4320	4330	4340	4350	4360	4370
2. STRUCTURAL OPERATIONS	**32045**	**31455**	**30865**	**30285**	**29595**	**29595**	**29170**
Structural Funds	29430	28840	28250	27670	27080	27080	26660
Cohesion Fund	2615	2615	2615	2615	2515	2515	2510
3. INTERNAL POLICIES	**5900**	**5950**	**6000**	**6050**	**6100**	**6150**	**6200**
4. EXTERNAL ACTION	**4550**	**4560**	**4570**	**4580**	**4590**	**4600**	**4610**
5. ADMINISTRATION	**4560**	**4600**	**4700**	**4800**	**4900**	**5000**	**5100**
6. RESERVES	**900**	**900**	**650**	**400**	**400**	**400**	**400**
Monetary reserve	500	500	250	0	0	0	0

Continued....

Table 1 Continued....

EUR million — 1999 prices — Appropriations for commitments	2000	2001	2002	2003	2004	2005	2006
Emergency aid reserve	200	200	200	200	200	200	200
Guarantee reserve	200	200	200	200	200	200	200
7. PRE-ACCESSION AID	**3.120**	**3.120**	**3.120**	**3.120**	**3.120**	**3.120**	**3.120**
Agriculture	520	520	520	520	520	520	520
Pre-accession structural instrument	1.040	1.040	1.040	1.040	1.040	1.040	1.040
PHARE (applicant countries)	1.560	1.560	1.560	1.560	1.560	1.560	1.560
8. ENLARGEMENT			**6.450**	**9.030**	**11.610**	**14.200**	**16.780**
Agriculture			1.600	2.030	2.450	2.930	3.400
Structural operations			3.750	5.830	7.920	10.000	12.080
Internal policies			730	760	790	820	850
Administration			370	410	450	450	450
TOTAL APPROPRIATIONS FOR COMMITMENTS	**91995**	**93385**	**100255**	**102035**	**103075**	**104995**	**107040**
TOTAL APPROPRIATIONS FOR PAYMENTS	**89590**	**91070**	**98270**	**101450**	**100610**	**101350**	**103530**
of which: enlargement			*4.140*	*6.710*	*8.890*	*11.440*	*14.210*
Appropriations for payments as % of GNP	1,13%	1,12%	1,14%	1,15%	1,11%	1,09%	1,09%
Margin	0,14%	0,15%	0,13%	0,12%	0,16%	0,18%	0,18%
Own resources ceiling	**1,27%**	**1,27%**	**1,27%**	**1,27%**	**1,27%**	**1,27%**	**1,27%**

Source: EU Interinstitutional Agreement, May 1999

Negotiations were opened in June 2000 but the EU common position on the financial questions related to agriculture was not finally decided until after the Brussels European Council in October 2002. This delay meant that negotiations on non-financial questions in agriculture also progressed more slowly. Pressure on the Union Member States from the candidate countries increased as frustration began to build. Finally the Commission produced the first official paper on financial matters since the agreement on the Berlin financial framework at the end of January 2002.[3]

A. The Commission's Information Note

The Commission's information note made a first attempt to present a realistic adjustment to the Berlin Financial Framework, using the assumption

[3] European Commission, Information Note: Common Financial Framework 2004–06 for the Accession Negotiations, SEC(2002) 102.

of the accession of ten countries on 1 January 2004. Here the Commission tried to steer a course between a hard line (consisting of saying that one should assume for 2004–06 the same figures found in Berlin for 2002–04, adjusted for ten rather than six countries) and a soft line (assuming that the 2004–06 Berlin figures should be retained and adjusted upwards for the larger number of countries), at the risk of pleasing no one.

The Commission's information note proposed significant changes in the negotiating position of the Union, without however breaching the Berlin financial framework.

The Commission went some way towards helping the candidate countries. Perhaps the most prominent policy change was the proposal to pay farmers in central and eastern Europe direct income subsidies. The Commission suggested that subsidies should be paid on a sliding scale starting with 25 per cent of the level in the old Member States in 2004 and rising in steps to reach parity in 2013.

The policy arguments on the EU side which had been used previously were apparently now no longer valid and the matter became a simple battle over the level of finance. Payment of 25 per cent of the EU-15 level of subsidy was estimated to cost an additional EUR1.2 billion. The reimbursement would only occur first in 2005 as payments are made in the year following the budget year in which the subsidies are allocated.

This proposal opened up the discussion about what level of subsidy was appropriate; at the same time it did nothing to defuse the argument about competitive distortions between the old and new members.

The Commission also sought to be helpful to the new Member States with improved proposals on finance for rural development. This included a higher rate of Community co-financing, the extension of the use of differentiated appropriations allowing for slower absorption in the new Member States, a higher proportion of Cohesion Fund spending in total structural fund allocations and measures to help with the restructuring of semi-subsistence farms.

The proposal to increase the size of Cohesion Fund spending to a third of total structural spending had the advantage of simplifying the procedure for using the funds and reducing slightly the proportion of national co-financing. These changes would not impact on the global financing of accession in the first years of membership up to 2006, though they would increase actual payments made in this period — but these are unlikely to reach the budgeted payments level.

The Commission also proposed specific financial transfers to co-finance the closure of the Ignalina nuclear power plant in Lithuania, the decommissioning of the Bohunice plant in the Slovak Republic and to finance development in the northern part of Cyprus.

A further significant concession was that the Commission proposed that no new Member State should be worse off in the first year of accession than in the last year of pre-accession. The early calculations of several of the candidate countries had suggested that they might indeed be net contributors to the EU budget in the first years of membership. The insistence of the Union on the payment of full contributions to own resources from the first day of accession combined with the expected slow absorption of structural funds and the refusal of the Union to pay direct income subsidies to farmers meant that in some cases the net contribution of the new Member States would have been very significant. This would have been indeed a very strange result for countries which on average have only around 40 per cent of the per capita GDP (at PPS) of the Union.

The Commission proposed that there should be a reserve created in the amended financial framework for 2004–06, which could be used for granting lump-sum budgetary transfers to countries which were threatened with becoming net contributors. It suggested that this reserve should remain within the overall margin of the Berlin framework and could amount to around EUR 800 million annually.

The new Member States had requested reductions to their own resources contributions in line with the expected slow build-up in the receipt of EU transfers. The Commission and the Member States, on the other hand, were adamant that any compensation given to the new Member States should be on the expenditure side of the budget rather than the own resources side. This reflected worries about opening a major discussion on the British budget rebate and on the Commission's preference to have a system which would be clear and limited in time; the arrangements agreed for Spain and Portugal had led to progressively smaller adjustments in the budget stretching over many years and were a budgetary nuisance. The idea to grant lump sum compensatory payments was to play an important role in the preparation of the final negotiation on the financial package.

B. The Methodology of Calculating Net Budgetary Balances

The proposal of the Commission to ensure that no new member state should become a net contributor to the EU budget in its first year of membership required a methodology to calculate expected net balances (payments appropriations). This was provided by the Commission in a note passed originally to the candidate countries in May 2002.

The Commission decided to propose an approximation to individual new member state budgetary balances on the basis of this methodology and to base lump sum compensatory payments on these estimates without any ex-post rectification. It became important therefore for the candidate countries to ensure that the estimates of receipts from the EU budget were as low as possible, in order to increase the size of the lump sum transfers.

The methodology proposed by the Commission on the expenditure side of the budget consisted of a set of assumptions concerning the absorption rate of both the remaining pre-accession funds and the agricultural, structural and other payments to which the new Member States would have access after accession. These assumptions were obviously contestable. Estimates of gross contributions to own resources were somewhat easier and less contestable, though still approximate.

The resulting preliminary calculations made by the Commission suggested that indeed the Czech Republic, Cyprus, Malta and Slovenia might be net contributors to the budget in 2004, while in addition Hungary might be worse off in 2004 than in 2003. Cyprus, Malta and Slovenia were calculated as being net contributors throughout the whole period 2004–06, while the Czech Republic was expected to still be worse off in 2005 than in 2003.

However the calculated amounts needed to ensure that all new Member States would be as well off in 2004 than in 2003 by no means exhausted the EUR 800 million suggested in the Commission's January 2002 paper. Hence both commitment and payment appropriations might be reduced even below the January figure.

C. The Brussels European Council and the EU Common Position on Financial and Budgetary Provisions

The proposals of the Commission remained simply proposals until the European Council meeting in Brussels on 24–25. October 2002. Several of the Member States had indicated that they could not agree to paying any level of direct income subsidy to farmers in the new Member States as this had been excluded in the agreement on the Berlin Financial Framework in 1999.

The debate went beyond the question of enlargement to that of the future of the Common Agricultural Policy (see below), with the net contributors to the EU budget on one side, against the countries which receive large agricultural subsidies from Brussels, notably France and Ireland. In the perverse way in which negotiations sometimes move, the countries most in favour of enlargement, Germany, Sweden, the Netherlands and the UK were against paying direct income subsidies to the new Member States because this would slow down the reform of the whole CAP, while countries traditionally less positive about enlargement, France and Ireland, were in favour of paying some level of subsidy as a guarantee that subsidies would continue in the longer term.

The Brussels European Council agreed to the Commission's January proposal on direct income subsidies, while at the same time agreeing that budgetary expenditure on market support and direct income subsidies in the period 2007–13 could not rise by more than 1 per cent per year in nominal terms over the level reached in 2006.

On the other hand the Council cut the proposed commitment appropriations for structural funds reserved for enlargement over the period 2004–06 from EUR 25.5 billion proposed by the Commission in its January note to EUR 23 billion. This was generally thought to be a tactical move to make room for concessions later in the negotiations.

This position was then confirmed in the EU Common Position on financial and budgetary provisions, agreed on 8 November 2002, which also approved the Commission's, slightly modified, methodology for calculating budgetary balances.

The candidate countries were then left with just one month in which to negotiate both the financial chapter and to finish the agricultural chapter.

D. The Negotiations at the Copenhagen European Council, December 2002

Negotiations after the adoption of the EU Common Position moved into a hectic phase, with a considerable amount of 'back-of-the-envelope' adjustments. Pressure on all sides was intense. As the economic downturn intensified, the Member States were under considerable pressure to restrict the 'cost' of the enlargement to a minimum. Yet they were also under pressure to help the new Member States, where even some of the toughest Member State negotiators realised that there was both a risk of serious budgetary crisis after accession and even possibly a refusal by the people to vote for accession in the referenda. The candidate countries' political leaders had by this time also realised that they faced a political crisis if the financial terms of accession were not improved and this situation even led at last to some coordination of positions between the candidate countries.

To break through the mounting confusion, the Danish Presidency of the Union proposed its own financial package, including detailed proposals for each candidate country. These packages were discussed in COREPER for the first time on 25 November only two weeks before the Copenhagen European Council.

The key new elements with respect to the EU Common Position were:

— Accession would now not take place in January 2004 but in May 2004. This would change very little in terms of receipts from the EU but would save the new Member States four months of contributions to own resources and therefore remove any remaining doubts about the budgetary balance being positive in the first year of membership.

— The possibility of 'topping up' direct income subsidies using funds reserved for rural development. The maximum level of subsidy in 2004, including this topping up, would be to 40 per cent of the level in the EU-15.
— The introduction of a 'Schengen facility' to finance the strengthening of the new external border of the Union
— A decision on the size of lump sum budgetary compensation for individual candidate countries
— It conceded certain specific national requests, such as reduced VAT rates on existing housing until 2007 in Poland and the hunting of Lynx in Latvia as well as the major transfers for nuclear decommissioning in Lithuania and Slovakia.

However the package only marginally increased the reference levels for certain agricultural products, which were a main area of discord between the negotiating parties.

The overall impact of the Danish proposals was to increase the level of commitments above the agreement in Brussels but the level in each of the three years 2004–06 remained below that suggested by the Commission in its January note and therefore below the Commission's interpretation of the Berlin Financial Framework. In payments the Danish proposal was well below the January package in all three years. The main reasons for this was the reduction at the Brussels Council of structural funds commitments by EUR 2.5 billion and the technical adjustments to the Commission's methodology for calculating budget balances, which reduced projected EU transfers in the first year of membership especially, thereby leaving more room for lump sum budgetary grants to be paid. The Danish proposal also raised considerably the payments for decommissioning nuclear facilities, both with respect to the January paper and the General Affairs Council proposals attached to the Presidency Conclusions at the Brussels European Council.

The potential budgetary problems faced by the new Member States in the first years of membership were by now understood by the Commission and many of the Member States. The Danish Presidency left open the question of lump sum payments to the new Member States in the first year of membership, although these were already more or less agreed in principle. The Schengen facility was also a direct subsidy to the budgets of the candidates, as this represented expenditure which would otherwise have to be met by the national budgets.

The negotiations at the Copenhagen European Council on 13–14 December 2002 concluded the financial negotiations, although leaving certain points unclear.[4]

[4] These unclear points were not so minor; the Polish Government discovered that part of the deal on topping up direct income subsidies for farmers, which had been negotiated at the Copenhagen summit, was ruled illegal by EU lawyers working on the Accession Treaty.

Overall the Copenhagen financial package was modest; modest in relation to expectations several years earlier; modest in relation to the Berlin Financial Framework; even modest in relation to the Commission's proposal in January 2002.

Table 2: Commitments and Payments Appropriations for Enlargement, 2004–2006

2004–2006	Berlin FF	Commission Jan 2002	Copenhagen
Commitments	42590	40160*	40952**
Payments	34550	28019*	27875**

* not including lump sum compensation payments
** including EUR 3.285 billion lump sum payments

However significant changes were made within the overall package, which made it more acceptable to the candidate countries.

— Except in Cyprus and Slovenia, the possibility of topping up direct income payments from both rural development allocations and from national tax sources up to a maximum total level of 55 per cent in 2004, rising to 65 per cent in 2006, was agreed. This of course meant no change in the overall financial package in terms of commitments, though it will raise payments appropriations. It also means that the phasing in period to 2013 was retained against opposition from several of the candidate countries.
— An increase in the level of the Schengen facility for certain countries bringing the total facility to almost EUR 750 million over the three years.
— The possibility for Poland and the Czech Republic to transfer commitments from the structural funds into budgetary subsidies in 2005 and 2006 — in the Polish case EUR one billion; EUR 100 million for the Czech Republic.
— Confirmation of the temporary budget compensation facility amounting to almost EUR 1.1 billion for 2004–06.
— Agreement to raise the reference levels for some agricultural products; these were important concessions for some of the candidate countries but with limited financial significance overall.

The negotiations at the Copenhagen European Council were essentially between the Polish delegation and the Union, the former being by far the largest candidate country and the most strident negotiator. The other candidates had nothing to lose in this system, as they received almost by right whatever the Polish delegation managed to negotiate for itself. The Council was therefore characterised by loud histrionics and many 'final offers'. The candidate countries needed a success as the start for the referendum campaigns on EU accession, while for the Union it was important to show financial prudence with responsibility for the European re-unification process.

The final Copenhagen commitment appropriations were as follows:

Table 3: Copenhagen Financial Settlement (Commitment Appropriations)

Maximum enlargement-related appropriations for commitments 2004–2006 (for ten new Member States)	**(EUR mio. 1999 prices)**		
	2004	**2005**	**2006**
Heading 1 Agriculture	1.897	3.747	4.147
Of which:			
1a — Common Agricultural Policy	327	2.032	2.322
1b — Rural development	1.570	1.715	1.825
Heading 2 Structural actions after capping	6.095	6.940	8.812
Of which:			
Structural fund	3.478	4.788	5.990
Cohesion Fund	2.617	2.152	2.822
Heading 3 Internal Policies and additional transitional expenditure	1.421	1.376	1.351
Of which:			
Existing policies	882	917	952
Transitional Nuclear safety measures	125	125	125
Transitional Institution building measures	200	120	60
Transitional Schengen measures	286	286	286
Heading 5 Administration	503	558	612
Total Maximum Appropriations for commitments (Heading 1, 2, 3 and 5)	9.952	12.657	14.958

In addition the following budgetary subsidy commitments were made:

Heading X (special cash-flow facility and temporary budgetary compensation) 2004–06 (for ten new Member States)	**(EUR mio. 1999 prices)**		
	2004	**2005**	**2006**
Special cash-flow facility	998	650	550
Temporary budgetary compensation	262	479	346

Source: Danish Presidency Conclusions, December 2002, Copenhagen

The conclusion of the Copenhagen European Council was a truly historic moment in post-Cold War Europe. It was not the moment to undertake a cool analysis of the outcome.

IV. AN ANALYSIS OF THE FINAL OUTCOME

A rough summary of the outcome of the negotiations on the financial settlement would be that it might not be ideal for the new Member States in the short-term, but that it is a good deal for the longer term. For the EU the judgment would be reversed: the long term is uncertain but the short-term deal is rather good. But from the point of view of the enlarged EU-25 as a whole, the deal leaves many questions unanswered.

Table 3 shows the short-term (2004–06) outcome of the negotiations as far as the EU budget is concerned. Table 4 attempts a longer term view of the EU budget to 2013. Table 5 shows the net balances for the new Member States.

A. The Impact on the EU-15

The impact of the final settlement on the budget of the Union between 2004 and 2006 will be relatively limited. Total commitments for enlargement over this period were agreed at EUR 40.9 billion (all figures at 1999 prices). Payments appropriations for the new Member States are expected to reach around EUR 27.9 billion, though this may be based on an optimistic assumption about absorption capacity. Estimated contributions to own resources from the new Member States will amount to EUR 14.7 billion. The net cost in payments to the EU budget between 2004–06 will therefore be only EUR 13 billion or around four per cent of total budget spending in these years.

The European Union therefore achieved its objective of reducing enlargement expenditure to a minimum during the current financial framework period. Appropriations for payment in the 2003 budget reached only 1.02 per cent of gross national income of the Union at almost exactly EUR 100 billion. The gross payments cost of enlargement will raise this by around 8 per cent, other expenditure remaining constant and payments in terms of gross national income will rise to around 1.04 per cent of GNI well below the upper limit for payments appropriations of 1.27 per cent of GNP.

The negotiations at Copenhagen changed very little in financial terms. The agreement to transfer some structural fund commitments and payments into budgetary subsidies for Poland and the Czech Republic will increase payments marginally in 2005 and 2006, but only to the extent that structural fund payments assumed an unrealistically high rate of absorption.

The most significant change in policy terms was undoubtedly the acceptance of the payment of direct income subsidies to farmers in the new Member States, which was agreed at the Brussels European Council in October 2002, and the Copenhagen concession that these could be topped up using rural settlement funds and national taxation. These decisions, apart from destroying the policy arguments against paying full income subsidies to farmers in the new Member States, are significant for the debate on the future of the CAP.

In the *longer term*, the financial agreement will lead to significant additional spending by the Union. If the future enlargement to Bulgaria, Romania and possibly Croatia is included as from 2007, the budgetary spending in 2013 should nevertheless still be well within the limit of 1.27 per cent of GNP in the Union (Table 4). The enlargement to Turkey should also lie within this period but this has not been included in these calculations.

The calculation presented in table 4 is rather rough but gives an idea of the possible development over the next financial perspective. It assumes the following:

— Economic growth in real terms in the old EU-15 expands by two per cent per year and in the new Member States by four per cent.
— By 2013 the new Member States (including Romania, Bulgaria and Croatia) will be receiving direct income subsidies to farmers at the same level as those in the EU-15.
— By 2013 they will also be absorbing four per cent of their GDP in structural fund payments.
— The current pre-accession payments are assumed to continue, but at a lower rate, being paid to the three candidate countries mentioned above. But they will cease prior to 2013.
— EU-25 expenditure on agriculture follows the formula agreed at the Brussels European Council in October 2003.
— Structural fund expenditure remains at 0.45 per cent of EU-GDP throughout the period.
— Other policies grow faster than GDP and average three per cent growth per year.
— Commitments appropriations and payments are assumed identical in 2013.

This calculation may underestimate spending in the Union. The agreement reached on CAP spending at the Brussels European Council limiting growth to 1 per cent in nominal terms from 2006 on, does not limit rural development spending. This could grow rapidly as direct aid for agriculture is complemented by growing assistance for rural areas. The pressure to relax the 0.45 per cent of GDP limit on structural fund spending may lead to some increase in this level, though no doubt the main contributors to the EU budget will be attempting to hold the line. The assumption that the real rate of growth of 'other policies' will be three per cent per annum may be conservative, above all on foreign policy and foreign aid and on justice and home affairs. Nevertheless as a central hypothesis in a period of considerable uncertainty, the assumptions on which table 4 are based look reasonable.

On these assumptions, the gross 'cost' of enlargement to the EU-15 in 2013 (in prices of 2003) will be roughly EUR 48 billion or just over 0.4 per cent of the EU-15 GDP. The net cost (gross cost less contributions to own resources) is likely to be around EUR 36 million or 0.3 per cent of EU-15 GDP. This is substantial but considerably less than many had imagined just a few years ago.

Table 4 shows that, on these assumptions, the EU budget in 2013 may still be well below the own resources limit of 1.27 per cent. It is likely to be of the order of 1.07 per cent of GDP.

Table 4: Schematic Budget Scenario EU Budget Scenario for 2013
(EUR bn; prices 2003)

	2003	2006	2013
GDP of EU-15 ass. 2% real growth	9558	10143	11651
GDP of EU-10/12 ass. 4% real growth	420	472	711
Enlargement costs — commitments: Total		15.8	48.5
— CAP (full DIS)+rural dev		4.1	14
— Structural funds (4% of GDP)		8.8	32
— Internal policies and admin.		2.0	2.5
— Budget transfers		0.9	0
Pm Pre-accession aid		1.4	0
Commitments EU-25/27	99.7		131.7
Payments as % of GDP	1.02	1.06	1.07
pmbudget contributions of EU-10		5.5	8

Source: own calculations

B. The Impact on the New Member States

Table 5 shows the final outcome of the negotiations for the ten candidate countries for the period 2004–06.

During this short term period two earlier worries are somewhat relieved. None of the new Member States will be net contributors in the first years of membership and most if not all of the countries will almost

Table 5: Net balances agreed at Copenhagen European Council

	CY	CZ	EE	HU	PL	SI	LT	LV	SK	MT	TOTAL
2003											
pre-accession aid	16	170	55	197	844	45	115	84	123	11	1,661
pre-accession aid in % of GNI	*0.13%*	*0.21%*	*0.77%*	*0.29%*	*0.40%*	*0.18%*	*0.75%*	*0.90%*	*0.44%*	*0.26%*	*0.36%*
2004	CY	CZ	EE	HU	PL	SI	LT	LV	SK	MT	TOTAL
total allocated expenditure	131	801	181	824	2,983	267	423	264	398	70	6,343
total own resources	-105	-623	-56	-554	-1,579	-187	-124	-70	-225	-43	-3,566
Net balance	27	178	125	270	1,404	80	299	195	173	26	2,777
Net balance in % of GNI	*0.21%*	*0.20%*	*1.61%*	*0.37%*	*0.60%*	*0.29%*	*1.82%*	*1.93%*	*0.56%*	*0.56%*	*0.55%*
% increase of net balance compared to 2003	*69%*	*5%*	*126%*	*37%*	*66%*	*76%*	*160%*	*133%*	*41%*	*130%*	*67%*
2005	CY	CZ	EE	HU	PL	SI	LT	LV	SK	MT	TOTAL
total allocated expenditure	191	1,255	266	1,342	5,068	370	674	402	647	119	10,334
total own resources	-160	-963	-86	-853	-2,454	-288	-191	-107	-350	-66	-5,518
Net balance	31	293	179	490	2,614	82	483	295	297	53	4,816

Continued….

Table 5 Continued....

	CY	CZ	EE	HU	PL	SI	LT	LV	SK	MT	TOTAL
Net balance in % of GNI	*0.24%*	*0.31%*	*2.23%*	*0.64%*	*1.08%*	*0.29%*	*2.83%*	*2.81%*	*0.92%*	*1.08%*	*0.92%*
% increase of net balance compared to 2003	*94%*	*72%*	*225%*	*148%*	*210%*	*81%*	*319%*	*252%*	*142%*	*363%*	*190%*
2006	**CY**	**CZ**	**EE**	**HU**	**PL**	**SI**	**LT**	**LV**	**SK**	**MT**	**TOTAL**
total allocated expenditure	**194**	**1,294**	**288**	**1,487**	**5,498**	**378**	**766**	**451**	**720**	**121**	**11,198**
total own resources	**-163**	**-988**	**-89**	**-873**	**-2,519**	**-296**	**-196**	**-110**	**-359**	**-68**	**-5,660**
Net balance	**31**	**307**	**200**	**614**	**2,979**	**82**	**570**	**341**	**361**	**53**	**5,538**
Net balance in % of GNI	*0.23%*	*0.32%*	*2.39%*	*0.78%*	*1.18%*	*0.28%*	*3.21%*	*3.12%*	*1.08%*	*1.03%*	*1.01%*
% increase of net balance compared to 2003	*94%*	*80%*	*263%*	*211%*	*253%*	*81%*	*395%*	*307%*	*194%*	*364%*	*233%*

(Source: EU Commission, December 2002–1999 prices)

certainly be better off in net terms in the first year of membership than in the last pre-accession year. It is still possible that the Czech Republic and even Hungary may not be better off in 2004, as the Table 5 calculations depend on assumptions about absorption capacity, which have to be realised. However the level of assumed payments has been reduced considerably since the first estimates were made at the beginning of 2002 and the figures now included are essentially advances which will be received in any case (though held in blocked accounts).

The results for 2004 show lower contributions to own resources and lower receipts than were expected some time ago. The lower contributions are the result of the delay in accession to 1 May 2004, with a saving of four months, contributions. The delay in the planned accession did not lead to any real problems for either party in the enlargement, allowing the financial position of the new Member States to be marginally improved and leaving some more time for ratification of the Accession Treaty. The low level of receipts is partly a result of direct income subsidies being received in the budget year after that in which they are paid out.

By 2006 all the new Member States should be comfortably net beneficiaries, although the size of the transfers as a percentage of GDP will differ considerably. The three small Baltic Republics have come out of the negotiations best on this basis. In the case of Lithuania it is a result partly of the special allowance made for the decommissioning of the Ignalina nuclear power plant, which was a specific demand of the EU and which will have severe economic and social implications for Lithuania. It is also understood that Lithuania will receive financial support for the solution of the Kaliningrad transit problem. The Baltic Republics are assumed to be able to absorb structural funds relatively quickly, have considerable agricultural populations but are relatively poor and therefore contribute somewhat less on the GDP key to own resources than some of the other countries.

At the other end of the scale are Slovenia and the Czech Republic, both of which have relatively modest agricultural sectors and have higher GDP per capita than the other candidate countries.

Poland, with over half of the population of all the new Member States together, will enjoy over half of the total net balance of the new Member States during this first period of membership. However this will have been achieved at the cost of the transfer of EUR one billion from the structural funds to a budgetary transfer, as mentioned above.

1. *Will there be a Budget Crisis in the First Years of Membership?*

The major question which hangs over all the new Member States is whether the budget settlement at Copenhagen will stave off a budgetary crisis in the first few years of membership. The answer cannot be generalised as the budgetary situation in the new Member States varies considerably.

For the national budget, the calculation of a country's net position with respect to the EU budget is important but not the whole story. While most of the political commentary has been on the net position of the new Member States, here we attempt to analyse the impact on the general government budget.

At least four elements of the accession process will affect the national budgetary process severely:

— The implementation of the acquis communautaire in the first years of membership will put a significant burden on the budget. In many areas investment and additional operating costs will not be able to be pushed through to the final consumer and will have to be borne by the state budget. This applies particularly to the environmental acquis but changes in other areas will also lead to additional spending.
— The receipt of structural funds implies the availability of national co-financing. While this will be lower in the cohesion funds, it may reach 30 per cent or more in the classic structural funds area. It is of course true that expenditure for infrastructure would eventually have to be made available, and in part at least from the national budget. Nevertheless accession will force the new Member States to make money available from the budget, unless of course they refuse to accept the available structural funds.
— The contribution to the EU budget will cost national budgets in the new Member States over EUR 5 billion annually — roughly 1.5 per cent of GDP and around six per cent of Government budgetary revenues. On the other hand many of the payments which will flow to the new Member States from the EU will be paid directly to final beneficiaries and other non-government agencies rather than to the budget.
— Some budgetary transfers must be pre-financed by the state budget and are recouped only later from the Union. This is particularly the case with direct income subsidies, where there is a six month delay in reimbursements.

These questions have been researched for Lithuania by Rasa Spokeviciute.[5] She concludes that the additional budgetary spending provoked by accession to the Union in 2004 will be of the order of ten per cent of 2003

[5] R Spokeviciute, 'The Impact of the EU membership on the Lithuanian budget', SEI working paper No 63, 2003.

budgetary revenues. This calculation does not include the costs of implementing new EU acquis.

Table 6: Impact of Accession on the Polish General Government Budget, 2004–06 (EUR bn. 1999 Prices)

	financial flows with EU			total expenditure			budgetary impact		
	2004	2005	2006	2004	2005	2006	2004	2005	2006
Pre-accession aid	970	823	509	1116	946	585	-146	-123	-76
Agriculture and rural development	353	1361	1714	1058	1716	2143	-542	-64	-105
Structural and cohesion funds	576	1296	1601	725	1621	1996	28	103	149
Internal policies + Schengen facility	130	141	139	169	212	278	-39	-71	-139
Budget transfers	443	550	450	0	0	0	443	550	450
Total EU financial flows to Poland	2472	4171	4413	3068	4495	5002	-256	395	279
Budget contribution	1579	2454	2519	1579	2454	2519	-1579	-2454	-2519
loss of tariff revenues**							-420	-764	-795
Net gain							-2255	-2823	-3035
GDP in EUR bn.							210	218	227
net gain as percentage of GDP							-1.07	-1.29	-1.34

Source: own calculations based on data from World Bank, IMF, European Commission and Polish Government

Definitions:

1. 'Financial flows from with EU' are payments appropriations drawn down in a specific year or payments made to the EU
2. 'Total expenditure' is Polish general government budgetary expenditure, including payments received from the EU which are paid out to final recipients; this includes co-financing of structural funds and rural development and topping up of direct income subsidies from the national budget and rural development funds
3. 'Budgetary impact' is the total impact of flows to and from the EU including the substitution of some domestic budgetary expenditure by EU assistance

** loss of tariff revenues above the level of the common external tariff. Loss of CET equivalent tariffs are included in the budgetary contribution

Continued…

Table 6 Continued....

Assumptions:

1. Poland absorbs only 70 per cent of the annual structural funds assumed by the EU and 70 per cent of cohesion funds in 2004 rising to 90 per cent in 2006
2. Poland tops up direct income subsidies to 55 per cent of EU-15 level in 2004, 60 per cent in 2005 and 65 per cent in 2006
3. 50 per cent of cohesion fund spending is substituted expenditure: 70 per cent of the structural fund co-financing is substituting for budget expenditure
4. this calculations ignores second order gains in budgetary revenue from increased spending resulting from accession
5. no allowance is made for financing the implementation of the acquis beyond that already in the budget for 2003
6. GDP grows in real terms by four per cent per annum

In Poland the situation will be similar, although the budgetary subsidies agreed for each year from 2004–06 will help to reduce the burden of accession on the budget. Table 6 attempts to show the impact of accession on the general government account.[6]

This table highlights some points of general applicability:

— While the whole contribution to own resources of each new member state will come from the national budget, not all the payments received by it will be paid into the budget account. An obvious example of this latter point is payments received directly by universities and other institutions from the EU research funds.

— In addition, apart from the budgetary subsidies, most of the inflows to the budget are paid out again to final recipients. This is the case for instance with direct income subsidies for farmers, where the state also has to pre-finance the subsidies, which are transferred from Brussels only after they have been paid out by the national agency. Structural fund transfers are also tied to specific projects and programmes and are drawn down from the budget as required. Advances paid to the recipient country are held in an account which prevents them being used for other purposes than payment of future calls on structural funds.

— The outflows from the national budget are usually larger than the inflows from the EU, because the recipient country has to co-finance EU expenditure, as mentioned above. For the

[6] The budgetary situation in many new Member States is complicated because of the lack of consolidation of the budget, with the existence of many substantial extra-budgetary items, which however are properly obligations for the government. Here we look however at general government receipts and expenditure rather than the narrow definition of the central government budget.

Cohesion Fund resources the assumed level of co-financing in Table 6 is 15 per cent, for the remainder of the structural funds and for rural development funding the level is 30 per cent. In certain instances in the past, Member States have refused structural fund financing, because they did not want to have to find the co-financing out of national budget funds.

— Also on the negative side for the budget, the loss of customs revenues will be quite serious. The level of tariff protection in the EU will be lower than that at national level today. The reduction of tariffs to the EU level will be a straight loss to the budget, while the tariffs collected by applying the Common External Tariff will comprise part of the national contribution to the EU budget.

— Finally the cost to the budget of implementing the Community acquis after membership is difficult to determine but is potentially very significant. This applies particularly to environmental directives but there are many other high cost areas too. The World Bank estimates that the cost of implementing the environmental acquis in Poland is of the order of EUR 47 billion. For the period 2004–06 they calculate roughly EUR 10.5 billion will be required, of which almost EUR 4bn will come from the general government account.[7] With state environmental expenditure at around EUR 400 million in 2000, this implies a major hike in budgetary spending. Some of this implementation will be achieved using the structural fund financing, but this will not be adequate to complete the whole post-accession adjustment process, particularly if the transport infra-structure programme is also to be completed by 2015 as planned.

— On the positive side however, some of the expenditure financed by Brussels will replace finance which would have been in the national budget anyway, so this expenditure is substituted for by receipts from the EU. In addition taxes will be paid on some EU expenditure or on revenues derived from these transfers, and thus there will be additional budget revenues in a second round of spending and taxing. These revenues are not considered in this table.

The overall impact of these different elements depends on the assumptions made about absorption capacity, the degree of substitutability of budget expenditure and the level of second round revenue gains for the budget.

[7] 'Poland: towards a Fiscal Framework for Growth', World Bank, January 2003.

On reasonably central assumptions, these calculations suggest that the impact of accession on the Polish budget is likely to be of the order of between one per cent and 1.4 per cent of GDP between 2004 and 2006. But this calculation ignores the cost of implementing the acquis, which could obviously add another point of GDP to the budget cost of accession, even assuming that the structural funds would cover some of the investment needed.

These calculations suggest that the impact of EU accession on the Polish general government expenditure in 2005–6 could be an increase in expenditure of the order of 2–3 per cent, or with the implementation of the acquis up to 3–4 per cent. In terms of the narrowly defined but normally quoted central government budget, the increase would be doubled to 4–6 per cent and 6–8 per cent.[8]

In Poland these increases in expenditure will come at a difficult period for the Minister of Finance, as he struggles to reduce the current large budget deficit, which reached 6.6 per cent of GDP in 2001 (general government deficit). While all recognise that budgetary consolidation is urgently required in Poland, both in the short term in order to get taxation down and economic growth accelerating and in the long-term to accommodate the large volume of EU transfers, the additional expenditure on accession related issues makes this consolidation more difficult.

These problems of budgetary management are posed for most of the other new Member States in the short-term as well. In 2002 the Czech Republic's general government deficit reached 9.1 per cent of GDP, while that in the Slovak Republic 7.4 per cent. Only the three Baltic countries have deficits below two per cent of GDP.

In the longer term the problem will indeed not be one of a penury of EU resources, as in the short-term, but one of successfully managing a very large flow of resources, exceeding four per cent of GDP. These transfers, if properly managed, will help to generate growth in the new Member States and support their efforts to close the income gap with the EU-15.

V. CONCLUSION

Three main conclusions can be drawn on the financial and budgetary impacts of the current enlargement of the European Union, assuming constant policies:

— For the European Union the final budgetary cost of enlargement is far lower than was assumed five to ten years ago. The Berlin

[8] While general government expenditure in 2001 was around 45% of GDP, the central government budget expenditure amounted to only 24% of GDP.

Financial Framework decided in 1999 was respected and the final deal is well within the limits set at Berlin. It is unlikely that the EU budget will grow significantly as a share of GDP over the coming decade

— For the New Member States the budgetary agreement poses both short-term financing problems and worries about the competitive position of agriculture, given the competitive distortion introduced by the EU–15 in favour of their own farmers
— In the longer term the budgetary outcome should be satisfactory. Much will depend on the capacity of the new Member States to manage large unrequited transfers.

However both agricultural and redistributionary policies may indeed change in the coming years in the Union. These changes could affect the budgetary position of the new Member States, both positively and negatively.

In the longer term however, success in terms of raising the economic growth rate and improving living-standards will depend more on the quality of policy in the new Member States than on the size of financial transfers from the Union.

8

The Impact of Accession on the Criminal Law and Criminal Procedure of the New Member States

JOHN R SPENCER*

I. INTRODUCTION

IT IS OF course a basic term for accession by new Member States that they implement in their systems the legislative *acquis communautaire*, including the *acquis* in relation to criminal justice matters.

Regrettably, it is not as easy as it might be to state exactly what this *acquis* is. Criminal justice falls largely outside the competence of the Community organs under the First Pillar, and is mainly a Third Pillar matter. As such, it is regulated by a collection of instruments, including Conventions and Framework Decisions, a number of which are not yet in force even in the existing Member States.[1] Furthermore, as law and order is a matter of high concern at the European as well as at the national level, the list of instruments keeps growing. The Council of the European Union published a list of texts in 1998 at the same time as a Pre-Accession Pact on organised crime was drawn up between Member States and a number of Candidate Countries,[2] and other instruments in the area of criminal justice have been added since. In December 2001 there was a proposal from the Commission for the acquis to be codified.[3]

In broad terms, the *acquis communautaire* in relation to criminal justice matters consists of legal rules that relate to three matters that are distinct, but obviously interrelated.

* Selwyn College, Cambridge.

[1] For example, the European Mutual Legal Assistance Convention. A serious practical problem for those interested in this area is discovering what instruments are in force, and what are not. SEMDOC (the Statewatch European Monitoring and Documentation Centre), which is available via Statewatch (www.statewatch.org), is helpful this respect.

[2] OJ 1998 C220.

[3] COM (2001) 645.

The first is legislation protecting human rights — and in particular, the European Convention on Human Rights and its various Protocols. This is a body of law that is designed to see that criminal justice comes up to certain minimum standards of fairness and independence that are universally thought necessary in a democratic country. As far as the EU is concerned, this obligation could be said to derive from Article 49 of the TEU, together with 6(1): 'The Union is founded on the principles of liberty, democracy, respect for human rights and fundamental freedoms, and the rule of law, principles which are common to the Member States'. In criminal justice matters, this body of law is largely 'defendant favourable'.

The second is a body of law designed to secure the effective repression of various matters which the EU collectively and the existing Member States individually find particularly worrying. These matters include frauds on the Community budget, corruption, organised crime, money-laundering, terrorism, trafficking in drugs, and trafficking in human beings. On these topics there now exists a rather confusing array of European Conventions, Framework Decisions, and other instruments. The immediate aim of these instruments is to extend the reach of the criminal law; compliance with them requires Member States, or some of them, to criminalise behaviour that was not criminal before, or if it was, to make it more severely punishable — and commonly to give their courts extra-territorial jurisdiction over it. It goes without saying that this body of law, unlike the first, is largely 'defendant unfavourable'.

The third is a body of law intended to ensure that trans-border criminal offences can be dealt with adequately. The basic problem here is well known and has often been described.[4] The basic idea behind the EU is the free movement of labour, capital and services. Whilst in general beneficial, an incidental unwanted side-effect is the free movement of crime and criminals, and a growth in crimes with a trans-national element. In a Union effectively without internal borders, but where each Member State has a criminal justice system that is an island entire unto itself, it is particularly difficult to deal with a crime where the defendant lives in country A, his co-defendants in countries B and C, the victims (or some of them) in country D, and the evidence to prove the case is scattered around all four of them. In recent years a stream of instruments have been designed to enable the criminal justice systems of the Member States to cope better with this problem — such as the European Mutual Legal Assistance Treaty of 2000. Since the dramatic events of 11 September 2001, the stream has rapidly become a flood. Early in 2002, a Framework Decision formally constituted Eurojust, an organisation of European public prosecutors

[4] See eg J Pradel and G Corstens, *Droit pénal européen* 2nd edn (Dalloz, 2002) §39.

designed to improve collaboration between national systems.[5] A European Arrest Warrant was provided for by a Framework Decision that was adopted on 13 June 2002 and will be applied as from 1 January 2004.[6] At the time this chapter goes to press, proposals are being formulated for a further Framework Decision on the mutual recognition of freezing orders, and on the mutual recognition of court orders for the seizure and production of evidence.

A number of agreements and legal instruments bind candidate countries to absorb and apply this criminal justice *acquis*. Foremost among them is the Pre-Accession Pact on Organised Crime mentioned earlier, which sets out fifteen 'principles'. Some of these principles are general, like Principle 1, 'We affirm our determination to co-operate fully in fighting all kinds of organised crime and other forms of serious crime', and Principle 12, 'We consider that corruption is one of the major threats to our societies … We therefore underline the need to develop in common a comprehensive policy against corruption in all its forms. To that end, we will organise regular consultations in common with the relevant bodies of the Council and the Commission …' Others are more specific, like Principle 2, under which the candidate countries agree to ratify a list of Conventions covering matters such as extradition, money-laundering, terrorism and trafficking in drugs.

To move the process forward, a range of mechanisms are in place to give the Candidate Countries practical help with bringing their criminal justice systems into compliance, and to ensure that the process of their doing so is monitored. With these arrangements, most readers of this chapter will probably be familiar already.

In broad terms, much practical help was delivered through Accession Partnerships, and the Phare Programme. Much of the help consists of training programmes for people involved in running criminal justice. Some of the help takes the form of 'twinning projects'. An example of these is the project entitled 'Strengthening the Public Prosecutor's Office' that has been running in Bulgaria since May 2001.[7] A group of judges and prosecutors from Bavaria are working together with a group of Bulgarian colleagues, in order to study the Bulgarian prosecution system and to make concrete and detailed recommendations — which are incorporated into a series of reports.[8]

Monitoring is carried out by a number of different agencies, with a certain amount of overlap in their functions. The Commission (Directorate

[5] Council Dec of 28 February 2002, 2002/187/JHA, OJ 2002 L63. S O'Doherty and A Gosine, 'Eurojust: a new agency for a new era' (2002) 152 *New Law Journal* 680.
[6] OJ 2002 L190/1. For the UK response, see the Extradition Act 2003, Part I.
[7] Twinning Project No BG/2000/IB/JH/01.
[8] For this paper, I have drawn on the second of these reports, a copy of which one of the participants kindly sent me.

General 'Enlargement') systematically monitors the progress of Candidate Countries towards meeting all the various criteria of membership. As part of this programme, it issues periodic reports on the different countries — and these reports incidentally cover matters relating to criminal justice, both generally, and in the context of human rights. To remain with Bulgaria, a report was issued in November 2000 commenting (inter alia) on reforms in the Criminal Procedure, the status and effectiveness of the Bulgarian judiciary, delays, the problem of corruption and attempts to fight it, the further problem of trafficking in human beings, judicial co-operation, conditions in Bulgarian prisons, and allegations of brutal behaviour of the Bulgarian police.[9] In the Council, COREPER set up an expert group in June 1998 to evaluate 'the enactment, application and effective implementation by applicant countries of the acquis of the European Union in the field of Justice and Home Affairs.'[10] This group also publishes periodical reports — some of which are made publicly available, others of which are not.[11]

Finally, in 2000 and 2001 OLAF (the official Community anti-fraud agency) sponsored a special study on the legal systems of nine Candidate Countries[12] with a view to establishing whether or not they would be able to provide adequate protection against frauds on Community finances. The study was entrusted to a group of experts, the nucleus of which was most of the working group that had drafted the *Corpus Juris* project,[13] to whom were added experts from the nine countries covered in the study. The leader of the group was the well-known Belgian lawyer, Professor Christine Van den Wyngaert. The final Report, which she prepared, was delivered to OLAF in the autumn of 2001. The practical organisation of the study was handled by the Europäische Rechtsakademie Trier (ERA), which published the Report as a special number in its series *Era-Forum*.[13a] The present author took part in this study; as will appear, he is indebted to the study for much of the information in this contribution.

So how has the process of assimilating the Community acquis relating to criminal justice gone? I propose to examine this question briefly, using the three-fold division mentioned at the beginning of the chapter: human

[9] Bulgaria 2000: Regular Report from the Commission on Bulgaria's Progress Towards Accession, 8 November 2000.
[10] OJ 1998 L191.
[11] See for example the Commission's progress report on Bulgaria, above n 9.
[12] Bulgaria, Estonia, the Czech Republic, Hungary, Lithuania, Poland, Romania, the Slovak Republic and Slovenia.
[13] M Delmas-Marty (dir), Corpus Juris, *portant dispositions pénales pour la protection des intérêts financiers de l'Union européenne* (Economica, 1997); M Delmas-Marty and J A E Vervaele (eds) *The implementation of the* Corpus Juris *in the Member States* (Antwerp, Intersentia, 2000).
[13a] *Era-Forum* 3–2001; Special Issue, *Study on Penal and Administrative Sanctions, Settlement, Whistleblowing and* Corpus Juris *in the Candidate Countries.*

rights provisions, 'get tough on crime' provisions, and provisions relating to mutual legal assistance and judicial cooperation.

II. HUMAN RIGHTS PROVISIONS

As regards the 'human rights' acquis, it can be said that the candidate countries have already gone far along the road — at any rate, in terms of what can be accomplished by legislation.

An odious feature of life in communist East Europe was the instrumentalisation of criminal justice. By this I primarily mean its manipulation by the government as a means of oppressing or eliminating those who disagreed with it: of which the classic example was Stalin's famous show trials in the 1930s; but I also mean its occasional manipulation in the opposite direction to enable those favoured by the government and its allies to break the law with impunity. A widespread reaction against this took place during the fall of communism and the return to democracy, and thereafter. In some countries, active steps were taken to seek out and rehabilitate those who had been the victims of government-inspired miscarriages of justice,[14] and to remove or sideline judges who were known to have been complaint to official pressure in cases with political overtones.

After the fall of the Iron Curtain, the newly restored democracies rapidly moved to ratify the European Convention on Human Rights. Bulgaria, Czechoslovakia (as it then was) and Hungary ratified in 1992, Poland in 1993, Romania and Slovenia in 1994; by 1997, the three Baltic States and Croatia had followed them. And unlike a number of well-established existing Member States (including the UK, Germany, Belgium and the Netherlands), all of these countries have subscribed not only to the Convention itself, but also to Protocols 1, 4, 6 and 7.

In connection with this, the new democratic countries systematically examined their criminal justice systems with a view to removing anything in them that formally conflicted with the requirements of the Convention. In consequence, there has been much re-writing of Criminal Codes and Codes of Criminal Procedure. In Hungary, for example,

> 'The great political changes of the late 1980s resulted in the first amendments to the criminal law in May 1989 when the Hungarian Parliament abolished the death penalty. In July of the same year 'socially dangerous parasitism' — a clearly ideological construct — was decriminalised. The legislation on political offences was amended in October 1989, when the very vague and imprecise criminalisations were abolished, and new

[14] I had a personal account of the process in Czechoslovakia from one of the people who, immediately after the 'velvet revolution', was employed by the new government to seek such cases out.

> precise and specific definitions were introduced. In October 1989 the criminal procedure was amended, to the benefit of the rights of the accused.'[15]

Throughout Eastern Europe, the process that began in the late 1980s is still continuing. In Hungary, for example, a new Code of Criminal Procedure came into force at the beginning of 2003.

In the context of the OLAF study I had the task of examining the provisions in the Criminal Procedure Codes of nine Candidate Countries governing criminal evidence, and I was struck by how liberal they were in a number of significant respects.

One remarkable example concerned the burden of proof. As every English criminal lawyer knows, the UK Parliament has the habit of reacting to moral panics and perceived threats to the security of the State by creating criminal offences — often very serious ones — in which the burden of proof on certain matters is reversed. For example, s 4 of the Explosive Substances Act 1886 (enacted in response to bomb outrages connected with political unrest in Ireland) makes it an offence punishable with fourteen years to possess explosives 'under such circumstances as to give rise to a reasonable suspicion' that they are to be used for an unlawful purpose, unless the possessor proves that he had them for a lawful purpose; and a further example is s 11 of the Terrorism Act 2000, which makes it an offence punishable with ten years' imprisonment for someone to belong to a proscribed organisation, unless he proves that it was proscribed only after he joined it, or that he has not taken part in its activities since it became so. Yet between them, the experts from the nine Candidate Countries in the OLAF study were unable to produce any criminal offence in their current Criminal Codes in which the burden of proof was similarly reversed.

Another sign of liberalism related to the status of the defendant's confession as a piece of evidence. The Criminal Procedure Codes of five of the countries in the study — Bulgaria, the Czech Republic, Slovakia, Hungary and Romania — impose a corroboration requirement on confessions by defendants. The consequence is that, unlike in English law, no person is to be convicted where the only piece of evidence against him is his own confession (even when it is made in the face of the court).

In some cases at least, rules of this sort that favour the defence have been enacted in reaction to abuses common in the authoritarian past, and there are instances in which reforming zeal appears to have been taken dangerously far. In 2000, a reform to the Bulgarian Code of Criminal Procedure actually changed the rules of criminal evidence in that country to make police officers incompetent as witnesses: a rule that the Bavarian

[15] K Kangaspunta (ed), *Profiles of criminal justice systems in Europe and North America* (HEUNI, Helsinki 1995), 94–95.

experts in the twinning project previously mentioned describe as being in contradiction to the universal rule in the existing Member States, and something that now amounts to 'a serious shortcoming of the Bulgarian criminal process'.[16]

It is not the case, however, that everything in Eastern European criminal justice has become a liberal paradise overnight, because the OLAF study did identify certain rather authoritarian features of the criminal justice systems of some of the Candidate Countries that were dubiously compatible with the European Convention on Human Rights. Some of these concerned the powers of the police. In all but two of the countries in the study, the police had power to search houses for evidence without obtaining a judicial warrant, and in one (Romania), official investigators could tap telephones without the authorisation of a judge.

In some countries a major issue is the independence and authority of public prosecutors, on which the OLAF study has the following to say:

> '... the role of the public prosecutor is, in most of the Candidate States, limited to the prosecution of criminal cases and to some extent the supervision of judicial investigations. Unlike in most of the current Member States of the EU, public prosecutors in most Candidate States are not an investigating authority themselves. There are some exceptions, such as Lithuania, Poland and Romania. In all other Candidate States, investigations are conducted by the police (or by administrative authorities), and are not directed by the public prosecutors. The latter act in a completely reactive capacity and are dependent on the input of the police. In many Candidate States investigating authorities function under the authority of the Ministry of the Interior and sometimes have a military organisation.
>
> There is no investigating judge in the candidate states, except in Slovenia. Instead, some candidate states retain the function of *Investigator*, which is a legacy of the communist past. The *Investigator* is a main authority for conducting preliminary investigations. He has powers that, in many current member states, are held by either the public prosecutor or the investigating judge. *Investigators* interrogate suspects, examine witnesses, conduct searches etc. The *Investigator* exists in Bulgaria, in the Czech Republic (where they are organised in a Bureau), in Lithuania and in the Slovak Republic....'

The idea of a investigator who acts without supervision from a prosecutor or judge is perhaps not particularly disconcerting for English lawyers, given that when the Crown Prosecution Service (CPS) was set up in 1985, a deliberate decision was made to leave the police free to investigate without CPS supervision or involvement — an arrangement that the Royal

[16] See above n 7 at 35.

Commission proposing the creation of the CPS had recommended on ground of principle.[17] However, it is unusual in Western Europe, where police investigations are usually carried out, at least theoretically, under the control of a judge or a public prosecutor. And as the OLAF study points out, guidelines issued by the Council of Europe[18] recommend that

> 'In general, public prosecutors should scrutinise the lawfulness of police investigations at the latest when deciding whether a prosecution should commence or continue. In this respect, public prosecutors will also monitor the observance of human rights by the police.'

III. 'GET TOUGH ON CRIME' PROVISIONS

Turning now to the part of the community acquis concerned with 'getting tough on crime', the Candidate Countries have been diligent in implementing it as well — and there seem to be few political obstacles to their implementing what has not been implemented already.

However, certain comparatively minor points do appear to cause some trouble. One of these — perhaps surprisingly — is the criminal liability of legal persons. Such liability is well established in the United Kingdom, where it was created more or less accidentally by case-law during the nineteenth and twentieth centuries.[19] So long has it existed in the UK that some reputable legal writers have now become sceptical about it, and question whether it really serves any useful purpose.[20] In Continental Europe, however, it is still comparatively new, and for some at least it has the attraction of the latest bright idea. In Brussels it has been warmly adopted by those responsible for making Framework Decisions in the area of financial crime, some of which impose requirements on Member States to create it in the context of particular offences.[21] This is not always easy, because in some existing Member States, such as Germany, criminal liability of legal persons is not generally accepted, and serious doctrinal objections are raised against the idea

[17] Royal Commission on Criminal Procedure (1981), Cmnd 8092. The Chairman of the Commission was Sir Cyril Philips, and the principle that the functions of investigating and prosecuting should be separated is sometimes called 'the Philips principle'.

[18] Recommendation 19 of the Committee of Ministers to Member States on the role of public prosecution in the criminal justice system (Adopted by the Committee of Ministers on 6 October 2000).

[19] For an account, see J Smith and B Hogan, *Criminal Law* 10th edn (London, Butterworths, 2002), 201–9.

[20] Having examined the arguments in favour, Professor Sir John Smith writes 'None of these reasons seems to be very compelling and the necessity for corporate criminal liability awaits demonstration': ibid, 207.

[21] See for example Art 5 of the Joint Action on Corruption in the Private Sector, OJ 1998 L358/2.

of introducing it; although the problem can be circumvented by labelling the offences committed by legal persons as 'administrative' rather than criminal — 'an approach which criminal lawyers have always considered to be *une sauce pour faire passer le poisson*.'[22] At the time of the OLAF study, none of the Candidate Countries concerned had yet amended their criminal law to enable legal persons to be convicted of criminal offences, although legislation to this end was being prepared in some of them. And as in some of the existing Member States, so in parts of Eastern Europe there are some who are opposed on doctrinal principle to the criminal liability of legal persons.

IV. PROVISIONS RELATING TO MUTUAL LEGAL ASSISTANCE AND JUDICIAL COOPERATION

The position is similar as regards the Community acquis governing mutual legal assistance and judicial co-operation. The OLAF study concludes as follows:

> 'On the subject of *extraterritorial jurisdiction*, all states comply with the *acquis communautaire* that exists on the subject...
>
> As far as *extradition* is concerned, a major obstacle seems to be the non-extradition of nationals, which is considered as fundamental in some candidate states. Other obstacles are that not all candidate states seem to be ready for direct transmission of requests and simplified extradition. These procedural forms, which are essential for day-to-day practice, will need to be available in the candidate states upon accession.
>
> On the subject of *mutual assistance*, the situation in candidate states seems, overall, to be quite satisfactory, leaving aside a number of problems that exist in individual candidate states... Like the current member states, they will have to implement the 2000 EU Convention on mutual assistance and to make sure that direct contacts with foreign judicial authorities are possible.'

Of course, a practical difficulty here is that, as mentioned earlier, the Community acquis in this area is itself in a period of transition; existing Member States as well as Candidate Countries have their work cut out to give effect to new Third Pillar instruments that are continually being produced.

Once again, however, there are occasional matters that look like causing unexpected difficulty. One, already mentioned, is the problem in

[22] OLAF study, n 13a; citing WC Van Binsbergen, 'Le droit pénal des Communautés Européennes', in H Rolin (ed) *Droit pénal Européen* (Brussels, Presses Universitaires de Bruxelles, 1970), 204.

some countries of changing the law to permit the extradition of their own citizens. Another is a particular problem relating to evidence gathered abroad. One of the reasons why it is difficult to prosecute in national courts for offences with trans-national elements is that, in some countries, it is difficult to persuade the criminal courts to admit evidence that has been gathered in another legal system. Some of the efforts currently being made to make it easier to prosecute for trans-border crimes centre on this problem, aiming to avoid it by introducing a principle of 'mutual admissibility of evidence': the rule that if a piece of evidence was legally collected in country A under the rules applicable to evidence-gathering there, it should in principle be admissible in evidence in the courts of country B or C or D. However, in several of the Candidate Countries — notably Poland, Hungary and Bulgaria — it is regarded as an important safeguard in a criminal case that the courts may only treat as evidence material that has been obtained by some organ of the national criminal justice system. In those countries, there could be resistance to establishing a principle of mutual admissibility of evidence.

Overall, it seems that the candidate countries are striving to implement the Community acquis in criminal justice matters in a way that is very encouraging. That said, it has to be accepted that enacting laws to give effect to international treaties and Third Pillar instruments is not the same as seeing that these laws are actually respected. The report from the Bavarian twinning project with Bulgaria stresses that the Bulgarian police force is still ill-equipped and comparatively ill-trained. Even where a given country has enacted all the necessary laws, it may take time for national practices to catch up with them.

V. CONCLUSIONS

In conclusion, I would like to ask the following question. What is the future for EU criminal law? And what will be the impact of the accession of the candidate countries upon it?

In some respects, I believe that the immediate future for EU criminal law will be increasing doses of what has been administered already. It seems likely that the stream of Framework Decisions and other Third Pillar instruments will continue to flow — and that, despite objections from parts of Europe accustomed to a more gentle tradition in criminal justice matters,[23] it seems likely that much of this will be directed towards trying to persuade Member States (both old and new) to be ever tougher upon certain particular forms of worrying trans-national criminality.

[23] For a contribution from Sweden, see P Asp, 'Harmonisation and cooperation within the Third Pillar: Built-in risks', (2002) 4 *Cambridge Yearbook European Legal Studies* 15–23.

But underneath this question of trans-national criminality there lurks a major issue of principle: whether the proper approach is 'vertical' or 'horizontal'. The 'vertical approach' is the notion that, in order to deal with at least certain types of trans-national crime, we need to create a centralised European prosecution agency with trans-national competence, equipped with a set of uniformly applicable procedural rules. This was of course the philosophy behind the *Corpus Juris* project, which recommended this approach for frauds affecting the Community budget, and it is the approach taken up by the Commission in its Green Paper on a possible European Public Prosecutor.[24] The horizontal approach is the idea that, with good will and much fine-tuning, it is possible to deal with the problem of trans-national crime effectively by leaving the separate national criminal justice systems of all the Member States to get on with it. This can be done, so it is said, by enlarging the jurisdictional boundaries of the national courts to enable them to deal with offences (or parts of offences) committed in other countries, by instituting a system of 'mutual recognition' of court decisions, and by setting up organisations (such as Europol and Eurojust) to help the national systems share information and to encourage them to co-operate with one another. At present, the Commission is in favour of the 'vertical approach', but the Council — representing the views of the governments of most of the existing Member States — are opposed to it and is placing all its faith and efforts in the 'horizontal approach'. This was the line adopted in the conclusions of the Tampere Council in 1999, of which the most obvious concrete manifestation of the approach is the creation of Eurojust. My personal view, for what it is worth, is that the horizontal approach is barely workable within a community of 15, and that with a community of 25 it will become completely impracticable. I suspect that an important effect of the enlargement process of criminal justice in Europe will be the eventual victory, at least in certain areas, of the 'vertical approach'.

That prediction I have made with hesitation. But I would like to close with a further prediction about which I feel much more confident. For EU lawyers, I believe that criminal justice is almost bound to be the 'new chapter' of their subject; and for criminal lawyers, the new chapter will almost certainly be the dimension brought to it by EU and comparative law.

[24] Green Paper on criminal law protection of the financial interests of the Community and the establishment of a European Prosecutor, COM (2001) 715 final.

9

EU Enlargement and EU Common Strategies on Russia and Ukraine: An Ambiguous Yet Unavoidable Connection

MARC MARESCEAU*

I. BACKGROUND

AN IMPORTANT PART of the preparatory work leading to the Treaty of Amsterdam concentrated on the second pillar's Common Foreign and Security Policy (CFSP). After complicated negotiations on the nature, function but above all on the institutional aspects of CFSP, agreement was also reached on a new provision, which was afterwards to become Article 13 TEU. This provision stipulates inter alia that the European Council 'shall decide on common strategies to be implemented by the Union where the Member States have important interests in common'. Notwithstanding the expression 'shall decide' used in Article 13, it does not seem to have been the purpose of the Article to create, through the new instrument 'common strategy', a new category of 'legally binding commitments'.[1] Indeed, practice shows that these strategies, as formulated in 'acts' of the European Council, are nothing more than external policy guidelines for certain countries or regions which need to be worked out through a variety of institutions, mechanisms and procedures. In doing so, a better coherence of the EU's activities must be achieved internally as well externally and here the all-embracing

* European Institute, Ghent University. This study was prepared within the framework of a IUAP-project with the Universities of Liège and Brussels (ULB).

[1] But see criticism by A Dashwood, 'External Relations Provisions of the Amsterdam Treaty' in D O'Keeffe & P Twomey (eds), *Legal Issues of the Amsterdam Treaty* (Oxford, Hart Publishing, 1999), 206, who interprets 'shall decide' in Art 13 in a sense that 'the European Council has been endowed with power *to take legally binding decisions*', a situation which he qualifies as 'constitutionally anomalous' since the function of the European Council is to provide the EU with the general political guidelines (emphasis added).

potential of the common strategy is certainly one of its strengths. However, the precise legal nature of a common strategy based on Article 13 remains unclear[2] and, further, the Article only stipulates that the common strategies 'shall set out their objectives, duration and the means to be made available by the Union and the Member States'. It is the Council which is in charge of the implementation of this strategy and the Council is also expected to make recommendations to the European Council. As will be mentioned later, one of the interesting features of the common strategies is that, while leaving the respective decision-making procedures in the three pillars intact, they allow for 'cross-pillar' activity to be developed.

At the 1998 Vienna European Council, as part of the chapter dealing with the implementation of the Amsterdam Treaty, the Council suggested that common strategies would focus on the neighbouring regions of the EU, in particular Russia, Ukraine, the Mediterranean region and the Western Balkans, but that the first to be developed would be on Russia. It was thought that it was in these regions that 'the EU has the common long-term interest and the greatest need for coherence and effectiveness', particularly 'in the context of enlargement and the development of the acquis'[3] and, clearly, in these proximity relations, those with Russia were of prime importance. The 'common strategy', as a new policy instrument under the second pillar, was itself not necessarily directly related with the enlargement process. The need for more coherence and effectiveness in EU foreign affairs was, and remains, also a necessity regardless of EU enlargement. But the enlargement process embracing so many countries in Europe strongly increased the need for such a comprehensive and coherent approach and explains why the first common strategy-'applications' of Article 13 EU Treaty concerned the relations with direct neighbours of the future enlarged EU. This new and at first sight refreshing intergovernmental instrument seemed to have a promising political future ahead.

At the 1999 Cologne European Council, the first European Council to be held after the entry into force of the Amsterdam Treaty, the Common Strategy on Russia (CSR) was officially launched for a duration of four years.[4] Strangely enough, and this notwithstanding the ambitious intentions of this new project, it smacked very much of a call in the desert. There are various not necessarily interrelated reasons that may help to explain this. Although in the preparatory drafting phase some contacts had been made with the Russian authorities,[5] this 'Common Strategy'

[2] Ibid.
[3] See Report of the Council of 7 December 1998, http://ue.eu.int/newsroom/LoadDoc.asp?MAX=361&BID=75&DID=56494&LANG=1.
[4] For text, see OJ 1999 L157/1.
[5] At the EU-Russia Moscow Summit of 18 February 1999 the EU informed the Russian side of the initiative to elaborate a Common Strategy on Russia, see Press Release 6118/99 (43).

was nevertheless very much a unilateral exercise.[6] Paradoxically, 'common strategies' are not really 'common' in the sense that they are the result of mutual consultations between the two partners, the expression 'common' refers to the positions of Member States. The objectives targeted are those that Member States of the EU identify from their point of view to be of high priority but in the end common strategies tend to present the picture of a 'shopping list' of themes rather than clear strategic objectives.[7] Even the High Representative for CFSP, Mr. Solana, has criticised the common strategy as an instrument '(that) did not cover new ground and instead tended to become inventories of existing policies'.[8]

Moreover, the various individual priorities are not necessarily identical with those of the partner country vis-à-vis the EU. The CSR is certainly no exception to this practice and Russian commentators have also observed that the preparation and launching of the CSR had passed almost entirely unnoticed in Russia itself.[9] In addition, and this is of course unfortunate, the moment of launching of this new EU policy instrument was not the most propitious. Russia had been, since 1998, in a

At the Second Meeting of the Co-operation Council EU-Russia of 17 May 1999, a few weeks before the adoption of the CSR, the EU informed the Russian authorities about the ongoing preparations. Russia, which seemed somewhat astonished by the procedure and method followed by the EU, informed the EU that it was preparing its own vision on partnership with the EU in parallel. The Co-operation Council noted, on the basis of the exchanged information, the largely converging views, see http://ue.eu.int/Newsroom/LoadDoc.asp?MAX=241&BID=102&DID=57689&LANG=1. Minister of Foreign Affairs Ivanov, after expressing his interest in the EU initiative, observed, not without a light laconic touch '(that) it must be borne in mind that this is a *common* strategy on which our work will be build' (emphasis added), see Minutes of the Second Meeting of the EU — Russia Co-operation Council, Brussels 17 May 1999, UE — RU 10001/00.

[6] On the preparation of the CSR, see in particular C Hillion, 'Institutional Aspects of the Partnership Between the European Union and the Newly Independent States of the Former Soviet Union: Case Studies of Russia and Ukraine' (2000) 37 *CMLRev* at 1224–45; same author, 'Common Strategies and the Interface Between EC External Relations and the CFSP: External Relations and the CFSP: Lessons of the Partnership Between the EU and Russia', in A Dashwood & C Hillion (eds), *The General Law of the EC External Relations* (London, Sweet & Maxwell, 2000) at 293–95; see also the very useful study by H Haukkala, 'The Making of the European Union's Common Strategy on Russia', in H Haukkala & S Medvedev (eds), *The EU Common Strategy on Russia: Learning the Grammar of the CFSP* (Helsinki, Finnish Institute of International Affairs — Institut für Europäische Politik, 2001) at 41–47.

[7] See Haukkala above n 6 at 65. The word 'strategy' for the EU policy instrument concerning Russia is inadequate and even misleading and H Haukkala & A Toivonen, 'The EU Common Strategy on Russia: In Search of the Foundations of European Foreign Policy'(2002) *Yearbook of Finnish Foreign Policy*, 58, do not hesitate to qualify the CSR 'as a result of a feeling of helplessness within the Union'.

[8] See Common Strategy Report, Council of the EU, 21 December 2000, 14871/00. He further refers to the 'Christmas tree approach' which has been followed for the drafting of the CSR.

[9] See the interesting contribution of Y Borko, 'The European Union's Common Strategy on Russia: a Russian View' in Haukkala & Medvedev above n 6 at 122: the launching of CSR was not regarded, as Borko puts it, 'as an event of major consequence'.

deep economic and financial crisis and the conflict in Chechnya was definitely not evolving in a good direction and, two months after the launching of the CSR in August 1999, eventually was to lead to the so-called second Chechen war. Last but not least, after the dissolution of the USSR, Russia had not been able to develop a clear and comprehensive policy orientation towards the EU. Certainly, a Partnership and Cooperation Agreement (PCA) had been signed in 1994, entering into force only on 17 December 1997,[10] and an Interim Agreement on trade and trade-related matters had been signed in 1995,[11] but both proved to be inadequate bilateral instruments for the purposes of governing the relations between the two sides. And, perhaps more importantly, Russia, at least before 1999, had hardly paid any attention to the EU's unprecedented ongoing enlargement process. A detailed study as to why Russia remained unmoved by this process for so long still has to be made but Baranovsky has already provided a very useful insight into various Russian attitudes towards EU enlargement which seemed or seem to be floating from a 'defensive' to 'co-operative' approach or are a mixture of both.[12] Of course, quick explanations for this state of affairs are the Russian domestic situation during the Nineties and, most obvious of all, the simultaneous threat of NATO enlargement, which was very much perceived as directly affecting Russia's security. In this constellation EU enlargement was seen in the first place as a domestic affair of the EU, which, if not necessarily something positive,[13] could largely be approached as a 'neutral' phenomenon. Vladimir Shemiatenkov, the former USSR Ambassador to the EC, is one of those in Russia who defended another thesis. In his view 'despite all the sweeteners of a *partnership*, it (EU enlargement) means the actual exclusion of Russia (and the Russians) from the zone of peace, stability and prosperity, which is ostensibly being built in Europe'. Seen in this perspective and notwithstanding the beliefs of the Russian President Yeltsin (who had stated that EU enlargement did not pose particular problems for Russia), Shemiatenkov argues that 'the enlargement of the European Union is even more detrimental to Russia's interests than the enlargement of NATO'. Russia 'has no reason to fear NATO military invasion but it has every reason to fear the long-term consequences of its relative economic

[10] For text, see OJ 1997 L327/1.
[11] For text, see OJ 1995 L247/1.
[12] See V Baranovsky, *Russia's Attitudes Towards the EU: Political Aspects* (Helsinki, Finnish Institute of International Affairs-Institut für Europäische Politik, 2002), 122–43.
[13] But for a positive approach, see Y Borko who calls a strong enlarged EU 'one of the cornerstones of stability in Europe' and 'from a strategic point of view, Russia is interested in this stability', see 'The New Intra-European Relations and Russia', in M Maresceau (ed), *Enlarging the European Union* (London, Longman, 1997), 380.

isolation from the rest of Europe'.[14] Be that as it may, when the EU's CSR was launched, there was no well-defined policy on EU enlargement in Russia, while for the EU itself the CSR came at a point in time when its enlargement process was already solidly established. The network of Europe Agreements with ten countries of Central and Eastern Europe (CEECs=Hungary, Poland, the Czech Republic, Slovakia, Romania, Bulgaria, Slovenia, Estonia, Latvia and Lithuania) had been completed. The Mediterranean candidate countries Cyprus, Malta and Turkey had developed privileged relationships with the EC through association agreements. Moreover, when on 1 May 1999 the Treaty of Amsterdam entered into force, the EU had already firmly incorporated the ten CEECs in the enhanced pre-accession strategy, which implied that accession partnerships and a reinforced financial assistance for pre-accession activity were also being made available to them. Furthermore, the EU had opened accession negotiations in 1998 with Cyprus, Hungary, Poland, the Czech Republic, Slovenia as well as with Estonia and by the end of 1999, at the Helsinki European Council (that is to say six months after the launching of the Common Strategy on Russia but simultaneously with the launching of the Common Strategy on Ukraine[15] (CSU)), it was decided to extend accession negotiations to the remaining five CEECs and Malta.

Seen against this background it might be worthwhile examining in this contribution, to which extent the EU enlargement process and the whole atmosphere created around it, which were already so omnipresent in the EU's external relations policy when the common strategies on Russia and Ukraine were conceived and launched, have influenced the wording, content and spirit of these strategies. Therefore, the context, objectives and structure of both common strategy instruments need to be analysed closely and compared in the light of the general topic of this book. Of course, it cannot be the purpose of this contribution to make a new detailed study of these strategies as such. The Russian and Ukrainian responses to the respective common strategies will be approached from the perspective of how these responses have coped with the enlargement phenomenon. This contribution will also briefly examine the implementation of the common strategies in view of the enlargement process.

Before going into detail, it should, as a preliminary remark, be observed that the EU position on Russia and Ukraine in the enlargement context may appear comparable, but they are not necessarily identical. There cannot be the slightest doubt about the fact that Ukraine is a

[14] V Shemiatenkov, 'The Relations Between Russia and the EU' (1997), *Revue des affaires européennes — Law and European Affairs*, 287.
[15] For text, see OJ 1999 L331/1.

'European State' within the meaning of Article 49 TEU[16] and that it could, if the other conditions of that article are satisfied, at one stage ask for EU membership and be incorporated into a new EU enlargement process. Of course, the EU must be willing to take Ukraine on board before this can happen and, for the moment, we are very far from this hypothesis. It is more difficult to imagine how Russia could ever become a member of the EU even if one day it would satisfy the political and economic conditions for EU membership. Simply the size of the country makes thinking about Russia's membership a surreal exercise at present. But what appears surreal at one moment in history may not necessarily last eternally. Legally speaking, should the Russian government ever wish to apply for EU membership at one stage, geo-political or simply geographical considerations in themselves would not constitute legal impediments to membership. Indeed, Russia would seem to satisfy the 'European State'-test of Article 49, certainly now that at the 1999 Helsinki European Council Turkey has explicitly been qualified as a candidate State. For the moment, however, Russia's membership of the EU remains a matter of pure speculation and the present reality offers a very different picture. Russia has unequivocally expressed the view that it does not envisage making any application for EU membership.[17] Russia is also politically and economically too far away from fulfilling the Copenhagen Criteria necessary for EU membership. But nobody can foresee how the EU will evolve and the enlargement process itself is not a neutral operation from the point of view of the EU's objectives, policies and institutional structures. Particularly if, for example, EU membership of Turkey ever becomes a reality, the perspective on the relations EU-Russia will necessarily need fundamental revision. Also, an evolution of the EU's enlargement policy towards Ukraine would undoubtedly directly affect the EU-Russia relations, especially if the future enlarged EU were then to embrace all or virtually all European States, except in the end Russia.

But apart from the possible or potential involvement of Russia and Ukraine in the EU enlargement process itself, there is, of course, the direct and indirect impact of this process on the current relations with the two countries while they remain on the sidelines. As opposed to the Russian approach, Ukraine, in an outspoken and formal way — even when sometimes contradictory signals may be given, as was recently demonstrated

[16] Art 49 TEU holds that 'any European State which respects the principles set out in Art 6(1) may apply to become a member of the Union'.

[17] See 'Medium Term Strategy for Development of Relations between the Russian Federation and the European Union (2000–2010)', Ministry of Foreign Affairs, Moscow, 1999, point 1.1, http://europa.eu.int/comm/external_relations/russia/russian_medium_term_strategy/index.

with its possible participation in a Single Economic Area with Russia, Belarus and Kazakhstan (see further) — opts for incorporation and participation in the EU enlargement strategy itself, something that is just one bridge too far for the EU. Therefore, the issue of new proximity relations of the enlarged EU is something very concrete and real for its two biggest neighbours. The EU now starts to realise this. While this study was being prepared and finalised, a growing influx of new reflections on the neighbourhood relations of the enlarged EU were coming in, particularly from the European Commission, to which its President, Mr. Prodi, seems to be particularly and visibly committed.[18] In the conclusions of this chapter we will make an attempt to link the analysis of the rules and practice of the common strategies here examined with this very recent evolution.

II. STRATEGIC PARTNERSHIPS WITH RUSSIA AND UKRAINE

The Common Strategy on Russia and that on Ukraine aim above all at developing 'strategic partnerships'. It is difficult to define in precise terms what is meant by the expression 'strategic partnerships' but, no doubt, it is used to indicate something that aims at promoting stability and prosperity while strengthening democracy, respect for human rights, rule of law and market economy. Actually, it could be anything as long as it does not come too close to EU membership itself. In other words, it is a nice formulation linking the adjective 'strategic' — a qualification which together with the noun 'strategy' is with great profusion being used in the official EU terminology — with 'partnership', another very attractive word in the EU vocabulary. However, as will be demonstrated, the combination of the two words to characterise the specific nature of the bilateral relations EU-Russia on the one hand and EU-Ukraine on the other, is manifestly overdone for what the contents of the common strategy in reality represents. But, notwithstanding its hollow content, or maybe precisely because of this, the partners of the EU have also incorporated this magic expression in their own discourse on the EU.

[18] The start for a public reflection on this matter was given by Mr Prodi at the Sixth ECSA World Conference in Brussels (5–6 December 2002) on 'Peace, Security and Stability, International Dialogue and the Role of the EU', where the Commission President launched the idea of developing around the enlarged EU 'a ring of friends'; on 11 March 2003, the Commission published a Communication on 'Wider Europe — Neighbourhood: A New Framework for Relations with our Eastern and Southern Neighbours', COM(2003) 104; see also C Patten & R Prodi, 'A côté de l'Union européenne, un cercle de pays amis', *Le Monde*, 19 March 2003. Before that, Commissioner Patten and High Representative Solana had jointly prepared a document called 'Wider Europe' which was distributed to the members of the General Affairs Council on 7 August 2002. At the General Affairs and External Relations Council of 18 November 2002 conclusions were approved on a 'New Neighbours Initiative', Doc 14183/02 (Presse 350), see further below.

Strategic partnerships as laid down in the CSR and CSU, respectively, have much in common and are thus largely comparable but there are also a few notable differences. One such difference is particularly relevant for our study since it has to do with the different degrees of presence of the enlargement dimension in the strategies themselves.

A. Common Strategy on Russia

1. *The General Objectives*

The first part of the Common Strategy on Russia is devoted to the 'vision of the EU for its partnership with Russia', the principal objectives and the instruments and means to implement the proposed policy. The second and third parts concern the areas of action and specific initiatives, but the various parts are all closely interconnected.

The EU 'vision' on the partnership with Russia is based on a number of main assumptions. A 'stable, democratic and prosperous Russia' is the first objective of the CSR. Second, Russia must be 'firmly anchored in a united Europe free of new dividing lines'. Both objectives are 'essential to a lasting peace on the continent'. The CSR therefore aims in the first place to consolidate and develop an open and pluralistic democracy, the rule of law and public institutions in Russia. Simultaneously, the EU will support the development of a prosperous market economy in Russia. These domestic policy objectives constitute the essential prerequisites for achieving the second objective, which is Russia's 'return to its rightful place in the European family'. Consequently, the CSR will strengthen the 'strategic partnership' between the Union and Russia and this reinforced partnership will be based on shared values. All this 'will help Russia to assert its European identity'. Naturally, Russia remains a crucial partner for promoting security in Europe and world-wide. The European Council 'recognises that the future of Russia is an essential element in the future of the continent and constitutes a strategic interest for the European Union'.[19] One of the principal CSR-objectives elaborates further the integration of Russia in a common European and social space. The EU is already Russia's main trading partner and Russia is a very significant energy supplier of the EU. The EU declares to support Russia's accession to the WTO as well as the establishing of a Common European Economic Space. It is interesting to note that the CSR explicitly refers to

[19] On this strategic dimension, see K Malfliet, 'Russia and Europe: Towards a Strategic Partnership' (2002) Chair Interbrew-Baillet Latour Working Papers at 15–23; see also H Timmermann & S Gänzle, 'The European Union's Policy towards Russia', in H Hübel (ed), *EU Enlargement and Beyond: the Baltic States and Russia* (Berlin, Berlin Verlag, 2002), 158.

Russia's 'geographical proximity'. Russia's proximity to the enlarged EU is seen as a 'common challenge on the European continent' which will need 'common responses'. However, this growing interdependence is not very visible in the CSR text itself where it comes to the proposed areas of action and specific initiatives. They reflect in the first place the EU's main preoccupations. Certainly, strengthening the rule of law and public institutions, civic society, consolidating economic reform and integration of Russia in the wider international economic context and strengthening co-operation with Russia in the field of security are recalled as fields of actions but the 'common challenges on the European continent' do concentrate heavily on areas such as the fight against organised crime, money laundering, illicit trafficking in human beings and drugs, and judicial co-operation. In particular, combating illegal immigration as well as envisaged co-operation in the field of readmission of own nationals, persons without nationality and third country nationals, including the conclusion of a readmission agreement, are high on the EU's CSR agenda. The same is true for Russia's visa policy, which the EU would like to see aligned to that of the EU, and for sanctions against immigrant smuggling. This is further elucidated in the part of the CSR on specific initiatives where the fight against illegal immigration and organised crime are mentioned as most prominent targets. Other fields of common importance and particularly sensitive in the EU are those related to ensuring nuclear safety, the handling of nuclear waste and environmental protection in general. By their very nature these areas quickly take on a transnational dimension and demand a common approach.

2. *Enlargement: The Difficult Removal of a Taboo*

Having set these objectives one might have expected that the CSR would have made an unequivocal link with the ongoing pre-accession process, especially where it refers to Russia's firm place 'in a united Europe free of new dividing lines'. However, this is not the case and this constitutes one of the main weaknesses of the CSR as originally conceived. For the drafters of the CSR it is almost as if EU enlargement is taking place on another planet. On the face of it this is, perhaps, not astonishing. Indeed, already in the various phases of the pre-accession process, before the launch of the CSR, the EU had avoided as much as possible any serious reflection on the effects of enlargement on the neighbours of the enlarged EU. As far as Russia is concerned the European Commission had produced in 1995 a — rather useless — Communication on the future of the bilateral relations EU-Russia, which did include a few lines on EU enlargement and its effects on relations with Russia.[20] The Commission recognised that 'as the effects of the process leading to enlargement begin to be felt by the Central and East European countries, it may be expected that the CIS countries will, for their part, intensify their search for closer links with the European Union'. The Commission went on to emphasise that 'since accession is not, in the European Union's view, an option for those countries' it was the network of PCAs that would provide the framework for establishing the necessary bridges.

The subsequent 1995 Madrid European Council's *Strategy for Future EU/Russia Relations* as well as the Council's *Action Plan for Russia* of 13 May 1996[21] fell short of making any reference whatsoever to the EU pre-accession strategy towards the countries of Central and Eastern Europe.[22] But the most striking illustration had still to come. On 15 July 1997, the European Commission published the long awaited comprehensive strategy document on enlargement called *Agenda 2000* together with its opinions on the applications from the countries of Central and Eastern Europe. Of course, in *Agenda 2000* it had been impossible to behave as if Russia did not exist, particularly, after Estonia had been included in the group of candidates with which, according to the Commission, accession negotiations could be opened.[23] Consequently, the European Commission was forced to acknowledge that 'the enlargement process (would) also require careful management in the Union's relations with the other partners in Europe and beyond, in order to ensure that it contributes to the overall objectives of strengthening international security and co-operation'.[24] Enlargement would 'benefit relations and co-operation with Russia, the Ukraine and other New Independent States' but it was also recognised that 'adverse effects could result from enlargement, were it to be perceived as raising new barriers in Eastern Europe'. The Union had to take steps 'to minimise such risks and to create conditions for exploiting

[20] See Communication COM(95) 223, 'The Future of Relations Between the European Union and Russia' at 6–7.

[21] Bull EU 5–1996, 2.3.1.

[22] See P Van Elsuwege, 'EU Enlargement and its Consequences for EU-Russia Relations: The Limits of a 'Fair Weather' Strategy' (2002) Chair Interbrew-Baillet Latour Working Papers at 7–8.

[23] In the Commission's Opinion on Estonia's application for EU membership the fact that Estonia has no border treaty with Russia is completely ignored. The discrimination of the large Russian minority in Estonia is briefly touched upon, but, notwithstanding the grave discrimination, the Commission came to the surprising conclusion that 'on the whole, the rights of the Russian-speaking minority (both with Estonian nationality and without) are observed and safeguarded', COM(97) 2006. In addition, the Commission saw it as something positive to use PHARE money to finance Estonian language courses for the Russian minority. For a criticism of this policy, see the author's 'The EU's Pre-Accession Strategies: a Political and Legal Analysis', in M Maresceau & E Lannon, *The EU's Enlargement and Mediterranean Strategies: A Comparative Analysis* (Basingstoke, Palgrave-Macmillan, 2001) at 18.

[24] Agenda 2000, 'For a Stronger and Wider Union', COM(97) 2000, Vol 1, 6.

fully the opportunities created by enlargement'.[25] The Commission accepted the idea that 'legitimate security and economic concerns' of the eastern neighbours of the enlarged EU could not be ignored and that inter alia 'the situation of Russian minorities in an enlarged Union' had also to be taken into consideration. Unfortunately, *Agenda 2000* failed to work out any of the various issues raised and the fact that less than one page of the voluminous document was dedicated to Russia was already indicative of the fact that the external effects of EU enlargement were, at that time, not, to put it euphemistically, a high priority. In the next crucial years of the enlargement process, the effects of this process on Russia continued to be largely ignored. One could not get away from the idea that EU enlargement was presented like the building of a miniature ship in a bottle, certainly a very delicate and most difficult exercise, but totally disconnected from the reality of the EU relations with Russia. Russia was outside the bottle and did not nor should have any say whatsoever in the EU's enlargement strategy. The enlargement process was already complex enough in its own right and did not need to be further complicated by a dash of Russian flavour. From a short term perspective this was understandable and defensible. Russia's domestic and external weaknesses of the Nineties made such an approach realistic and almost 'easy' to implement so that at the end of the road the EU enlargement process would become a *fait accompli*. Of course, at one stage, 'little' rear-guard fights such as those over the Kaliningrad issue or the question of Russian minorities in the Baltic States could not be swept under the carpet perpetually. But, on the whole, in order to make the eastward enlargement process feasible, credible and solidly established, it was absolutely necessary in the Nineties to avoid touching the Pandora's box of Russian interests and sensitivities in so far as possible. However, this policy was not without danger and could not be applied for long. Whether one likes it or not, enlargement does affect Russia and an EU enlargement policy leading to an alienation of Russia in Europe would be a disastrous strategy in the long run for the entire continent. In such a scenario enlargement would bring about the opposite of what it officially aims to achieve.

In the basic CSR 'document' or 'paper' — the child cannot be given a better name — 'enlargement' is mentioned only once and in so many words: in a sibylline statement proclaiming that enlargement will be beneficial and create new opportunities for Russia, enlargement is presented as a stimulus for qualitative improvement of the strategic partnership and reinforced relationship between the EU and Russia. However, what these benefits and opportunities really might be and

[25] Agenda 2000, 'The Challenge of Enlargement', COM(97) 2000, Vol 2, 14.

how they ought to be generated are not worked out further. They are taken for granted by the EU and the repeated announcement of this statement in previous and subsequent policy declarations of the EU creates the impression that it has become dogma in the EU enlargement strategy. Generally speaking, enlargement is invariably presented as something that is beneficial for Europe as a whole, in other words, also for those which are not included in the enlargement process itself. For example, the 1999 Helsinki European Council announced without further specification that enlargement brings 'stability and prosperity for the *entire European continent*' (emphasis added).[26] In the December 2002 Copenhagen European Council Conclusions it is recalled that the common determination of peoples of Europe to come together in a Union 'has become the driving force for peace, democracy, stability and prosperity *on our continent*'[27] and the strategic objective of enlargement is 'to overcome the legacy of conflict and division in Europe'. The Athens Declaration issued on 16 April 2003 at the occasion of the signature of the Accession Treaty reiterates the same idea.[28] Already at the 1997 Luxembourg European Council the launch of the enlargement process was presented as a new era 'finally putting an end to the divisions of the past'. Extending the European integration model 'to encompass *the whole of the continent*' was seen as 'a pledge of future stability and prosperity within *and beyond the new borders of the Union*'.[29] In an attempt at a comprehensive reflection paper on the enlarged EU's proximity relations, the European Commission published on 13 March 2003 a Communication called 'Wider Europe — Neighbourhood: A New Framework for Relations with our Eastern and Southern Neighbours'.[30] In this document, again, enlargement is presented as something which 'gives new impetus to the effort of drawing closer to the 385 million inhabitants of the countries who will find themselves on the external land and sea border, namely Russia, the Western NIS and Southern Mediterranean'.[31] It is one thing to proclaim something as truth, another to provide sufficient evidence. Thus far, and this is unfortunate, not one serious EU study can be mentioned which substantiates the official EU approach in a convincing way.

The failure to duly connect the need for a CSR with the EU enlargement phenomenon makes the reference to Russia's anchorage 'in a united

[26] Also in Agenda 2000, above n 25 at 12, the Commission holds that 'enlargement should increase security of the EU member States and *of the entire continent*' (emphasis added).
[27] Emphasis added.
[28] http://www.eu2003.gr/en/articles/2003/4/16/2531.
[29] Emphasis added.
[30] Above n 18.
[31] Above n 18 at 3.

Europe free of new dividing lines' something enigmatic. On the one hand, Europe will be 'united' within the enlarged EU but of which Russia will not be part and on the other, the enlarged EU will inevitably create new dividing lines in the European continent. As just mentioned, official EU discourse is increasingly keen to repeat that this is not to happen but one cannot get away from the idea that the very essence of belonging to the EU was and remains to be perceived by many in candidate countries precisely as a means and an expression of the ultimate differentiation towards those who remain outside this process, in particular Russia. In this logic, enlargement is principally shoving borders eastwards in Europe and part of a strategy to create a definitive and 'final' separation from Big Brother in the East. In other words, in this scenario, enlargement is, if not enhancing, then at best consolidating further division in Europe. Moreover, if these perceptions were to prevail and continue among some new Member States after enlargement, the new physiognomy of the EU could adversely affect the future EU relations with Russia globally. The fact that the CSR has been unable to address these fundamental issues properly, notwithstanding this inextricable but discretely kept link between enlargement and the CSR, explains why the part of the CSR devoted to the EU's vision of the partnership with Russia was a blatant demonstration of a lack of vision and originality. This ambiguity in the CSR-approach was further enhanced by the fact that the core of the relationship between the EU and Russia, also after introduction of the CSR, necessarily remains the 1994 Partnership and Co-operation Agreement. So far, this Agreement, notwithstanding its nice title and its praiseworthy aim of promoting the integration of Russia into a wider area of co-operation in Europe, has had only very limited results — and surely this is not only the EU's responsibility — but contrary to what the EU has long proclaimed, it can by no means be considered a substitute for the EU's enlargement policy towards the countries of Central and Eastern Europe. Clearly, the strong emphasis on the PCA in the CSR is yet another illustration of the inherent weakness of the CSR itself. If indeed the PCA was intended to play such an essential role, what then was and is the very meaning and purpose of the CSR?

If from the point of view of contents and quality of policy-making the PCA has not proved to be an instrument adequate to govern the mutual bilateral relations and if its contribution to promote integration of Russia in the wider area of co-operation in Europe has remained minimal, its institutional structures on the contrary have played a very useful role. That alone is already a good justification for its existence. One of the PCA's main results lays in the field of political dialogue or dialogue *tout-court*, since it provides for an institutional framework that allows the Contracting Parties to meet regularly at various levels and in various formats. The most visible of these joint meetings is the EU-Russia Summits which take place in principle twice a year,[32] composed of, for the EU, the Head of Government of the EU Member State holding the EU Presidency, the President of the European Commission, the Commissioner for External Relations and the High Representative for Common Foreign and Security. Russia is represented by the President and Ministers responsible for areas related to EU relations. Besides the Summits there are the annual meetings of the Co-operation Council at ministerial level, and the various meetings of the Co-operation Committee and subcommittees. High as well as lower level joint meetings have proved to be indispensable channels to air some of the most important political and economic concerns in the bilateral relations, including those related to the effects of enlargement, even if initially the joint PCA institutions were not foreseen for that purpose and even if originally the EU was perhaps not particularly eager to discuss this matter within the PCA framework. Legally speaking, however, it would appear that Article 102 PCA with Russia, which holds that the Parties 'agree to consult promptly through appropriate channels at the requests of either Party to discuss any matter concerning the interpretation or implementation of this agreement and other relevant aspects of the relations between the Parties', created a sufficient basis for such a discussion.[33] A word of caution is needed regarding the Co-operation Council's implementing role within the PCA framework combined or not with the CSR. The Co-operation Council and indeed the other joint instances created by the PCA cannot take legally binding decisions. As opposed to acts from the Association Council operating, for example, within the framework of the Europe Agreements,[34] the Co-operation Council within the PCA structures may only 'make appropriate recommendations, by agreement between the representatives within the Co-operation Council of the Parties' (Article 90 PCA).

At the 1999 Helsinki EU-Russia Summit, Russia was briefed on the EU's enlargement process 'which was now picking up speed' and both parties welcomed the fact that detailed discussions on this topic had already previously taken place at the PCA Co-operation Council. They furthermore agreed 'to continue such discussions on a regular basis in the relevant PCA bodies',[35] a statement that has been recalled at virtually all

[32] See Art 7 PCA with Russia.

[33] The Russian position on this point, as expressed by Ambassador Likhachev, see *Agence Europe*, 20 February 1999, is in our opinion correct.

[34] For example, Art 106 of the Europe Agreement with Hungary states that the Association Council 'shall have the power to take decisions in cases provided for therein'. Such decisions 'shall be binding on the Parties which shall take the measures necessary to implement the decisions taken'.

[35] For text, see http://www.bits.de/EURA/Helsinki.html. For an analysis, see K Schneider, 'The Partnership and Co-operation Agreement (PCA) between Ukraine and the EU — Idea

the subsequent EU-Russia Summits. At this point it might be worthwhile examining briefly how the EU-Russia Summits and in particular how the Russian side have coped with the enlargement process as such in such meetings.

Already at the first Summits, after the entry into force of the PCA, those of Birmingham and Vienna in 1998, EU enlargement was very briefly touched upon but this theme was obviously not the masterpiece of the meetings. Enlargement appears to be mentioned almost incidentally and does not seem to draw any further attention.[36] The following Summit, that of Moscow of 18 February 1999, which announced that a CSR was being prepared, as mentioned above,[37] also referred to the enlargement process which 'had entered a substantive phase'. These developments, that is to say enlargement on the one hand and CSR on the other, 'will help to strengthen the stability and the prosperity of the European continent as a whole'. This familiar reference to enlargement in subsequent Summits is becoming gradually influenced by the growing awareness by the Russian authorities that it is not all gold that glitters in the EU's official enlargement discourse. At the 29 May 2000 Moscow Summit, for the first time, explicit reference was made to the need to discuss in the framework of the PCA bodies, not only the impact of enlargement on Russia's trade interests but also the special issues existing in the Kaliningrad region. It must be said that before this meeting, within the framework of the Third Meeting of the EU Russia Co-operation Council on 10 April 2000, Russia had already made clear that enlargement was either directly or indirectly affecting Russian interests, insisting strongly that this be discussed in parallel to the negotiations on enlargement and that these discussions be completed before enlargement takes place.[38] But Russia also continued to accept the idea that enlargement would bring benefits and at the 30 October 2000 Paris EU-Russia Summit enlargement is seen as a phenomenon which will 'boost exchanges between an enlarged European Union and Russia and between Russia and the applicant

and Reality', in L Hoffmann & F Möllers (eds), *Ukraine on the Road to Europe* (Heidelberg, Physica-Verlag, 2001) at 66.

[36] At the 15 May 1998 Birmingham Summit, the relevant passage in the Joint Statement reads as follows: 'we discussed the enlargement of the EU, the establishment of economic and monetary union in the EU and the launch of the euro'. This is very similar to the passage in the Joint Statement of the 27 October 1998 Vienna Summit where it is held that 'we discussed economic prospects in the EU as well as the preparations for the introduction of the Euro and the EU enlargement process'. The Statement goes on by saying that 'these developments would have important consequences on which we would continue to exchange views'.

[37] Above n 5.

[38] Minutes of the Third Meeting of the EU-Russia Cooperation Council of 10 April 2000, UE-RU 1001/01, Annex 9.

countries'. The same line of thought is followed at the 17 May 2001 Moscow Summit but it is also explicitly said that the consequences of enlargement will have to be addressed 'including the movement of people, goods and services'.

A real turning-point in the formulation of Joint Statements of EU-Russia Summits seems to be the 3 October 2001 Brussels meeting. From then onwards indeed any mention of the benefits of enlargement for Russia is immediately followed by a reference to its challenges and drawbacks. A degree of worry becomes discernable in the statement that enlargement 'should not mean drawing any more dividing lines in Europe, but should forge even closer links between the enlarged Union and the Russian Federation, thus contributing to peace and prosperity of our citizens'. The 29 May 2002 Moscow EU-Russia Joint Statement summarises adequately the current perceptions of both sides on EU enlargement when it holds that

> 'the pending EU enlargement will open new prospects for our relations but at the same time will possibly create new problems, including in the sphere of trade, economic co-operation and human contacts'. The two Parties 'agree to discuss more actively the essence of the Russian concerns in the framework of the PCA'.

Taking into account the legal and political consequences of EU enlargement, Russia and the EU also agreed at that Summit to continue joint work with a view to reaching mutually acceptable solutions for the Kaliningrad region. This was considered to be of key importance for the development of a strategic partnership between the Russian Federation and the European Union and for strengthening the atmosphere of good neighbourliness and mutual understanding. At the 11 November 2002 Brussels EU-Russia Summit, a very strategic summit just before the December 2002 Copenhagen European Council, a compromise could be reached resulting in a Joint Statement on transit between the Kaliningrad region and the rest of the Russian Federation.

The Kaliningrad issue is indeed one of those prototype examples where enlargement directly and adversely affects Russian interests. Here, enlargement cannot simply be presented as a pure blessing for Russia since it creates very serious obstacles for, among other things, movement of persons from Kaliningrad to mainland Russia and vice versa. While after independence of the Baltic States, no visa was required for Russian citizens travelling in particular through Lithuania, the application of the Schengen regime now makes travelling much more complicated. In the pre-accession process of the Nineties the EU has done everything possible to ignore for as long as possible the existence of Kaliningrad as a Russian enclave, exclave, oblast — whatever it may be called — and, it must be said, has managed to do so remarkably well. It is only after growing and sharper insistence from the Russian side in various fora, such as Joint Summits or Co-operation Councils and through statements from the Russian Foreign Affairs Ministry, that the EU has reluctantly started to 'discover' the problem. The first overt but tardy recognition of the effects of enlargement on Kaliningrad was the well-known Communication on Kaliningrad of the European Commission of 17 January 2001.[39] It is not the proper place here to analyse in detail the Commission's position and how on this matter in general the EU and Russian views have evolved.[40] The fact is that the Joint Summits have been instrumental in creating the dynamics for finding a solution to the problem and the Joint Statement of 11 November 2002 is the best illustration of this. Certainly, the nature of such 'an understanding' remains from an EU law point of view somewhat uncertain, since it is difficult to visualise which EU institution has really committed itself and more than that it is very problematic whether at such summits the EU representation with its complex composition has treaty-making capacity. The Joint Statement is therefore not an 'agreement' in the legal sense of the word and it has above all a political value even if contents or parts of its contents create the impression of being formulated in a legal manner. The final terms of the Joint Statement of 11 November 2002 indicate that Russia's position of principle that visa requirement for transit over EU territory — Lithuania — was unacceptable has been watered down and that Russia has finally accepted the so-called 'Facilitated Transit Document' and the 'Facilitated Rail Travel Document'. These documents, although not called visa, very much resemble the visa. Transit of Russian citizens travelling between Kaliningrad and other parts of Russia by land will only be possible on condition of such a Facilitated (Rail) Travel Document. No doubt, by accepting the principle of such documents for Russian citizens, Russia has put much water in its wine, all the more since Russia also had to recognise that the transit regime 'will not infringe upon the sovereign right of the Republic of Lithuania to exercise the necessary controls and to refuse entry into its territory'. Russia, for its part, obtained that Lithuania's national border controls 'shall be applied in a flexible manner in order not to disrupt the traditional flow of transit passengers by rail'. In addition Russia also accepted that before 30 June 2003 a readmission agreement with Lithuania 'covering persons of all nationalities' be in place. This was obviously a

[39] COM(2001) 26.

[40] For in-depth analysis on the Kaliningrad problem within the context of EU enlargement, see L D Fairlie & A Sergounin, *Are Borders Barriers? EU Enlargement and the Russian Region of Kalingrad* (Helsinki, Finnish Institute of International Affairs & Institut für Europäische Politik, 2001); J Baxendale, S Dewar & D Gowan, *The EU & Kaliningrad: Kaliningrad and the Impact of EU Enlargement* (London, The Federal Trust, 2000).

politically sensitive matter, the more since at the moment of acceptance of the Joint Statement of 11 November 2002 the agreement between Russia and Lithuania on the State border had not yet been ratified but, interestingly enough, in the first half of 2003 ratification did take place and agreement between Russia and Lithuania was also reached on transit and readmission. Clearly, the 'guide-lines' laid down in the Joint Statement appear to have been closely respected. The Facilitated Transit Document will be valid for three years and will only cost five Euros. The holder will have the possibility to make multiple transit journeys. On 12 May 2003 the readmission agreement was formally signed and a few weeks later already ratified by the Russian State Duma and Federation Council.[41] The readmission agreement lays down the conditions and procedure of admission and return of not only citizens of the Contracting Parties but also of third States.[42] A readmission agreement in general is also, and this already for years, very high on the EU's agenda of the bilateral relations with Russia (see further). Of course, the interesting question from the purpose of our study is whether the CSR has contributed to solving the attempt to solve the Kaliningrad question in the EU enlargement process. The answer is of great simplicity: the CSR's role has been so minimal that it can simply be ignored. It was only in the Work Plan of the Belgian Presidency of July 2001 that Kaliningrad was first explicitly mentioned (see further). Subsequent Work Plans did no more than reiterate that a solution had to be found but nothing at CSR-level appears to have emerged to help solve this problem.

B. Common Strategy on Ukraine

1. *Background*

A Partnership and Co-operation Agreement with Ukraine was signed on 14 June 1994 ten days before the signature of that with Russia.[43] It is not always easy to see clearly into Ukraine's ultimate objectives of its

[41] See *Pravda*, News and Analysis on-line 18 and 28 June 2003, http://newsfromrussia.com/main/2003/06/18/48366.html and http://english.pravda.ru/main/2003/06/25/48654.html.
[42] The financial cost for the introduction of the Facilitated Transit Document and Facilitated Rail Travel Document will be covered by the EU. On 28 February 2003, a financing memorandum providing Lithuania with 12 million Euro was signed. Under the terms of this memorandum transit documents should be issued smoothly, border security at border crossing points should be improved and effective control of transit trains should be ensured, see http://europa.eu.int/comm/external_relations/north_dim/news/ip03_301.htm.
[43] For text, see OJ 1998 L49/1. For an analysis, see G Sasse, 'The EU Common Strategy on Ukraine. A Response to Ukraine's *Pro-European Choice?*', in A Lewis (ed), *The EU & Ukraine. Neighbours, Friends, Partners* (London, The Federal Trust, 2002), 213.

relations with the EU.[44] Between sometimes contradictory statements and approaches there is nevertheless one tendency which seems to prevail and which clearly opts for the following strategy: the PCA is a step towards a more ambitious association agreement, which, in turn, will prepare for Ukraine's accession to the EU. Hence, Ukraine's view on EU enlargement is fundamentally different from that of Russia since Ukraine has this very outspoken stand in favour of a firm anchorage in the European structures with membership of the EU as a final goal. But the EU's perception of Ukraine's place in Europe is a bit more complex, if not ambiguous, as was already illustrated in 1996 by the Commission's *Action Plan for Ukraine*.[45] The *Action Plan* was an indirect response to a demand and statements made by the Ukraine authorities on Ukraine's integration into the EU. The Plan proposed support for economic and social reform, integration in the European security architecture, support for regional co-operation, assistance in reforming the energy sector and the deepening of the bilateral contractual relations. However, the EU refused to make the slightest move towards inclusion of Ukraine in its enlargement strategy and conceded only that 'over the longer term, it (was) a matter for the EU to take note of the request of the Ukraine authorities to secure a firmer anchorage in the European structures and possibly membership in the EU'. Obviously, for the EU, Ukraine's EU ambitions were far too premature.[46] Ukraine had first to put order in its own house and since the domestic political, economic and social situation was by no means optimal, this certainly would take time and then the situation could be re-evaluated later. Clearly, not much had to be expected from the EU concerning possible EU membership of Ukraine.

2. *EU Enlargement and Ukraine's Specificity*

The Common Strategy on Ukraine launched in December 1999 did not lead to a fundamental review of this approach. The first part of the CSU text deals with the vision of the EU on the strategic partnership with Ukraine. For the EU the points of reference are: support for a stable,

[44] For a comprehensive overview, see O Pavliuk, 'Ukraine and the EU: The Risk of Being Excluded', in I Kempe, *Beyond EU Enlargement, Vol. 1: The Agenda of Direct Neighbourhood for Eastern Europe* (Gutersloh, Bertelsmann Foundation, 2001), 65.

[45] See Commission 'Action Plan for Ukraine', COM(96) 593; see also resolution European Parliament, OJ 1996 C104/226. Before that, the EU had on 28 November 1994 defined a Common Position on Ukraine based on Art J.9 TEU in which the EU pledged 'to develop a strong political relationship with Ukraine' but no further indication was provided of how this would be further worked out.

[46] See also Commissioner H van den Broek during visit to Ukraine 11–13 September 1996, *Together in Europe*, 15 September 1996.

open, pluralistic democracy and shared values. Freedom, independence and stability of Ukraine 'rank among the greatest achievements in the new Europe rid of old dividing lines'. An important and original feature of the CSU is the great emphasis on Ukraine's 'regional importance' in Europe. Geography, size and strategic location 'give Ukraine a unique position in Europe and makes it a determinant factor'. 'Ukraine's European aspirations' are explicitly acknowledged and its 'pro-European choice' welcomed. No doubt, the EU when preparing the CSU had taken note of Ukraine's first comprehensive policy paper on the EU and EU enlargement of 11 June 1998 called *Strategy of Ukraine's Integration to the European Union*.[47] With this Strategy Paper Ukraine had anticipated the EU's own CSU and it was, so to speak, Ukraine's common strategy on the EU. At first sight it may appear astonishing that in the CSU no explicit reference is made to this Ukrainian policy document. The reason for this silence is almost certainly the immense divergence of perception between the two parties as regards the final objectives of the relations EU-Ukraine. Ukraine's Strategy Paper starts from the assumption that EU membership of Ukraine's neighbours Poland and Hungary creates a totally new geopolitical situation which must necessarily lead to a foreign policy orientation of Ukraine whereby resolute integration in the European political, economic and legal field is the only vital option possible. In this view, as already mentioned, Ukraine's integration in the EU must first pass through an association agreement with the EU but the ultimate goal of this association policy is, not less not more, full-fledged EU membership. Some of the main targets in this process towards integration include legal approximation to EU law, economic integration in and intense trade development with the EU, European security, political consolidation and strengthening democracy. As expected, the CSU's answer to Ukraine's strategic policy options just mentioned remains very vague and only expresses the EU's commitment 'to support a successful political and economic transformation in Ukraine', facilitating Ukraine's 'further rapprochement' with the EU. Consequently, 'a successful, stable and secure Ukraine is in the best of interest of the EU'. But again, nowhere is reference made to possible incorporation of Ukraine in the enlargement process itself. The CSU only acknowledges — but for that statement not much geo-strategic thinking is needed — that as a result of enlargement 'some future Member States will share an external border with Ukraine'. In addition, and similarly to what has been said about Russia, it is also taken for granted that the enlargement process — naturally and automatically — 'will further enhance economic dynamism and political stability in the region, thus increasing the possibilities for

[47] For text, see http://ukraine-eu.mfa.gov.ua/cgi-bin/valprint_miss.sh?1p030101.html.

co-operation with Ukraine', a stand which, is increasingly being challenged by Ukraine, particularly because of the unavoidable negative effects on movement of persons.[48]

A striking but interesting difference between the CSU and CSR in the light of our topic is the short but specific section in the CSU on support for strengthening co-operation between the EU and Ukraine 'within the context of EU enlargement'. However, this part lacks imagination and is overtly disappointing for Ukraine. Three different actions for strengthening co-operation are proposed. The EU will support Ukraine's integration in the WTO and the establishment in the future of an EU-Ukraine free trade area, as already foreseen in the PCA, and investment protection will be stimulated. This part of the CSU is very similar to its counterpart in the CSR, where, however, reference to enlargement is lacking. The second area for co-operation in the context of EU enlargement is that of justice and home affairs. Co-operation in this field should include combating illegal immigration, trafficking in human beings, border security, fighting organised crime, money laundering and illegal trafficking in weapons and drugs. The EU will also seek adjustment of Ukraine's visa policy 'through the introduction of visa requirements in accordance with EC provisions'. The formulation here is almost word for word identical to that in the CSR. Finally, regional and cross-border co-operation with neighbouring countries of Ukraine will be encouraged and TACIS will support such initiatives. Development of infrastructure networks will be stimulated and there is a strong emphasis on border management. This dimension in the CSU policy is therefore also closely interrelated with the already mentioned development of justice and home affairs. Once more the contents of this section of the CSU is almost the same to that in the CSR. In other words, the explicit reference to 'the context of enlargement' does not bring anything value added to Ukraine's European aspirations.

Clearly, the identification of the specific actions for Ukraine in the light of the EU enlargement are very much inspired by the direct EU concerns. In order to achieve a 'safe' enlarged EU a degree of understanding from and co-operation with the neighbour is absolutely indispensable. This

[48] See, for example, Statement Ukrainian Minister of Foreign Affairs, Mr A Zlenko, at Conference 'Managing the Borders of the Central and East European States in the Context of European Security', 1 November 2002, http://ukraine-eu.mfa.gov.ua/cgi-bin/valprint_miss.sh?1p030209.html; Head of Ukraine Mission to the EU, Mr R Shpek, at Joint Meeting European Parliamentary Delegations for Ukraine, Moldova, Belarus and Russia, 13 February 2003 http://ukraine-eu.mfa.gov.ua/cgi-bin/valprint_miss.sh?1p040303.html; also statement of meeting of 9–10 October 2000 of EU-Ukraine Parliamentary Co-operation Committee; Press Communiqué Ukrainian Delegation on results of Fourth EU-Ukraine Co-operation Council Meeting of 26 June 2001, http://ukraine-eu.mfa.gov.ua/cgi-bin/valprint_miss.sh?1p04030205.html.

explains why the most important CSU initiatives are to be found in the field of justice and home affairs and border management, which, in fact, means organising effective border controls. Improving co-operation in the field of illegal immigration, in particular, regarding the readmission of own nationals, persons without nationality and third country nationals, including the conclusions of readmission agreements, is not only very high on the EU Common Strategy agenda but on that of the EU agenda itself. Here, Ukraine's geographical location is indeed really pre-eminently strategic. Another explicit reference regarding specific actions concerns integration of Ukraine in the WTO but again this can, as such, hardly be seen as a genuinely specific strategy resulting from the ongoing enlargement process since it was already one of the main objectives of the PCA. Consequently, the global conclusion is simple: there is nothing in the CSU reflections on the EU-Ukraine relations in the context of EU enlargement indicating that Ukraine's European expectations have been taken into consideration.

C. Responses to the Common Strategies

1. *The Russian Middle-Term Strategy Paper: A Punctual Reaction*

As mentioned before, the CSR came at a point in time where Russia lacked any comprehensive vision on its relations with the EU and even more so on EU enlargement. Of course, and also for this reason, the unilateral character of the CSR could not be left unanswered and led to a prompt Russian reaction which took the form of a Memorandum of the Ministry of Foreign Affairs called 'Middle-term Strategy for Development of Relations between the Russian Federation and the European Union (2000–2010)',[49] officially presented at the Fourth EU-Russia Summit of 22 October 1999. Moreover, in the Joint Statement of this Summit both sides expressed 'their readiness to examine how to intensify their co-operation further on the basis of these *two* documents'(emphasis added).[50]

It is obvious that for the drafting of the Russian Memorandum the line of thought of the CSR had been closely followed, notwithstanding the fact that the CSR was only explicitly mentioned twice.[51] Even if the Russian Strategy Paper incorporated several of the main objectives of the CSR as own goals, making them really 'common', there was also what Youri Borko defines as 'a reserved attitude to the CSR'. This probably explains

[49] For an unofficial English version see: http://www.eur.ru/eng/neweur/user_eng.php?func=apage&id=53.
[50] For text: http://www.bits.de/EURA/Helsinki.html.
[51] Y Borko, above n 9 at 121.

why there is no thorough assessment of the CSR as such. One reason for this cool love was 'the general worsened state of relations between Russia and the Union at the time of drafting the Russian strategy'.[52] Another explanation might also have been that the CSR simply did not deserve a serious Russian evaluation because the CSR was itself a document too general in content and with a poor methodology. Later, from 2000 onwards, under President Putin, interest at the official level in EU affairs would steadily grow[53] and, with an increasing frequency, references to 'EU expansion' can indeed be found in various Russian foreign policy statements. In the global *Foreign Policy Concept of the Russian Federation* of 28 June 2000,[54] for example, relations with the EU are considered to be of key importance for Russia and in the Russian view they continue to be based on the PCA. Interestingly enough, in this document, the EU's CSR is not mentioned at all but

> 'concrete problems, primarily the problem of adequate respect for the interests of the Russian side in the process of the EU expansion and reform, will be dealt with on the basis of the Strategy of the Development of Relations between the Russian Federation and the European Union, approved in 1999'.

According to Minister Ivanov, there is growing awareness in Russia as well as in the EU that the implications of enlargement need to be addressed and that it is necessary to work jointly to solve problems resulting from enlargement. In the words of the Foreign Minister, there is a common understanding that the EU enlargement process must not create new barriers on the road for co-operation Russia-EU but, on the contrary, it should deepen the relations as the boundaries come up even closer to Russia.[55] It is precisely the lack of a *joint* common strategy that adversely affects the efficiency of the EU policy towards Russia and therefore the CSR itself. At the 2000 Third EC-Russia Co-operation Council the Russian side proposed to harmonise the EU and Russian strategies and to come up with one single plan of action. This sensible suggestion, for a reason which is difficult to explain, has not been taken up seriously by the EC.[56] This is probably also one but not the exclusive reason for the weakness of the CSR.

To date the 1999 Middle-term Strategy Paper remains the most comprehensive Russian official document on the relations with the EU. It

[52] Y Borko, above n 9 at 122.
[53] See I Kempe & W van Meurs, 'Strategic Challenges and Risks of EU Eastern Enlargement', in Kempe, above n 44 at 15.
[54] For text: http://www.russiaeurope.mid.ru/RussiaEurope/concept.html.
[55] Speech Minister Foreign Affairs, PACE Standing Committee Meeting, 26 March 2002, St. Petersburg, http://www.russiaeurope.mid.ru/RussiaEurope/speech15.html.
[56] Minutes of the Third Meeting of the EU-Russia Co-operation Council, 10 April 2000, UE-RU 1001/01, Annex 16.

is one of the first and certainly not the last illustration of the growing Russian awareness of the role of the EU. The starting point of the analysis is that Russia's national interests must be safeguarded. Therefore, Russia must enhance its role and image in Europe and in the world. Russia is interested in developing a 'strategic partnership' with the EU in European and world affairs and the PCA, the CSR as well the Strategy Paper are all instrumental to achieve this.[57] Far away is indeed the time when Yeltsin's Prime Minister Chernomyrdin caused embarrassing consternation in Brussels, declaring that Russia 'would do everything to prepare itself for accession to the EU'.[58] The Strategy Paper now defines Russia as 'a world power situated on two continents' and 'Russia should retain its freedom to determine and implement its domestic and foreign policies, its status and advantages of an Euro-Asian state and the largest country of the CIS, independence of its position and activities at international organisations'. Seen in this perspective, partnership with the EU will primarily concentrate on collective security in Europe, the creation of a Russia-EU free trade zone and a high level of co-operation and confidence in politics and the economy as a whole. The Strategy Paper also refers to 'the construction of a united Europe without dividing lines' and 'the interrelated and balanced strengthening of the positions of Russia and the EU within an international community of the 21st century'. It further recognises that the PCA remains the major legal and institutional basis for partnership between the two parties. All this resembles very much the EU discourse and terminology.

In general, Russian views on EU enlargement are not samples of oversophistication.[59] This stems probably from a lack of proper understanding of and insight into what the EU is all about. Moreover, coordination of views among various Russian Ministries dealing with EU affairs is also not the strongest side of Russian administration. Seen in this perspective the Russian Strategy Paper, notwithstanding its sometimes poor structure and formulation, is probably from a Russian perspective already an achievement. It should be recalled that it does not explicitly reiterate the official Russian position that EU enlargement is an internal matter of the EU but that it draws attention to the 'ambivalent impact' of the EU enlargement process on co-operation with Russia and on Russian interests. Consequently, Russia requests consultations before enlargement takes place on extension of EU agricultural, technological and anti-dumping policies, EU visa and border regimes and EU preferences to

[57] See also Joint Declaration at occasion of the Paris EU-Russia Summit of 30 October, see Press Release 12780/00 (406).
[58] See *Agence Europe*, 19 July 1997.
[59] See I Leshoukov, *Beyond Satisfaction: Russia's Perspective on European Integration*, Zentrum für Europäische Integrationforschung, Discussion Paper, 1998 at 4.

developing countries competing with Russian exports to the countries of Central and Eastern Europe and the Baltic States. In other words, it may well be that enlargement brings about some trade advantages for Russia, for example, as a result of the decrease of customs tariffs, but it is also to be expected that enlargement could lead to trade substitution to the detriment of Russian exports, particularly in new Member States. Consultations are also requested in order to safeguard, in the interest of stability, security and co-operation in Europe, the rights of the Russian-speaking population in the Baltic States. The ultimate paragraph on the effects of EU enlargement is nothing less than a barely concealed treat. As a 'reserve option' the Strategy Paper does not even rule out a refusal 'to extend the PCA to cover those candidate-countries that, in spite of the existing agreements, do not ensure fulfilment of the generally recognised norms'. It must be said that since the publication of the Strategy Paper, things seem to have simmered down and at subsequent joint meetings EU-Russia no allusion is made to the 'refusal option' and at the prestigious St. Petersburg EU-Russia Summit of 31 May 2003, in a nice symbolic gesture, the heads of State or Government of all the candidate States had also been invited. Finally, in the Strategy Paper, attention was explicitly drawn to the fact that Russia, also wanted to secure protection, including under international law, of the interests of the Kaliningrad region as an entity of the Russian Federation and of the territorial integrity of Russia. As already mentioned, a compromise on this issue was found at the Brussels EU-Russia Summit of 11 November 2002.

2. *Ukraine's 'European Choice': A Strategy for Economic and Social Development for 2002–11*

As opposed to the reception of the CSR in Russia there was already in Ukraine the 1998 Strategy of Integration which had, as mentioned before, anticipated the EU's Common Strategy. Therefore, an immediate Ukraine reaction was less compelling as compared to the situation created by the CSR vis-à-vis Russia. It was only in 2002 that Ukraine adopted a new conceptual framework for a *Strategy of Economic and Social Development for 2002–2011*.[60] In this new policy paper the main objectives of the strategy of integration to the EU as laid down in 1998 were reiterated, that is to say that first associated status with the EU should be obtained as a step towards the ultimate goal of EU membership. The 2002–11 Strategy Plan proposes a work scheme with the following phases: 2002–03 should lead to WTO membership; 2003–04 should bring negotiations and signature of an association agreement with the EU as well as the negotiation on a free trade area; 2002–07 should entail an approximation of laws programme

[60] For text http://ukraine-eu.mfa.gov.ua/cgi-bin/valprint_miss.sh?1p030202.html

bringing Ukraine legislation in conformity with EU law; 2005–07 should lead to the creation of a customs union with the EU; 2007–11 should bring about the implementation of the association agreement and compliance with the Copenhagen conditions for EU membership. By the year 2011 the internal preconditions for Ukraine's accession to the EU should be created.

Targeting association as a step towards accession to the EU in a sense encompasses the whole economic and social development policy of the country. On paper it appears that virtually everything done domestically in whatever policy area is seen in pursuit of this target. Underlying this radical line of thought is the perspective of possible accession to the EU, which has in all Central and Eastern European applicants for EU membership been experienced as a very important if not the most important incentive and catalyst for vital and urgent social, economic and political transformation. It is difficult for the EU to contradict this since the EU has itself consistently held the same position with regard to the political and economic transformations in the candidate countries.[61] Moreover, this is exactly the approach that the EU has adopted towards the countries of South East Europe where, through Stabilisation and Association Agreements, the prospect of EU membership is offered to those countries that implement the necessary political and economic reforms and engage in regional co-operation.[62] Therefore, the Ukraine Strategy 2002–11 believes in the following dynamics of interaction: for economic and social development, the geopolitical objective of EU membership is indispensable while for EU membership economic, social and institutional transformation are essential. Consequently, the substantive part of the strategic economic and social development priorities basically comes down to an elaborated working scheme for the adoption of the entire acquis communautaire. It is obvious that the 2002–11

[61] See eg European Commission, 'Towards the Enlarged European Union. Strategy Paper', COM(2002) 700: 'in striving to fulfil the EU's accession criteria and adopting the EU's regulatory framework, candidates have been able to accelerate domestic reforms at the same time as they have been preparing for EU membership'. In the 2001 Strategy Paper 'Making a Success of Enlargement', the Commission is even more outspoken where it holds that 'the enlargement process has contributed decisively to achieving political stability, economic progress and social justice', COM(2001) 700. R Prodi, speaking at the Sixth ECSA World Conference (above n 18), recognises that 'the goal of accession is certainly the most powerful stimulus for reform we can think of' but hopes that such benefits can also be obtained through strong proximity relations links with neighbours of the enlarged EU, even when there is no perspective of EU accession; in a same sense also W Kok, *Enlarging the European Union, Achievements and Challenges. Report to the European Commission*, 26 March 2003, European University Institute, Florence, 64.

[62] The offer of prospective EU membership to these countries serves 'as the anchor for reform in the Western Balkans in the same way the accession process has in Central and Eastern Europe', see Second Annual European Commission Report of 26 March 2003 on 'The Stabilisation and Association Process for South East Europe', COM(2003) 139.

Strategy cannot be interpreted as a specific reaction to the CSU. Its ultimate objectives and scope are fundamentally different from those of the CSU and this also explains why there is hardly any reference at all to the CSU.[63] But also the EU's reaction to Ukraine's European Choice is very cautious. The impression prevails in the EU that the real problems of Ukraine in terms of political and economic transition are concealed behind an unattainable magical objective namely that of EU accession. In Ukraine, the fact of not being able to reach this aim in the near future helps to explain and perhaps also to justify serious failures in the domestic transition process. President Kuchma appears already to live with the idea that the target date of 2011 for Ukraine's EU accession cannot be met.[64] Maybe it is the awareness of this reality which has led Ukraine to envisage the signing of an agreement on the Single Economic Area with Russia, Belarus and Kazakhstan.[65] It is difficult to believe that with this agreement Ukraine is fundamentally reorienting itself 'eastwards' and its first choice remains 'a European choice'. Nevertheless the feeling of

[63] The CSU is mentioned only once — almost in a hidden way — under the heading 'Creation of preconditions for Ukraine's full-fledged EU membership' where the CSU, together with the PCA, the 2001 Fifth EU-Ukraine Summit and the EU's 2001 Action Plan in the Field of Justice and Home Affairs are enumerated. The CSU is qualified as 'important for establishment of relations between (Ukraine) and the European Union'.

[64] See Declaration at Press Conference in Surgut, 12 February 2003, *Forum*, 12 February 2002, http://eng.for-ua.com/news/2002/02/12/131416.html.

[65] After the completion of the draft of this contribution the agreement was signed on 19 September 2003. It will be interesting to follow the ratification and implementation process of this agreement. Its signature already caused serious concern even among members of the government fearing that it could hit the relations with the EU (see 'Ukraine ministers seek to change treaty', *Financial Times*, 16 September 2003). The substance of the agreement is confined to proclaiming the general objectives of the basic principles of a single economic area, that is to say free movement of goods, services, capital and labour but it lacks an institutional infrastructure to implement these principles. Above all, there is no legal and judicial framework created to organise the single economic area. The first impression is, therefore, that the agreement of 19 September 2003, as such, does only provide a weak basis for the creation of a single economic area. That being said, the fact that it was signed by Ukraine signals a deep discontent, frustration and probably also bitterness about its relations with the EU. It is to be seen whether the EU's New Neighbours Initiative (see Conclusions) will offer an alternative for Ukraine's European 'wishful thinking'. Also, Commissioner Verheugen is not crystal-clear on Ukraine's dilemma. On the one hand it would, according to him, be wrong to understand the (EU) policy of new neighbourhood as a kind of choice that Ukraine has to make between its relations to Russia or other NIS and its relations with the European Union since 'Russia is also part of the new neighbourhood policy'. Therefore, 'we encourage Ukraine to develop close neighbourly relations with all its neighbours including Russia while sticking firmly to the strategic partnership with the EU at the same time' (see Speech 'New Neighbourhood between the EU and Ukraine. From a vision towards reality', Kiev, 12 September 2003). On the other hand Verheugen, while understanding Ukraine's need to maintain a high level of economic cooperation with its Eastern neighbours, advises his Ukrainian interlocutors 'to be cautious at the same time and to ensure that the foreseen Single Economic Space is fully compatible with Ukraine's existing obligations and its European integration aspirations' (see Delegation of the European Commission to Ukraine, Kiev, Press Release, Ref: 2411, 12 September 2003).

frustration about the EU position on Ukraine probably explains at least in part the latter's return to a dose of 'Realpolitik'.

D. Implementing Common Strategies

1. *Institutional Mechanism*

The institutional framework governing the implementation of the common strategy is not particularly transparent and besides the interaction mentioned earlier between European Council and Council, nothing about how implementation of the common strategy ought to be organised is mentioned in the EU Treaty itself. As a general rule it is up to the Council to ensure unity, consistency and effectiveness of action by the Union (Article 13 TEU) and it is in each of the respective common strategies themselves that mechanisms are provided for implementation and review. These implementing rules are the same for the CSR and CSU. The Presidency plays the leading role since each incoming Presidency must ensure that a work plan and priorities for implementation of the common strategy are presented to the Council, on the basis of the various areas of action and taking into account the specific initiatives defined in the common strategy document. In the European Council Declarations related to the CSR and CSU it is recalled that as regards adopting the classical second pillar instruments such as joint actions, common positions or any other decisions on the basis of the Common Strategy the Council can act by qualified majority but that for acts adopted outside the scope of the Second Pillar the appropriate relevant rules will be applied. This procedural clarification constitutes at the same time an explicit confirmation of a 'cross-pillar' potential.

At least once a year a global review and evaluation report on implementation is submitted to the European Council. Since no joint institutional structures are provided under the common strategies themselves, the various existing institutional frameworks of the PCA are, in the first place, the main channels allowing for the necessary communication and interaction with the partner. Moreover, no specific financial means have been made available and TACIS remains the most important financial instrument to finance EU supported activities in Russia or Ukraine. All this helps to explain why so little has been achieved under the EU's Common Strategies for these two countries.

2. *Common Strategy on Russia*

Between the first CSR Work Plan presented on 19 July 1999 under the Finnish Presidency and the Greek Work Plan of 18 January 2003 — the last to be considered for the purpose of this contribution — the general priorities have hardly changed. The main areas of action throughout almost four years of operation of the CSR have been: 1) consolidation of democracy, rule of law and public institutions in Russia; 2) integration of Russia in a common European economic and social area; 3) strengthening stability and security in Europe and beyond; 4) addressing common challenges on the European continent.

Under the head of promoting democracy, the EU has again and again emphasised the need for reforms of the judiciary, consolidation of civil society, freedom and pluralism of the press. In virtually every Work Plan since 1999 references have also been made to the situation in Chechnya. Russia is asked to respect human rights and to find a political solution to the problem but no such reference is made without at the same time mentioning the need of full respect of the territorial integrity of the Russian Federation. However, the impact of CSR on helping to address the Chechnya crises, and even more so after 11 September 2001, has been non-existent. The issue of Russia's integration in a broader European and international framework passes in the first place through WTO-membership. EU support for Russia's accession to the WTO was already acknowledged in the CSR text of 1999 and is, since Russia is not a WTO member yet, logically, still reiterated in the 2003 Greek Work Plan. It is a clear indication that on this point little progress has been made. Of course, satisfying WTO conditions is in the first place something for Russia itself and at the moment of writing serious adjustments have still to be made on the Russian side. But besides repeating every six months in each new CSR Work Plan or in joint statements of EU-Russia Summits that the EU will support Russia's efforts to join the WTO, little more than lip service seems to have been paid to Russia's WTO accession.[66] Parallel to the discussion on membership of the WTO, attempts have been made to bring the EU and Russia closer together in the economic field. Two initiatives need particular mention. In the PCA, Russia is recognised as no longer being a State-trading country but 'a country with an economy in transition'. In addition, 'continued progress towards a market economy (would) be fostered by co-operation between the Parties'. However, notwithstanding these good intentions, Russia continued to be treated as a State-trading country from the purposes of application of the EC anti-dumping legislation and this led to bitter Russian complaints on discriminatory treatment. It is true that

[66] As a matter of fact the EU's position on Russian domestic energy prices, arguing that price differentiation leading to a much higher price for foreign customers amounts to an indirect subsidy to Russian industry, is one of the various serious obstacles to Russia's WTO accession, see R Behr & A Jack, 'Russian talks on WTO entry stall over energy', *Financial Times*, 19 February 2003.

Council Regulation 905/98 of 27 April 1998 had amended the EC anti-dumping regime but an important burden of proof continued to be imposed on Russian producers. At the EU-Russia Summit of 29 May 2002 the EU declared its intention to grant Russia full market economy status, a political commitment which was legally implemented via Council Regulation 1972/2000 of 5 November 2002.[67] Furthermore, at the May 2001 EU-Russia Summit the initiative was launched to study the establishment of a Common European Economic Space (CEES) and a High Level Group (HLG) was set up to do the preparatory work.[68] The HLG presented its formal plan in October 2003.[69] The idea is that the CEES would promote legislative approximation and regulatory convergence, indeed an absolute must for Russia as a country at the side-line of the enlarged EU.[70] It is hoped that this will help to stimulate the investment climate in Russia and be beneficial for the development of bilateral economic relations. The CEES has strongly been praised by the political leaderships from both sides as a very important concept and, if implementing planning can be achieved, it may indeed be a good idea. In the Greek Work Plan, for the first time, mentioning is also made of examining the possibility of launching an initiative for the creation of a Common European Social Space where, for example, support for public health could take a prominent place.

Co-operation to strengthen stability and security in Europe and beyond is an area where various initiatives have been developed but they also, as so many other CSR-actions, seem to find their origin in other initiatives rather than the CSR itself. The section of the CSR on common challenges on the European continent has probably been the most active one because of the very high domestic priority of the EU on illegal migration, international crime, drugs, money laundering, etc. The Work Plans of the various Presidencies have continuously stressed the need for cooperation in these fields. An embryo of the CSR framework is developing in the field of Justice and Home Affairs (JHA), at first sight, partly inspired from what had been initiated with governmental contacts under the Structured Dialogue for the Countries of Central and Eastern Europe within the pre-accession process.[71] That means that on the margins of a formal Council of Ministers of JHA, the Ministers of the Interior and

[67] OJ 2002 L305/1.
[68] See Decision Cooperation Council of 15 February 2002, Doc EU-RU 1005/01.
[69] See Press Release Nr: 13990/03 (6/11/2003) http://ue.eu.int/pressData/en/er/77845.pdf
[70] For a Russian perspective, see I Ivanov, *Common European Economic Space: A View from Russia*, (Moscow, Foundation 'East-West Bridges', 2003).
[71] For an in depth analysis of the practice of 'structured dialogue' in the pre-accession process, see B Lippert & P Becker, 'Structured Dialogue Revisited: the EU's Politics of Inclusion and Exclusion', (1998) 3 *European Foreign Affairs Review* 341.

Ministers of Justice, the Commissioner for Justice and Home Affairs together with the Ministers for the Interior and of Justice of the Russian Federation meet to discuss issues of common concern.[72] Maybe one of the most important subjects in this context is related to the development of the common EU policy towards immigration and asylum. One of the key elements to this policy is the conclusion of readmission agreements with third countries. Already the basic texts of the CSR contain, as mentioned before, a clear reference to the need for such an agreement with Russia and also the Work Plans of various EU Presidencies have systematically referred to this as a leading priority. On 30 March 2001 the EU presented a draft agreement to the Russian authorities and at the Fourth Meeting of the EU-Russia Co-operation Council of 10 April 2001 Commissioner Patten insisted on negotiating such an agreement as quickly as possible: such a move would be considered very beneficial in building confidence between the two parties.[73] However, consultations at expert level were only formally opened on 23 January 2003.[74] Originally, Russia had other priorities, which also explains why no such agreement has yet been signed with the EC so far. Russia invoked, among other things, the need for adequate border management, in particular efficient border control at the Eastern borders.[75] An important first step in this direction is the already mentioned readmission agreement signed between Russia and Lithuania. From a Russian perspective it looks more and more as if the negotiations on a global readmission agreement with the EU will have to be seen in a broader context of Russia's possibility of signing similar agreements with Asian countries from where illegal migrants may be originating[76] and also in the light of the Russian demand for facilitating travel of Russian citizens to the EU, in particular the increasingly outspoken Russian request of abolition of visa.[77] This, in the context of the EU proximity policy to be developed after enlargement, is less exorbitant than at first sight may appear. Of course, visa free travel would mean that

[72] The idea was suggested in Spanish Work Plan, 22 January 2002, Doc 5534/02 NIS 20 COEST 2 PESC 21. Such a first meeting took place in Luxemburg on 25/26 April 2002, see Doc 7991/02 (Press 104).

[73] See Minutes on the Fourth Meeting of the EU-Russia Co-operation Council of 10 April 2001, UE-RU 1001/02, Annex 23.

[74] See Press Communiqué, Delegation of the European Commission in Russia, 23 January 2003, http://www.eur.ru/eng/neweur/user_eng.php?func=main.

[75] See Minutes of the Troika meeting of 10 April 2002 of the Strategic Committee on Immigration, Frontiers and Asylum and Representatives of Russia, Council of the EU, 12 April 2002, Doc 8061/02 JAI 65 ASIM 9 RELEX 61.

[76] See also interview with Vladimir Chizkov, Deputy Minister of Foreign Affairs, in *Vremya Novostei*, 'Our Goal is a Visa-free Agreement with the European Union', *Daily News Bulletin*, Ministry of Foreign relations, Moscow, 4 December 2002.

[77] See also statement to the press by President Putin at the St. Petersburg EU-Russia Summit of 31 May 2003, Ministry of Foreign Affairs, Moscow, *Daily News Bulletin*, 2 June 2003.

Russia applies norms and standards on movement of persons and migration applicable in or comparable to those in the EU. This would require considerable investments in human resources, infrastructure, etc. in other words cannot be organised overnight. Anyhow, it is to be expected that the EU will not obtain a readmission agreement without having to pay a price … Finally, it should be mentioned that a noteworthy example of increasing co-operation between the EU and Russia in the field of the third pillar but not directly related to our topic is that on combating organised crime. An Action Plan was adopted by the EU-Russia Co-operation Council of 10 April 2000.[78]

In the first years of implementation of the CSR, references to EU enlargement have been avoided as much as possible. There are no such references in the Work Plans of the first two years of CSR application. The Belgian Work Plan of 10 July 2001 was the first explicitly to refer to enlargement and this was a noteworthy innovation in the Presidency's Work Plan practice.[79] In the Belgian Work Plan, 'Discussing the impact of EU enlargement process' is explicitly mentioned as a specific area for CSR action. It is stated that the impact of enlargement will be discussed in the PCA bodies 'in order to give Russia fully transparent information on the enlargement process and point out how Russia could best benefit from the opportunities provided by enlargement'. In the same Work Plan, also for the first time, reference to the Kaliningrad problem in the EU enlargement strategy was made. Subsequent Presidency Work Plans reiterate the same approach but nothing indicates in the Work Plans and yearly Evaluation Reports or any other CSR instrument, that the CSR in itself has contributed to addressing the effects of enlargement on Russia in any way.

3. *Common Strategy on Ukraine*

As far as the CSU implementation is concerned, the distance between the first Work Plan of the Portuguese Presidency of 18 January 2000[80] and that of the Greek Presidency of 17 January 2003[81] is short. The first Work Plan noted that the PCA remained the basis for developing the relations with Ukraine and in the Greek Work Plan also the PCA is still 'the cornerstone' of the relations EU-Ukraine. The first 'Work Plan' was not really a work plan in the sense that it set clear targets for the EU. The part

[78] Minutes of Third Meeting of the EU-Russia Co-operation Council, UE-RU 1001/01. For a detailed analysis of the legal nature of this Action Plan and particularly its 'cross-pillar'-dimension, see Hillion above n 6, 1230–34.
[79] Doc 10718/01 NIS 57 COEST 24 PESC 288.
[80] Council 18 January 2000, Doc 5434/00 NIS 17 COEST 2 PESC 22.
[81] Council 17 January 2003, Doc 5408/03 NIS 6 COEST 2 PESC 20.

on strengthening co-operation within the context of EU enlargement did not incorporate anything that was not already included in the basic CSU text itself. In short, the Work Plan and following Work Plans did not reflect a true working strategy and, as was already recognised in the introductory part of the first plan, the CSU served in the first place to implement the PCA.[82] The objectives of the CSU enumerated in the various Work Plans from one Presidency to another have hardly changed, which is also understandable since priorities do not change every six months. Consolidation of democracy, rule of law and public institutions, including respect of human rights were then as they remain today, top priorities. Actions for strengthening civil society and the free functioning of the media have been important references throughout the implementation of CSU. The treatment of the enlargement dimension, in the sense of the impact of enlargement on Ukraine, has clearly been lacking inspiration in the various Work Plans and did little more than reiterate the EU's support for accession of Ukraine to the WTO. It was through direct bilateral trade negotiations, and not really as a result of Common Strategy activity, that on 17 March 2003 agreement was reached on a bilateral package for Ukraine's accession to WTO.[83]

One of the most important activities strongly promoted within the Common Strategy framework has been that of cooperation in the field of Justice and Home Affairs. Ukraine has been willing to accept some of main EU concerns as 'shared' concerns. An illustration of this is the fact that, on 12 December 2001, Ukraine endorsed the EU Action Plan on Justice and Home Affairs.[84] The Plan provides for an accompanying framework, called 'scoreboard', to define and monitor the set annual priorities. The main targets are migration and readmission, border management, visa, organised crime, terrorism, law enforcement, strengthening the judiciary, rule of law and good governance.[85] On 11 November 2002, for the first time, an EU-Ukraine Ministerial Troika on Justice and Home Affairs meeting took place and confirmed the set priorities. It was, among other things, also agreed to explore the possibility of establishing central contact points to exchange information on organised crime,[86] but the most important priority was assigned to migration and readmission. On this last matter Ukraine expressed its willingness to start negotiations

[82] Doc 10018/00 NIS 85 COEST 12 PESC 300.

[83] See Press Release European Commission, 17 March 2003, IP/03/390.

[84] Doc 14228/01 COEST 36 JAI 150.

[85] For an updated version with timeframe and further details, see EU-Ukraine Scoreboard on Justice and Home Affairs, updated on 11 October 2002, Doc 13343/02 NIS 124 JAI 225.

[86] See Conclusions of meeting, Doc 14433/02 JAI 257 NIS 142.The Greek Presidency has taken the initiative for a Joint Declaration on this matter by the Ministers for Justice and Home Affairs. The initiative is largely based on the CSU, see Doc 5361/1/03 REV1 CRIMORG 3 NIS4, 14 February 2003.

on expert level but emphasised that at the same time it wished to conclude similar agreements with Russia and Belarus.[87] Ukraine wants also a greater liberalisation of the EU visa regime. The linkages between readmission and the visa regime as well as with the need for bilateral readmission agreements with neighbours[88] are not very propitious to the quick conclusion of a readmission agreement with the EU.

Contrary to the EU's approach towards South East Europe, which benefits from the Stabilisation and Association Policy leading where possible to Stabilisation and Association Agreements, there is no intention to offer Ukraine the status of 'potential member'.[89] First, the current enlargement process will have to be accomplished and consolidated before changes can be envisaged. Of course, Ukraine's internal political and economic problems, lack of democratic accountability and widespread corruption do not contribute to offering an attractive pre-accession atmosphere. But another reason why the EU will be very cautious to go in that direction is related to the position of Russia. Speculations as to the future accession of Ukraine to the EU only make sense when the enlarged EU-Russia relations are free from ambiguity and truly stabilised. Moreover, on the enlargement issue, the bilateral relations Russia-Ukraine are obviously of crucial importance and Ukraine's possible EU accession could only be conceivable in a triangular relationship based upon agreement among the EU, Ukraine and Russia. In other words, EU enlargement incorporating Ukraine at one stage would need prior and full accord from Russia.

The ambivalence of Ukraine's position on the margins of the EU enlargement process is also clearly demonstrated by the wording of the Joint Statements issued after each EU-Ukraine Summit. Generally speaking the Joint Statements reiterate 'the classics' of the EU enlargement strategy: enlargement is a process 'reinforcing political and economic integration and stability in Europe' and it offers an opportunity to increase trade between the enlarged EU and Ukraine.[90] Also, the PCA does remain the basis for further rapprochement of Ukraine to the EU: in other words, the PCA's 'full potential' should be used.[91] The CSU is mentioned in the 2000 and 2001[92] Joint Statements but not in that of 2002.

[87] See Minutes Fifth EU-Ukraine Co-operation Council of 11 March 2002, Doc UE-UA 1053/02.

[88] Minutes Meeting Troika Strategic Committee on Immigration, Frontiers and Asylum and Representatives from Ukraine, Doc 8062/02 JAI 66 ASIM 10 RELEX 62.

[89] See statement Commissioner Verheugen, in 'Kiev's hopes for gaining EU membership dashed', *Financial Times*, 17 September 2002.

[90] See for example Joint Statement of 15 September 2000, http://ukraine-eu.mfa.gov.ua/cgi-bin/valprint_miss.sh?1p04030103.html.

[91] See Joint Statement of 11 September 2001.

[92] In the Joint Statement of 11 September 2001 'the relevant administrations (are encouraged) to continue to co-operate closely ... with a view to ensuring a successful implementation of the Common Strategy'.

The enlarged EU necessarily implies that Ukraine commits itself to an intensified process of legal alignment to the norms and standards applied by the EU.[93] Legal approximation is considered to be 'one of the key elements for an intensified relationship between Ukraine and the EU'.[94]

The problem with these Joint Statements is that they send out conflicting messages. The EU wants to stress 'strategic partnership' which, as already mentioned before, does not aim at envisaging EU membership. Thus, for example, the end sentence of the Joint Statement of the Summit Ukraine-EU of 4 July 2002, whereby account is taken of the progress made by Ukraine towards democracy, the economic performance of Ukraine 'and its strong pro-European choice as well as EU enlargement (choice)' must not be understood to mean that the EU also supports Ukraine's membership of the EU: the pro-European and enlargement choice of Ukraine will contribute to 'a new and strengthened dimension *of our strategic partnership'* (emphasis added).[95] Ukraine, for its part, is realising that the negative effects of not being included in the enlargement process only becomes increasingly apparent. These effects are in the first place political: Ukraine will have to assume willy-nilly the role of 'buffer-state' alongside the enlarged EU. Understandably, the message that EU enlargement brings peace and stability 'for the entire European continent' is not very attractive for Ukraine which sees its European future in the long run within the EU itself. This is also made clear in the March 2003 *Joint Report on the Implementation of the Partnership and Cooperation Agreement Between the EU and Ukraine* where on the enlargement issue the two parties, after acknowledging their eagerness to make full use of this process, 'were unable to agree on how to describe the situation in this report in more detail'. Ukraine expressed its concern that as a result of enlargement a visa regime was introduced by its neighbours, cross-border trade reduced and that enlargement might further adversely affect cooperation, business activities, cultural exchange, tourism. The EU, for its part, reiterated its official and traditional view that new opportunities created by enlargement were outweighing possible disadvantages: 'EU enlargement, by giving a new dynamic impulse to prosperity and economic development in Central Europe, should entail considerable potential benefits for the direct new neighbours, in particular Ukraine'.[96] The obvious problem is that in the period of the pre-accession process for the countries of Central and Eastern Europe and particularly during the four years of application of the CSU, the EU has not been able to offer any substantiated strategy to

[93] Ibid.
[94] Joint Statement of 4 July 2002 and also Joint Statement of 11 September 2001.
[95] Joint Statement of 4 July 2002.
[96] For text see: http://europa.eu.int/comm/external_relations/ukraine/into/pcarep2.pdf, 3 and 9.

countries like Ukraine to ease their growing frustrations. This is a great responsibility for the EU and explains why now, almost *in extremis*, a variety of new suggestions are being launched on the proximity relations of the enlarged EU. And, as already mentioned, it also explains why Ukraine creates the impression of wanting to review its ties with its eastern neighbours.

E. Common Strategies and New Neighbour Initiatives: A Conclusion

The CSR and CSU, as formulated in the basic texts of 1999, apply for a period of four years and both expire in 2003. The Greek Presidency has not opted to do away with the Common Strategies but proposed to prolong the CSR, expiring under its Presidency, for another year. This leaves all further options open and the idea was that in this extension period the ratification of the Accession Treaty, the activities of the European Convention and the 2003 IGC would all be rounded off. It may indeed be difficult to reflect on replacing and fundamentally reviewing an ailing CFSP-instrument like the Common Strategy as it operates today while such other important political and institutional activities are underway, which, moreover, may directly or indirectly affect the relations with Russia and Ukraine.

In any case, it is certainly difficult to agree with the Swedish Presidency's and the Council's assessment of the Common Strategy made after two years of operation, that, in particularly the CSR, 'has proved to be an important instrument for guiding the European Union in relations with Russia'.[97] The end balance of even four years of CSR activity is indeed particularly meagre. The Strategy's extremely weak institutional structure with its strong emphasis on the Presidency, which changes every six months, has affected its strength and possible impact. With every new Presidency the Common Strategy ritual where a new Work Plan is formally proposed, leaves very little place for creative thinking and most of the proposals for CSR or CSU action have been externally 'imposed' on an *ad hoc* basis rather than being the result of a well-conceived strategy towards these countries. But the main substantive weakness was the EU's existential fear of properly addressing the enlargement issue in its relations with Russia and Ukraine. The EU's lack of vision combined with an almost exclusively inward-looking and 'self-protective' approach where so-called 'common challenges on the European continent' are addressed, have not helped to give the Common

[97] See Council Report of 11 June 2001 to the European Council on the Implementation of the Common Strategy of the European Union on Russia, Doc 9805/01 NIS 44 COEST 17 PESC 226.

Strategy its necessary *élan*. One cannot therefore be astonished to see that virtually no concrete achievement in the relations EU-Russia or EU-Ukraine can truly be qualified as a Common Strategy result. The Common Strategy's biggest 'achievement' is semestrial stock-taking of areas where actions are desirable and what has been done in these areas. This, in itself, is a useful exercise and the comprehensive inventory of problems and issues has helped to see better interconnections, as well as perhaps the necessity for a more coherent EU approach. However, at the moment of writing these conclusions and on the eve of the grand enlargement, the relations between the EU and Russia seem to be poor and deteriorating. Both parties have their share of responsibility for the present state of affairs. This chapter has mainly focused on the shortcomings of the EU policy towards Russia. The closer the enlargement date comes nearer, the more Russian nervousness becomes explicit. In this context the discriminatory treatment of the Russian minorities in Latvia and Estonia, which the EU was unable to address properly and effectively during the pre-accession phase,[98] and which was with great care avoided in the CSR, remains an understandable point of reference of Russian criticism of the EU enlargement.

The fate of the Common Strategies is now very much in the hands of the New Neighbours Initiative, which was formally launched at the 18 November 2002 General Affairs and External Relations Council (GAERC), of the European Convention and ultimately the 2003–04 IGC. As far as the work of the Convention on this matter is concerned, attention seems to have concentrated rather on semantics than on substance and one of the proposals is to replace the expression 'common strategies' by 'European decisions of the European Council on strategic interests proposed and objectives of the Union'.[99] On the other hand a specific article of the proposed Constitutional Treaty lays down the legal and political basis for a possible 'special relationship' between the Union and neighbouring States.[100] But from a substantive point of view the EU Foreign Ministers call on the European Commission and the High Representative to prepare proposals on how the relations with the 'new neighbours' have to be organised in the light of the coming EU enlargement may be more interesting. The mentioned GAERC Conclusions[101] concentrate on the relations with Ukraine, Moldova and Belarus and

[98] For a criticism of the EU policy in this respect, see our contribution 'Quelques réflexions sur l'origine et l'application de principes fondamentaux dans la stratégie d'adhésion de l'UE', Mélanges Professeur Jean Raux, 2004 (in print).

[99] See Art III–194 in Draft of 18 July 2003, CONV 850/03.

[100] See Preliminary Draft Constitutional Treaty, 28 October 2002, CONV 369/02, later refined in Draft Art 42, CONV 649/03 of 2 April 2003, becoming Art 56 in Draft of 18 July 2003, CONV 850/03.

[101] For text, see Doc 14183/02 (Presse 350).

suggest a differentiated approach 'considering each country's distinct political and economic situation, potential and aims'. The EU's approach will obviously be very much determined by the countries' own progress in the field of political and economic reform. In this 'New Neighbours Initiative' (NNI) Russia's position as 'a key partner' is nevertheless somewhat ambiguous. According to the Council, there should be a strong commitment to deepening relations with Russia 'in conjunction with' the development of new initiatives but the NNI concerns in the first place Ukraine, Moldova and Belarus. On the GAERC's call the European Commission has published its response[102] in the already mentioned Communication on 'Wider Europe-Neighbourhood' aiming to develop 'a zone of prosperity and a friendly neighbourhood — a *ring of friends* — with whom the EU enjoys close, peaceful and co-operative relations'.[103] In short, the Commission's main thesis is that 'the EU's neighbourhood should benefit from the prospect of closer economic integration with the EU'. The Commission is of the opinion that 'in return for concrete progress demonstrating shared values and effective implementation of political, economic and institutional reforms, including in aligning legislation with the acquis, the EU's neighbourhood should benefit from the prospect of closer economic integration with the EU'. The most innovative and certainly most challenging suggestion is that to this end 'Russia, the countries of the Western NIS and the Southern Mediterranean should be offered the prospect of a stake in the EU's Internal Market and further integration and liberalisation to promote the free movement of persons, goods, services and capital (four freedoms)'. Several of the suggested areas for closer co-operation and/or integration can in one way or another also be found in the various Common Strategy Work Plans and a lot of water will still have to flow under the bridge before, for example, free movement of persons can be contemplated. But the fact that the Commission has also dared to incorporate this objective may be an indication of the growing awareness of the need to monitor closely the external effects of EU enlargement. In the aftermath of enlargement, the feeling of isolation and frustration by the neighbours may be the strongest on this issue and the EU should take seriously the demands for visa free travel under certain conditions as part of an EU confidence building strategy. After all, it is the EU which is involved in enlarging and it is easy to understand the Russian or Ukrainian concerns and sensitivities on this matter. Moreover, such a strategy will be the best guarantee for genuine improvements and modernisation of the national laws in the field of migration, border controls, etc. in the enlarged EU's neighbours

[102] At the moment of writing the High Representative's views had not yet been published.
[103] For references, see above n 18.

themselves. It is a positive signal, even if it is expressed in very vague and cautious terms, that at the 2003 St. Petersburg Summit the EU and Russia 'agreed to examine the conditions for visa-free travel as a long term perspective'.

In the Commission's Communication a new type of agreement, called 'Neighbourhood Agreements', is envisaged to organise the new form of relations in the post-enlargement phase. Whatever such agreements might be, it is interesting to note that the Commission does not seem to make the sharp distinction between Russia on the one hand and the other three countries concerned on the other. Certainly, it would be an unforgivable mistake to disconnect Russia from the other Eastern European new neighbours unless Russia itself would want this to happen. The success of the EU's new orientation will largely if not exclusively depend on the neighbours' willingness and capability to play the game. The most probable test-case will be Ukraine whose ambitions go far beyond what the EU is proposing.

Finally, it is difficult not to notice that no explicit reference to the Common Strategies has been included in the Council's New Neighbours Initiative nor in the Commission's 'Wider Europe — Neighbourhood' Communication. It is almost inconceivable that this could be the result of simple inadvertence. Whether this must be interpreted as silent confirmation of an unannounced death still remains to be seen but it would appear that, whatever the EU's institutional outcome may be, a fundamental substantive and procedural review and reorientation of the Common Strategy instrument are indispensable for its own survival. If, as suggested, 'Neighbourhood Agreements', particularly with Russia or/and Ukraine, were to be signed the existing 'Common Strategy/ies', as separate and all-embracing instrument(s), could well be disposed of and its objectives integrated in these agreements. This is not the same as saying that the European Council should always be precluded from taking *ad hoc* decisions on 'strategic interests and objectives' — to use the terminology of Draft Article III–194 of the Constitutional Treaty — in specific matters not, or not sufficiently, covered by 'Neighbourhood Agreements'. If complementary to such agreements, the successor of the common strategy, might in the future still have a role to play also in the EU's neighbourhood, but this will depend on the precise scope and content of such agreements.

Final Remarks

ALLAN ROSAS*

IT IS A privilege to be able to offer some 'final remarks' for this Conference publication devoted to EU enlargement. There are two personal experiences I can draw upon. First, my country of origin, Finland, was among the three countries that joined in the latest, fifth round of enlargement. Second, I have dealt with external relations, enlargement included, during my more than six years with the European Commission and its Legal Service.

From my own personal perspective, the eight and a half years that have elapsed since Austria, Finland and Sweden joined the EU have passed very quickly. On the other hand, it seems as if these countries have always been EU members. I believe that many people from the present candidate countries will have the same feeling when their countries have been EU members for more than seven years. Time will have flown quickly, but at the same time EU membership will appear well-established and a natural part of every-day life.

Allow me to offer some personal thoughts which may draw some inspiration from both my past experience with the 1995 enlargement and the more recent enlargement negotiations, and the discussions in this volume. I shall address three sets of problems: 1) the ability of candidate countries to adopt and implement the *acquis* and other requirements of membership, 2) the ability of EU institutions to cope with an increased membership, and 3) the ability of the EU to win the hearts and minds of the populations of both candidate countries and current Member States (or the problem of legitimacy). I am not convinced that the first challenge will be the overriding one. It may well be that it is the third challenge which is the hardest nut to crack.

To start with the ability of the new Member States to adjust to EU membership, there is no denying that it will not be easy to implement something approaching 100,000 pages of *acquis*, often consisting of very complex legal areas and texts, to change, if need be, administrative cultures and practices, and to convince judges and others to accept EU law as an every-day part of domestic law and domestic legal life. But on the

* Court of Justice of the European Communities.

whole, a lot has already been done, and the remaining problems will gradually be overcome, by co-operation, training, and determination. I have had the pleasure of co-operating with a number of lawyers from some of the candidate countries, and this already during the 1970s and 1980s. Also during the difficult years, one could discern strong legal traditions and convictions on which to build. A lot still needs to be done as far as the training of judges and the strengthening of the judicial system are concerned. Such efforts should now be intensified. Personally, I would look very much into the question of legal education and training, and developing further co-operation between law faculties, centres of EU law, professional training institutions, and the like, among all the 25 countries involved. It goes without saying that in a Union of 25, it is more of a challenge to preserve the coherence and unity of the EU legal system than, say, in the original Community of six.

Let me now say a word about the second set of problems, the ability of EU institutions to cope with a Union consisting of 25, or maybe more, Member States. This, I feel, is even more of a challenge. Some problems are less serious. For instance, I do not foresee any insurmountable problems for the institution I have the honour of serving, the Court of Justice, including the Court of First Instance. There will be more cases, surely, but also more judges. In so far as the size of a population has a bearing on the number of requests for preliminary rulings, it should be noted that an enlargement with ten new Member States would imply an increase of the EU's total population by only 20 per cent, while it would bring a 75 per cent increase in the number of judges.

In any case, the Treaty of Nice provides for some mechanisms to counter an increasing case load, such as the establishment of judicial panels to relieve the Court of First Instance from certain categories of cases, combined with a further transfer of jurisdiction from the Court of Justice to the Court of First Instance. The mounting case load and the length of proceedings are of course difficult problems, but they are generic problems not caused by enlargement alone. As to translations and interpretations, space, and other practical problems, there will be a lot of headaches, but nothing that will pose insurmountable problems for the functioning of the EU courts.

How to preserve, and if possible increase, efficiency in the EU legislative and decision-making process will pose a much bigger problem, and one specifically linked to enlargement. While it is true that, especially with the Treaty of Nice, and the outcome of the work of the constitutional Convention, the great bulk of decisions can be taken by qualified majority in the Council, there would still be areas where unanimity is required. Giving a veto power to one Member State out of 25, not to speak of 35, is not the same thing as preserving it in a small club of six (if we are comparing with the original situation of 1958).

Let me take as a concrete example one of my hobby horses, EU external relations and notably the question of mixed agreements. As you know, a mixed agreement requires the consent not only of the EC but of all the Member States separately. Already today, this process can take up to five or even ten years, from signature to conclusion. Also, the management of mixed agreements poses a host of problems of a legal and/or practical nature. This has to be looked into, to help making the EU even a bit more efficient and credible in its external relations. The proposals of the constitutional Convention go in the right direction, for instance in so far as international trade policy is concerned.

On this and other institutional issues, I am cautiously optimistic. The idea that enlargement will slow down, or even paralyse, integration may prove to be wrong. If we look at the past, a Community of six did not produce constitutional reform (apart from the case law of the Court of Justice), but instead the Luxembourg compromise, which was a step back. Only after rounds of enlargement were important modifications brought about: the Single European Act, Maastricht, Amsterdam, Nice and more recently the work on a new constitutional instrument. When you are very few, you can still 'afford' to keep it more or less as an intergovernmental club. The more Member States, the more there is a pressing need to strive for the Community method, and majority voting.

The constitutional Convention and the ensuing Intergovernmental Conference will hopefully make meaningful progress on these institutional issues. But the importance of the on-going constitution-making in my view goes beyond the question of institutional reform. I now come to my third, and last, set of problems concerning questions of legitimacy, and the need to win the hearts and minds of the peoples of Europe. I am avoiding the notion of 'democratic deficit', as I do not know what that means, preferring notions such as legitimacy, identification, and popular perceptions.

It is here, I think, that the fundamental problem lies. A genuine, strong and coherent popular support for European integration is lacking, or at least it is hard to detect. The negative outcomes of referendums, twice in Denmark and Norway, and once in Ireland, and the close calls in France (Maastricht) and Sweden (accession) are not just 'accidents' but in my view symptomatic of a more general problem. And as far as the candidate countries are concerned, it is my impression that many have thought of EC accession as a political or security policy gesture akin to NATO membership, combined with access to EU funds. When people realise that there is a host of obligations to undertake, and adjustments to accomplish, but perhaps less money than expected, frustration or scepticism may enter into the picture.

There are no easy fixes, and more money to 'Euronews', or more brochures, will not suffice. One step that needs to be taken is to obtain a more simple and coherent constitutional document. One should not necessarily assume that constitutions are terribly important for ordinary people. But there is a case for arguing that a proper EU constitution would have a certain symbolic as well as educational value. The existing constitution has been developed in various stages, and almost by stealth. Most people do not have a clue of the nature and extent of existing EU powers in different fields. All this should now be put down on one piece of paper, and in a more succinct and coherent fashion. Various elements of confusion, such as the EU/EC/Communities/Euratom mess, should be eliminated. Some may think that people will be shocked to learn what is already on the books, or what is envisaged for the future. I do not share this view. A proper constitutional document would encourage, not discourage. While every citizen would probably not hold such a piece of Europe in his hand, things could be different as far as teachers and opinion leaders are concerned.

But this is not enough. The role of the citizen, and of civil society, should be highlighted also in developing substantive rules. The new Constitution should include radical solutions to enhance citizen involvement. I am not — and this may come as a surprise — necessarily envisaging new legal remedies giving access to courts and judges. What I have in mind is more in the nature of popular initiatives giving access to a privileged political procedure, increasing the powers of the European Ombudsman, improving administrative procedures and transparency, making the Charter of Fundamental Rights legally binding, strengthening the rights of EU citizens, and so on and so forth. The work of the constitutional Convention should bring about some improvements in this regard. In this context, one can also refer to the role of national parliaments, not as a 'third' chamber (as has been proposed by some) but by emphasising their role as EU institutions, for instance in the monitoring of the application of the principle of subsidiarity.

Without wishing to dramatise, I feel that the future of the EU will to a large extent depend on whether we will be able to meet such challenges. The fundamental problem, to conclude, is not caused by enlargement, but is related to the legitimacy of, and popular perceptions about, the integration project itself, both in the existing 15 and the 10 new Member States. It is our historic duty to succeed.

I am convinced that the new Member States will bring in fresh blood and new ideas and, on a personal note, I look very much forward to cooperating with old and new friends and colleagues from these countries, both at the Court of Justice and in relation to their national courts and legal institutions in general.

Index